Media and Tourism

MEDIA AND TOURISM

Ms. Shallini Gupta

CENTRUM PRESS
NEW DELHI-110002 (INDIA)

CENTRUM PRESS
H.O.: 4360/4, Ansari Road, Daryaganj,
New Delhi-110002 (India)
Tel: 23278000, 23261597, 23255577, 23286875
B.O.: No. 1015, Ist Main Road, BSK IIIrd Stage,
IIIrd Phase, IIIrd Block, Bengaluru-560085 (INDIA)
Tel: 080-41723429
Email: centrumpress@gmail.com
Visit us at: www.centrumpress.com

Media and Tourism

First Edition, 2012
ISBN 978-93-81293-90-4

PRINTED IN INDIA

Printed at Tarun Offset, Delhi

Contents

Preface

In addressing the connections between the media and tourism this collection breaks new ground. There are a multitude of tourist practices and an extended range of media. We are, therefore, immediately engaged in a process of multiplication. Tourism studies and media studies both address key issues about how we perceive the world. They raise acute questions about how we relate local knowledge and immediate experience to wider global processes, and they both play a major role in creating our map of national and international cultures. Adopting a multidisciplinary approach, this book explores the interactions between tourism and media practices within a contemporary culture in which the consumption of images has become increasingly significant.

A number of common themes and concerns arise, and the contributions included are divided between those: written from media studies awareness perspective, concerned with the way the media imagines travel and tourism written from the point of view of the study of tourism, considering how tourism practices are affected or altered by the media that attempt a direct comparison between the practices of tourism and the media. Incorporating case study material from England, the Caribbean, Australia, the US, France and Switzerland, this significant text, ideal for students of media and tourism studies, discusses tourism and the media as separate processes through which identity is constructed in relation to space and place.

Author

1

Introduction

Tourism has long been recognised as an agent of change, generally perceived along a positive-negative continuum. Such change is usually noted in terms of socio-cultural, economic and environmental elements. In many cases, the extent of the impact is a direct function of the number of visitors. Simply speaking, more visitors can bring more money, but also create more pressure on the environment and their associated communities. When a movie or popular television series is filmed on-site in an existing town or region, increased visitation to those sites often follows. As with many cases of increased tourism, those film sites that are in fragile environments and communities tend to see the most dramatic changes. Filminduced tourism is of particular interest in terms of community development, as many of the more popular television and film sites are in small communities, particularly in rural/regional areas. In this thesis, one such community in Australia is considered by looking at the physical changes to the town and beliefs held by residents as well as visitors in terms of the overall effect of a popular television series.

TOURISM AND COMMUNITIES

Many researchers have contributed to our understanding of the positive and negative impacts of tourism on communities. In particular, the economic impacts are well documented, however in more recent times the socio-cultural elements are becoming more widely acknowledged. Singh relate this pattern of change towards tourism and communities in terms of Jafari's four tourism platforms of advocacy, cautionary (such as considering primarily the negative socio-cultural impacts), adaptancy (pro-community compromise) and knowledge-based (research-focused community development) platforms. This interesting framework has been used to trace the overall trends in community development and tourism, while allowing us to recognise that not all communities have followed the path at the same rate. There remain many communities in both developed and developing countries that appear to remain 'stuck' in the more confrontational advocacy-cautionary range. The presence of these two platforms within community groups can result in significant levels of irreconcilable conflict.

The socio-cultural effects of tourism in terms of cultural impacts, tourist-host interactions and tourism development. They have not been identified as either positive or negative, as in many cases such identification is an arbitrary position based on an individual's personal views, circumstances and position in the community. While important to consider, the complexities behind such prescriptive designation is not in the scope of this introductory discussion on tourism and communities. Many of these effects are not the sole province of tourism, however as tourism becomes considered more and more a means for regenerating declining communities and responding to some of the consequences communities face from globalisation, building tourism is becoming a significant development strategy.

Communities are also faced with many issues surrounding the increasing pace of change. As well as creating specific issues and impacts, tourism also facilitates and even increases rates of change (Murphy and Murphy, forthcoming). Film-induced tourism has the potential to increase the pace of change, particularly where such tourism has not been anticipated or planned for. The primary aim of this thesis is to examine elements of change by outlining the process undertaken to test the hypothesis that Film-induced tourism increases the rate of physical change in a community, and to identify the range of attitudes towards change between stakeholders. The case of the Australian television series, Sea

Change and the Victorian coastal village of Barwon Heads where it was filmed, provides some evidence of this issue of change and its consequences. In the particular case outlined in this thesis, the physical changes are illustrated, followed by an outline of the changes that were noted by residents and regular visitors to the town. Finally, the attitudes of these stakeholders towards such change are considered by looking at one particular development that had initially polarised the community.

THE SEA CHANGE STORY

Over a two year period from 1998 to 2000, three 13 episode series of the Australian comedy-drama Sea Change were screened on Australian television (with the first series being repeated immediately prior to the screening of the second). It featured quirky characters and a small (usually) friendly community, tinged with the obligatory 'love interest' (between the lead characters Laura and Diver Dan, and later, Max) and rapacious self-serving developer. The series was extremely popular, with a reach1 in Australia's five capital cities of 43 per cent, the highest being in Melbourne (a few hour's drive from Barwon Heads) at 46.2 per cent.

It continually ranked highly in its timeslot and won numerous awards such as the Most Outstanding Drama Series for 1999 and 2000 in the Australian TV Week Logie Awards, as well as numerous individual awards for the actors. Almost immediately, visitation increased to the small seaside village of Barwon Heads where it was predominantly filmed, known as 'Pearl Bay' in the series. Barwon Heads is a quintessential Australian holiday seaside village, some 20 km from Geelong, Victoria's largest regional city, and 100km from the state's capital, Melbourne. It has traditionally hosted a high level of family and budget holiday-makers, with visitation levels peaking in the summer holiday month of January.

THE RESEARCH APPROACH

In order to test the hypothesis introduced earlier and to provide some analytical depth, a longitudinal study of Barwon

Heads was undertaken over four years, from 1998 to 2001 inclusive. By adopting a qualitative, primarily participant-observation based approach, such changes could be observed and recorded. Personal diary notations and photographs were used to track and record physical changes. In order to ascertain the perceived effects of the physical and attitudinal changes of regular visitors as well as local residents, a series of interviews and surveys were undertaken throughout the period when Sea Change's influence was at its greatest–shortly after the series commenced to some 18 months after it finished screening on Australian television.

Triangulation was achieved by taking a multi-perspective approach that included surveys and interviews as well as the aforementioned participant-observation. A self-completion survey was mailed to a random sample of Barwon Heads' residents, as well as further self-completion mail-back questionnaires of visitors that were made available at strategic places in the township during 1998, 1999 and 2000. Consequently, issues and attitudes from both residents and visitors were identified as they arose. The issues were then developed in follow-up interviews in 2001. These interviews regarding the changes to the town and Park were conducted with people at Barwon Heads during the 2001 Spring school holiday break, resulting in 23 responses from residents and 56 from regular visitors to the town.

The questions focused on the impacts of Sea Change on the town, the series and opinions of what had become a controversial restaurant development at the site of one of Diver Dan's home, and what they saw as similarities between the town and the fictional series. Apart from some basic demographic questions, the responses in all of the surveys and interviews were unprompted, allowing for a broad range of responses and a more in-depth qualitative study. Acceptable response levels to open, unprompted questions are dramatically different from that of closed questions. In Pearce from a Canadian study by Keogh in 1990, compares such rates on responses towards impacts of tourism. Keogh's study suggests what could be considered a reasonable (or 'interesting') response rate from unprompted open questions as being far fewer than for the closed questions. In addition, the open question provides opportunities for unexpected responses, which is the essence of research. The study demonstrates that acceptable rates of response to open questions should be considered in terms of the type of question and response given, not merely frequency. This is important for the survey research discussed in this thesis, much of which was approached using open questions.

LIMITATIONS

Participant-observation, a form of qualitative research, has been criticised as being biased through the influence of the researcher, both during the research and the interpretation of the results. Yin proposes the use of triangulation in such cases. This has been applied in this study through keeping detailed photographic records along with diaries of the personal observations and, where relevant, community, tourism and business leaders were approached formally and informally. Finally, the series of questionnaires and interviews conducted with residents and visitors provide further triangulation. Nevertheless, as with all research, the interpretation of the findings is based on my own expertise, background and knowledge.

SIMILARITIES BETWEEN BARWON HEADS AND PEARL BAY

The physical changes to Barwon Heads are outlined and illustrated pares after some consideration of the perceptions of the primary stakeholder groups of residents and regular visitors, regarding perceived any similarities between the fictional series and the actual town. In a survey undertaken in Easter 2001, residents and regular visitors were asked about the similarities between Barwon Heads and the fictional town of Pearl Bay. Their responses to the open question seem to revolve around what they considered to be the particular nature of a small coastal town, which was closely linked to the people and their personalities. What is most interesting here in the difference between visitors and local residents is where the latter displays a much higher denial rate about any similarities between the series and the town. This is not surprising as much of the participant observation research showed that there was a general resistance towards being 'pigeonholed' into a quaint, quirky caricature, especially when the media was striving to do exactly this. A report by ABC TV on a controversy surrounding the development of the restaurant at Diver Dan's home irritated the locals, many of whom felt they were inappropriately represented through inferred links with the characters in the series.

Nevertheless, of those who saw some similarities between the series and Barwon Heads, there was general consensus between the locals and visitors. The only notable discrepancy was the perception from the local residents that it was the small town size that was the most significant similarity between the series and the town. While being the smallest reported similarity, the characters (people and personalities) portrayed in Sea Change have nevertheless remained a strong element of interest in the township. Considering that 61% of locals saw no similarities a third of those residents who acknowledge some similarity is a strong response. This raises the notion that it is the characters as well as the Australian scenery that holds the greatest key to film-induced tourism for this type of programme.

Such quirky series tend to be character-driven, with these results supporting that notion, compared with than the power of the Australian countryside as seen in movies such as The Man from Snowy River, Crocodile Dundee and various 'Ned Kelly' movies that tended to use the uniqueness of the bush as a character in its own right. While visitors were still attracted to the site, it can be argued that they are motivated by the stories and characters rather than the scenery. This proposition is discussed further in Beeton. In any service industry, and even more so with tourism, the attitudes of the various parties are extremely important as they influence the nature of the exchange and relationship between them all. The perceptions of relevance of the fictional series to the actual town is important as it may influence expectations and behaviour of tourists emulating the fictional film. However, it is also important also to determine the actual situation, which is now considered in terms of the physical changes that took place.

HOW SEA CHANGE CHANGED BARWON HEADS

After a state of decline, with many shops and services closing down, followed by a period of stagnation, the physical nature of the town itself experienced rapid change after the commencement of Sea Change, evidenced by an increased presence of visitor services such as cafes and restaurants as well as soaring housing prices. It is difficult to isolate Sea Change as the only cause for the most obvious changes, such as those to the main street shopping precinct; however the TV series has been acknowledged by the local community and tourism industry as a major contributor.

There were certainly some physical changes that came about as a direct result of the series, particularly at the Barwon Heads Park camping ground where it was filmed. Over the first twelve months since the commencement of airing Sea Change on television, the main street shopping strip experienced some dramatic changes. In 1998, shops were vacant and closing down, in particular basic residential services such as the green grocer, butcher and baker. While those actual shops did not re-open, as of January 2000 all shop-fronts were occupied.

The main shopping precinct now boasted a predominance of tourist services as opposed to the general services that had been lost. In place of a defunct butcher's shop, closed Chinese restaurant and vacant new shops were now two new cafés, a bar and restaurant, a second-hand book shop, gift shop, Indonesian import shop, an additional fish and chip shop, a take-away chicken shop and a second surf shop. For general services such as banking, hardware supplies, groceries, meat and large supermarket shopping residents and visitors to the area were required to travel to the neighbouring town of Ocean Grove, some five kilometres away. However, it is in the Barwon Heads Park and camping ground where some of the more obvious and, at times, problematic changes have occurred. This area is the site of the most recognisable aspects of Sea Change, namely the residences of the main romantic leads, now known as 'Laura's Beach House' and 'Diver Dan's Shed', as well as a further site of the home of second series lead, Max. From Barwon Heads Park, the images of fishing boats, the bridge over the Barwon River (which is central to the narrative) and the tidal views feature significantly in the series, and were more than merely a visual backdrop to much of the action.

These aspects are also among the main attractions for campers and other recreational visitors to the Park. The prominent signage at the entrance of the park is the first indication of change, and one of the most evident and lasting elements of the Sea Change legacy, along with directional signage from the main road. During an intense period of participantobservation research in Barwon Heads Park, while staying in the cottage used as Laura's residence in the series on a site visit, which is situated in the government-owned and operated camping ground with a predominance of caravan and camping sites, so there is no fencing around the cottage. Tourists were continuously taking photos of the cottage, while others ran up onto the veranda to peer through the windows at all times of the day and night.

This created a great deal of stress and insecurity, especially at night time, whereas in the past this had never been an issue when I had stayed there, even when being the only resident in the Park. That this was not a one-off experience was confirmed by the Park Manager, who recounted stories of single women leaving the cottage early due to a strong sense of insecurity. It was at this time that Park Management erected notices that read, "Visitors are requested to respect the privacy of the beach house residents". Park Management emphasised their concern over these privacy invasions (which continued regardless of the signs), suggesting that the signs may not be sufficient, and they may need to eventually fence off the site. This would restrict public access to the foreshore walk which may contravene regulations surrounding the management of camping grounds on public land. The increasing number of visitors wishing to view and photograph the cottage and its surrounds was also imposing on campers adjacent to the cottage. By mid 2001, a second cottage had been built next to 'Laura's', with plans to build a third. While the threatened fencing had not happened, earthworks and vegetation plantings were added to discourage people from walking right up to the cottages in order to gain some privacy for guests was not able to test their efficacy personally as the cottages were booked out for over six months in advance.

A further group of 'Sea Change Cottages' in a different area of the park had also been constructed. They (or the site) had nothing directly to do with the series, yet management saw obvious marketing benefits in using the reference. In an in-depth interview, the manager also explained that the camping site at the end of the park next to the Bluff is now the most popular camping site, as the tea-tree was cleared to provide views of the mouth of the Barwon River for the shooting of the third series where it was used by the romantic lead who replaced Diver Dan, Max, as his home. Unlike Laura's Cottage and Dan's Shed, which already existed, the actual building in the series was purely temporary (due to the sensitive environmental nature of the site), being constructed out of two shipping containers, which were easily dismantled. The nature of the temporary building for Max's 'home' in the park is also illustrated.

PERCEPTIONS OF AND ATTITUDES TOWARDS CHANGE

It is recognised that people's attitudes and perceptions can be behind many of the issues of conflict and power relations that arise in relation to community development and change. While we often consider attitudes towards the more social elements, the physical changes brought about through tourism in general, and filminduced tourism in particular, tend to be neglected in terms of residents and visitor attitudes. In the case of Barwon Heads, there is a group of regular visitors who have been holidaying in the area for generations. They have a strong sense of ownership and vested interest, however have little or no direct influence over the future of the town. This group is an important community stakeholder group, and such disenfranchisement and neglect can be disastrous in the long term. It was this group that formed the majority of responses to the interviews conducted in September 2001. The interviewees' comments regarding the impact that they felt the series has had on the town.

All but one respondent were aware of the series, so the comments are based on their own personal observations and are the result of open-ended, unprompted questioning. Regardless as to whether they felt that Barwon Heads was similar to Pearl Bay as depicted in the series (27 per cent overall saw no similarities), all those interviewed (visitors and residents) believed that it had an effect on the town. This is important as it indicates the level and range of changes the perceived influence of film-induced tourism and the changes it can bring about. Comments were more favourable than negative, indicating that Barwon Heads was not suffering the negative effects seen at towns in the United Kingdom affected by film-induced tourism such as Goathland, the film-site for the UK TV series, Heartbeat.

Some of the typical comments from locals and visitors include "Put on to tourist maps–before may not have known where Barwon Heads is"; "It's good for the tourism industry and real estate"; "Always busy; more upmarket shops; helped real estate prices"; "It put it on the map, whereas Ocean Grove used to overpower it. No longer the 'small sister'–has come of age. Good for business". With what may be considered as a small sample size of 23 local residents, such a proportion would not be considered significant under a parametric quantitative research paradigm.

However, as noted in the part on the research approach, due to these comments being unprompted, they are significant. In addition, in qualitative methodology it is often the exception that is of interest. Local residents were particularly aware of the role that Sea Change played in raising the awareness of the town as well as the added benefit of spreading visitation throughout the year, away from the peak summer and school holiday times. Real estate price increases were seen more as a positive than negative aspect, even though a relatively small proportion of the residents commented that it was not good, especially for young people trying to purchase a home. Their comments include: "Increase in interest throughout the year–used to be dead in winter"; "Been great for Barwon Heads. All shops are open–weren't a few years ago", "On our knees before they came… New lease of life–houses now selling for $100,000–couldn't sell at all before then".

There were only a few negative comments from the locals interviewed, primarily along the lines of: "Real estate too high, so local young people can't afford to buy homes". Visitors also noted the increase in the number and 'quality' of shops and cafes as well as the increase in year-round visitation, possibly reflecting the time of year of this survey–while it was in a school holiday period, it is still traditionally a quiet time at Barwon Heads. Consequently, they would have been more aware of increased visitation at that time.

CHANGING ATTITUDES TOWARDS CHANGE

More important than actual changes are the attitudes towards that change. When visitor interviews were conducted at Easter 2000, a restaurant development that incorporated Diver Dan's Shed was under construction, prompting many negative comments regarding the changes to the site, which was particularly unattractive and fenced off at that stage, just under half wanted the place to be left alone. This was also an issue for locals, evidenced in the survey conducted in April 1999. Results from the September 2001 interviews indicate a more positive outlook to the development, from visitors as well as locals, even though some, especially residents, felt it was too expensive, commercial and tourist-focused, as illustrated by comments such as: "Doesn't entirely meet working class–more for tourists not locals", "It's too expensive for locals and exclusive–not locally friendly".

There was also some actual turn-around in opinions, with a small number of locals and a fifth of visitors admitting that they were originally against it, but now support the development. "Originally thought it would never be good, but now think it looks great"; "I was originally against the building–but now don't mind it. I sit down there a bit". While small, the direction of the change is worth noting as these were once again unprompted responses and can represent an even greater shift. This shift in attitude of regular visitors is also interesting in that this group, along with newer residents, had been most resistant to change.

The photos of the site demonstrate the extent of the development and the retention of the shed's façade which was a region of concern of many protests. The front part of Dan's shed has been retained and incorporated into the restaurant–it has not been re-painted, rather left with the 'distressed' façade that is now so familiar to millions of Australians. These photos show the 'before and after' versions of the site development. If we take these attitudes and correlate them with Jafari's aforementioned platforms, the overall position of the community at Barwon Heads is in the second 'cautionary' platform. Some 'adaptancy' is evident, however the move into a knowledge-base in terms of film-induced tourism and community development is non-existent. For Barwon Heads to truly embrace and develop in this field, the knowledge of individual groups and stakeholders must be expanded.

WHEN FICTION AND REALITY COLLIDE: IMPLICATIONS FOR COMMUNITY PLANNERS

The elements of the Barwon Heads study outlined in this thesis demonstrate the complex nature of film-induced tourism in small communities. Film-induced tourism has significant effects, but they are not easy to isolate due to its integrative nature. Many of the changes seen in Barwon Heads may have occurred without Sea Change–the region was experiencing economic recovery after a severe downturn, and buyers who could no longer afford other seaside areas were also moving in. However, Sea Change certainly accelerated the pace of change; a point agreed to by tourism and community leaders. In addition, the perceptions of stakeholders such as residents and regular visitors can change at an uneven rate, making them difficult to predict. Yet, perceptions are important, as they influence the nature of social interactions between and among residents, regular visitors and tourists. Resentment towards visitors and between community members can create an environment that is poor in terms of social capital. This will most likely ultimately translate into economic paucity as the region becomes less and less attractive to visit and live in. However, as demonstrated with the restaurant development, opinions regarding change can alter over time, so careful thought must be applied in these circumstances, particularly when one group may be applying undue influence.

Simply bowing to the most prominent opinion may not be appropriate. As noted by Hall, understanding the power relations in a community is crucial to its development. While not highly evident in this study to date, film-induced tourism that is characterdriven has the potential to 'encourage' a place and its people to emulate those characters, which may result in an alteration of the nature of that community. There was some indication of a few of the Barwon Heads shopkeepers consciously taking on elements of the characters, however this was quite limited.

Ultimately, any change to the community will most likely depend on how long the influence of the series persists, and in the case outlined in this thesis, whether it has encouraged people to make their own 'sea change' to Barwon Heads. Nevertheless, regardless as to whether this does remain in the public consciousness, the impression created by such a popular series will last in some form or other for many years. The Sea Change cottages, caravan park signage and restaurant at Diver Dan's remain concrete reminders for visitors and residents. So, what does all this mean in terms of community planning and development? As it is usually not the primary reason for filming a TV series or movie, film-induced tourism is an incidental/accidental outcome, which is different to most more conscious forms of tourism development.

Film directors and producers are primarily concerned with getting their movie or series filmed, not how this will translate into tourism in the future. This, however can change when they are involved in a long-running TV series that will require some goodwill from residents and other stakeholders. In the case of Sea Change, the on-site filming of the series was over approximately four blocks of time with extended breaks in between, not a long-term ongoing process as for series such as the UK produced Heartbeat that has been regularly filmed at Goathland since 1991.

Regardless, the limited understanding by local councils, community developers and destination marketers of some of the intricacies of the legacies of such 'unplanned' tourism can result in under-realised benefits, or at the worst unplanned social and environmental degradation. Once again, the call goes our for pro-active community planning, not simply reactive responses. Local government in particular must become more aware of not only the potential of tourism, but also the impacts it may have and issues that may arise–attracting visitors is only the start. By the time these issues become apparent, it is often too late to correct them.

2

Examining the Role of Zoos and the Media

INTRODUCTION

The increased prevalence of educational material in the media means that the role of zoos in providing education is being called into question. Indeed, there are claims that zoos have become "educationally redundant", given the role of other public communication avenues such as television, newspapers and radio. In particular, several authors claim that wildlife documentaries now play an increasing role in achieving public education of wildlife related issues. Therefore the aim of this thesis is to examine the role that zoos play in public education. The approach taken is to examine learning that occurs at an Australian zoo, and to determine the role that the zoo plays in providing information, as compared to that learnt from other sources such as documentaries. A case study approach is taken, utilising Werribee Open Range Zoo near Melbourne.

THE HISTORY AND ROLE OF ZOOS

The history of keeping and displaying animals for recreational purposes has received extensive coverage in the literature for many years. An examination of this literature reveals that while animals have been kept in captivity for thousands of years, the role of these collections has transformed over time. As Markwell argues, institutions such as zoos 'serve to construct and present nature in particular ways just as to particular historical and cultural contexts'. Originally, private animal collections were symbols of the affluence, power and prestige of their owners. While the first modern zoos, which presented animals for public viewing in a park-like setting, were founded in Europe in the 1700's, it was not until the 1800's that the appeal of zoos became more widespread, following the opening of the London zoo in 1828. Originally London Zoo was based on a philosophy of scientific interest, whilst also offering recreational experiences.

For the Victorian zoogoer, they 'wanted only to satisfy their curiosity and merely look at specimens of exotic wild animals', while to the zoologists, these visitors 'were merely the source of the means by which they could pursue their scientific interests'. Since the 1800's zoological societies such as the Zoological Society of London and the New York Zoological Society have been citing public education, scientific research and species preservation as benefits of having zoos. However, it was not until the 1950s and 60s, that a reduction in national rivalry and an increase in international cooperation resulted in the formation of the World Zoo Organisation, and a formalised commitment to the objectives of conservation, education, research and recreation. However, the rise of the animal rights movement in the 1970's meant that the ethics of keeping animals in captivity were given more consideration and the debate over the justification for zoos has now been raging for several decades.

THE DEBATE OVER THE ROLE OF ZOOS IN PUBLIC EDUCATION

Sommer may have been one of the first to question the educational objectives of zoos. However, the foundation of this debate is arguably the publication of Dale Jamieson's stage "Against Zoos" in Peter Singer's book on animal rights, in which Jamieson assesses the achievements of zoos in the same four domains–education, conservation, recreation and research. As the title suggests, Jamieson is particularly critical of zoo practice and sceptical of their achievements and argues that there is no moral justification for the existence of zoos. In response to Jamieson's object, Chiszar published "For Zoos" which contains a rebuttal of many of Jamieson's arguments and several assertions about the achievements of zoos. Needless to say, Jamieson responded in 1995 and the debate continues until this day but has expanded to include many other commentators. A result of the academic debate is that zoos have begun to introspectively evaluate their role in society and the service they provide.

This internal evaluation has led zoos to reposition themselves to increase and promote their involvement in public education and in-situ conservation, because under scrutiny, justifications such as recreation, and ex-situ conservation and related research appear to lack substance. It is generally accepted that education is one of the key roles of the modern zoo.

Broad and Weiler's review of literature concerning the history of zoo education identifies four key objectives or outcomes:

- An educational experience that is recreational, enjoyable and satisfying;
- The cognitive learning of facts regarding animals, and about the function and management of the zoo or exhibit;
- The development of positive attitudes including a concern for and commitment to wildlife conservation; and
- Behavioural outcomes, including appropriate on-site behaviour and longterm environmentally responsible behaviour.

These objectives or outcomes are not necessarily unrelated, as enjoyable learning experiences can in fact be designed and delivered in ways that influence attitudes and behaviour. It is also likely that there is some degree of linearity to these objectives. Indeed, Hungerford and Volk identify awareness and knowledge of issues as a precursor to environmentally responsible behaviour. This framework has been operationalised by zoos, for instance, by Melbourne Zoo in their design of Trail of the Elephants exhibit. The importance of general zoo education and the more specific educational objective of fostering environmentally responsible behaviour is evidenced by the extent to which the zoo community has embraced this objective at an international, national, and organisational level. Internationally, The World Zoo Conservation Strategy states that conservation education is 'a specially important element of zoo education'. In Australia, the theme of the 2003 ARAZPA2 Conference-'Education-The Key to Conservation' demonstrates how important this role is to the local zoo community.

However, despite some authors arguing that zoos have, or have the potential to play, a significant role in relation to public education and zoos stating that they have a strong focus on education, some people believe zoos have not demonstrated their success in achieving their aims. Consequently, there have been many calls for further research examining the education achievements of zoos. Furthermore, despite the actual or potential educational benefit that zoos may have, an additional issue is whether zoos' role in public education is necessary given the alternative educational sources that are available through other media. As Hancocks asserts, the media have been informing the public on threats to wildlife for well over two decades. Likewise, Beckmann argues that 'interest in wildlife has been fostered by the mass media, particularly television'.

Margodt claims that it is 'often argued that zoos have become educationally redundant because of the many nature programmes on television', whilst other commentators refer to the media more broadly as performing a public education role. For instance, Sommer contends that before technological media advances, the role that zoos played in providing a visual encounter of, and learning opportunities about animals had merit. However, he goes on to argue that this role has been made redundant by the availability of animal imagery in wildlife documentaries, books and magazines.

Similarly, animal welfare organisations WSPA and The Born Free Foundation examined zoos' claims to be 'conservation centres' aimed at saving endangered species. Their report concludes that 'most zoos do little to educate people about how the public can help to conserve wild species and that many zoos cause considerable physical and psychological animal suffering'. Furthermore, it is argued that zoos have been undermined as a 'source of education and inspiration', because 'high quality information about wild animals and the issues affecting them is widely available from television, video, books and radio. In addition, Jamieson questions whether confining animals is necessary to educate people and wonders whether the same educational outcomes could be achieved through other avenues such as 'films, slides, lectures and so forth'.

Even some zoo visitors have shown support for claims that zoos may be redundant, as Shackley found in an empirical study, that 21% of zoo visitors felt that television and radio wildlife programmes do make visits to the zoo redundant. In contrast to claims that zoos are educationally redundant, Andersen argues that zoos do provide an important educational role and that documentaries can be misleading. He suggests that with developments in enrichment and exhibit design, the behaviour of animals in zoos has become more natural than that of 10-15 years ago, and concludes that 'the value of zoos as a place to learn has increased enormously'. He contends that viewing animals in a zoo context is much more representative than images viewed in documentaries and other media.

To demonstrate his point Andersen argues that lions in a zoo rest and sleep for most of the day, as they would in the wild, and therefore visitors observing lions in a zoo see a more realistic representation of lions, than those watching a TV documentary, where lions are shown being active for the majority of the time. Several other distortions in documentaries, such as speed, light, size, and distribution have also been identified by the popular documentary presenter David Attenborough, who acknowledges that 'there is precious little that is natural, in that sense, in any film'. Despite strong arguments both supporting and criticising the educational value of zoos, there is a dearth of empirical research supporting either side. There is also a lack of research into the comparative roles of zoos and the media in providing public education. The research reported in this thesis forms part of a larger project critically examining the role of zoo education in fostering environmentally responsible behaviour, in the context of captive wildlife attractions, and with particular reference to Zoos Victoria.

While the focus of this project is the achievement of both short and long-term environmentally responsible behaviour visitor awareness or knowledge of threats to wildlife and/or their habitats have been identified as an important precursor to visitors undertaking environmentally responsible behaviour. Therefore, initial data collection focused on identifying the extent to which visitors to Werribee Open Range Zoo were able to recall hearing information about threats during their zoo visit. Furthermore, due to the debate regarding the educational redundancy of zoos, this study also addressed the research gap by examining whether visitors were exposed to new information regarding threats, or information they have already been exposed to from different sources, such as the media.

THE CASE STUDY

Three properties are managed by Zoos Victoria; Melbourne Zoo, WORZ and Healesville Sanctuary. WORZ is located approximately 35 kilometres south-west of Melbourne and has an annual visitation of approximately 200,000 people. It first opened to the public in 1983, having originally been established as an agistment property for the Melbourne Zoo. The entry fee to WORZ includes a 50 minute bus tour with personal commentary. The bus tour is the only means of accessing a large proportion of the zoo.

METHODOLOGY

Face-to-face structured interviews were administered at the WORZ exit, during a six week period in June and July, 2004. A total of 144 visitor interviews were completed, at a response rate of 85%. A further three visitors were not eligible to undertake an interview as they had not been on a bus tour and the focus of the interview was on information communicated to visitors during the bus tour. A systematic, stratified sample was used in selecting visitors for interview. Systematic sampling reduced any bias from the researcher in the selection of individuals, by using a next person basis to approach visitors as they neared a predetermined point by the exit to the zoo. Stratified sampling ensured interview times were drawn from a range of strata, with data collected at different times of the day, on weekdays and weekends, and during school holiday and non-holiday weeks.

Interviews were undertaken with visitors aged 18 years and older. Interviews were used to collect data relating to visitor demographics and recall. Visitors were initially asked if they could recall hearing any information on threats as part of their tour, and those that could were subsequently asked what the information was and whether they had already known this information. If they had heard the information before, they were asked about the source of their knowledge, and were encouraged to list as many sources of information as they thought appropriate.

RESULTS

The survey group consisted of 144 respondents. Sixty two respondents were repeat visitors and 82 were first time visitors. Of the repeat visitors, the average time since their last visit was 3.8 years however this varied considerably between respondents. The vast majority of respondents were from Australia with only eight respondents indicating that they lived overseas. Of the Australian residents, 87% were from the local state of Victoria, with the remainder living in other states, notably Queensland and New South Wales/Australian Capital Territory. Respondents were asked if they could recall hearing any information on threats as part of their tour. Of the 144 respondents, 113 could recall and 31 couldn't recall hearing such information.

There were no differences in ability to recall hearing threats between males and females school holiday and non school holiday visitors and repeat and first time visitors. Those

113 visitors that could recall hearing threats were then asked whether they had known about the threats prior to hearing them on the bus tour. Five different In each of the five possibilities, the educational role of the zoo is labelled.

Four different labels are used:

1. Redundant-where the role of zoos is educationally superfluous because other sources have already fulfilled this role
2. Effective-where the zoo has provided the respondent with new information on threats to animals and/or their habitats that can be recalled
3. Enhancing-where the zoo has clarified or provided more specific details regarding pre-existing information known from other sources
4. Ineffective-where information on threats was not given, was not heard or if it was heard, could not be recalled.

The 47 respondents felt that while they had heard information about threats on the bus tour, they had previously known this information, and so had learned nothing new. Despite stating that they could recall hearing information on threats, a further nine respondents were unable to recall what the information was. Forty three respondents and felt that they had learned at least some, if not all new information regarding threats on the bus tour. A further 14 respondents indicated that the information provided on the bus tour enhanced their previous understanding rather than providing them with new information.

A total of 77 respondents indicated that they had previous knowledge of some or all of the threats they recalled from the bus tour. These 77 were asked to identify the source of their knowledge, and their responses were collated and placed into nine categories that emerged from the data. A summary of responses. Television was mentioned as a source of information on threats by 42% of respondents who indicated that they had previous knowledge of some or all of the threats they recalled from the bus tour. Documentaries, and television channels that almost exclusively run documentaries, accounted for the next highest proportion of respondents with 29%. In total, general media or specifically identified media sources accounted for 67% of responses.

A large proportion of these media sources were television and wildlife documentaries. Non media sources of information totalled 24% of responses. The remaining 9% of responses were listed in the "Everywhere, general knowledge, just know" category and it is not known how respondents became aware of the information.

It is possible that the information could have been derived from media or non media sources or both. It is also evident that there is some overlap between the nine categories. For instance, it is likely that most documentaries are viewed on television. Similarly, television, radio and published material could be subsets of media.

DISCUSSION

The results revealed that the educational role of the zoo can be considered redundant for 33% of respondents, effective for 30%, enhancing for 10% and ineffective for 28% in regard to teaching the public about threats. The study also examined the learning sources of those respondents who indicated that they had previous knowledge of some or all of the threats they recalled from the bus tour. Media communication avenues, particularly television and wildlife documentaries were the main sources of that knowledge. These findings support claims in the literature that wildlife documentaries play a role in achieving public education of wildlife related issues.

The combination of:

- Visitors for whom the zoo was educationally redundant with
- The prevalence of responses indicating that television and wildlife documentaries were sources of previous knowledge, provides some support for the assertions made by Sommer, WSPA and the Born Free Foundation and Margodt, that television and documentaries are one of the primary sources that negate the educational role of zoos.

However, whether the educational role of zoos is in fact redundant for visitors who had previous knowledge of all of the threats they recalled from the bus tour is an issue that can be debated. Although we have labelled the zoo's educational role as being redundant for some visitors, it could be argued that by hearing information again, their existing knowledge was reinforced. To directly refute the contentions of redundancy, this study has shown that the zoo's educational role was effective or enhancing for 39.6% of respondents. The question might be asked: for zoos to justify their existence on educational grounds, what percentage of visitors must learn new information during their visit, and must learning occur about every issue communicated? Due to the exploratory nature of this study and that only one particular category of information was examined, it is impossible to state whether this level of effectiveness is adequate.

A further question arises as to whether any level of educational benefit is an adequate justification for the existence of zoos. This at least in part a moral evaluation, requiring the benefits of keeping animals in captivity to be compared to any negative impacts on the animals. For Jamieson who has a 'moral presumption against keeping wild animals in captivity', it may well be that the perceived benefits, educational or otherwise, will never outweigh the perceived negative impacts. In comparison, for Chiszar who believes that 'professionally managed zoos and aquariums do not inflict harm upon animals', the issue is that zoos be well managed to ensure there are benefits and no negatives.

A third position is that individual animals in zoos can be considered as ambassadors for their species and that any negative impact on the individual animals within zoos is outweighed by the benefits realised by their wild counterparts through conservation and education. Following on from this, the classification of zoo's educational role as ineffective is also debateable. While a visitor may not learn about threats during their zoo visit, it is suggested by Kerr that a zoo visit may stimulate an interest in wildlife, which leads visitors to watch documentaries or to read objects about wildlife, which they may not have done otherwise. Hence zoo visits may induce learning at a later stage rather than during the zoo visit. Instead of zoos being considered educationally redundant or ineffective, an alternative view is that their may be a symbiotic relationship between wildlife documentaries and zoos. For example, while not specifically referring to learning, in an empirical study of zoo visitors, Shackley found that 65% felt that wildlife programmes enhance enjoyment of a zoo visit, and she goes on to suggest that zoo visitors 'want to see animals which have recently featured in television wildlife documentaries'. In addition, visitors may be inspired to seek out further information as a result of the zoo visit or they may have previous knowledge enhanced, as our results have demonstrated.

The role of zoos as reinforcement, enhancement or inducement agents does not appear to have gained attention in the literature. It may be beneficial for zoos to position themselves as performing these roles. Given the rise of media communication avenues to this point, it seems unlikely that the educational overlap with zoos will decrease and so reinforcement may well be a role that zoos are in a position to undertake. To do this, it may be beneficial to link public education messages to those being conveyed in the media, particularly those found in documentaries and on other television shows. In addition to the impact that wildlife documentaries may or may not have on the public education role of zoos, several authors claim wildlife documentaries also influence wildlife tourism and ecotourism more broadly.

Therefore, wildlife documentaries have induced participation in other leisure/tourism pursuits that provide opportunity for learning. For instance, Swarbrooke claims that the growth in ecotourism is at least partly due to television programmes about wildlife and specific habitats. This raises a final philosophical point: if zoos are considered educationally redundant because of the prevalence of other sources of educational information, then does it follow that other cultural institutions and leisure pursuits are also educationally redundant?

CONCLUSION

This study has largely corroborated assertions that wildlife documentaries and television are providing similar information as zoos. However, assertions made about zoos being educationally redundant due to the media appear to lack substance. Various media/zoo relationships have been posited for the most part arguing that the sources of information should be considered as complimentary. In a world where there is ever increasing pressure on wildlife and their habitats, providing and reinforcing information pertaining to threats could be considered vital to their survival. If providing this information through multiple avenues can reach a wider audience, then all mechanisms should be considered valid. However, to be most educationally beneficial, it would be ideal for zoos and the media to join forces and cooperate in this campaign.

3

Teaching Tourism, Image and Media Relationships

INTRODUCTION

Tourism is an industry very much dependent on discretionary decisions. The trade offs potential tourists are considering can be as diverse as deciding between different destinations, to buying a new television or even house, going to a musical at the local theatre, to saving for retirement. In this environment it is image and perceptions that determine what the choice will be made between, and more importantly what the choice will be.

Increasingly noted is the role of the media in providing this image. This is obviously a very important aspect of tourism, conceptually, and for destination and business management.

This thesis presents considerations and reflections on the development and implementation of a unit expounding the relationships between tourism, image and the media. In the presentation of this the conceptual foundation for the relationships will be briefly introduced, followed by the pertinent aspects of the relationships between tourism, image and the media.

The structure of the unit will be presented, including assessment outlines, objectives and outcomes. Then a discussion of reflections on the tourism, image and media unit and future undertakings will be presented. Finally considerations, implications and conclusions will be provided.

CONCEPTUAL FOUNDATION

The relationship between tourism and image has received a lot of coverage in the tourism literature.

The extensive relationship between image and tourism has been presented in the literature for its role in:

- Creating expectations;
- Marketing strategy and market segmentation;
- Destination selection;
- As a form of consumption;
- Construction and reinforcing images of people and place;
- Effects on prospective markets

Conceptually the investigation of these roles provides great insights into the field of tourism. Additionally there are enormous practical implications of these roles of image. This perspective is very much functional, though it is acknowledged and appreciated that the power of image presentation and interpretation creates or reinforce gazes, and in this there is a critical cultural interpretation and definition of what image is, means and does. To briefly expand and clarify, a functional perspective focuses on the function of image, and especially the importance in marketing and destination selection.

This perspective also focuses on the formation of image from the individual's perspective. This initially started in the role for planning and marketing though, as a greater understanding of the significance of destination image has occurred, there has been an orientation towards processes of image formation and building an understanding of the specific parts of image that influence decision-making. It must be noted that the critical cultural perspective related to representation and the cultural, political or social context within which they take place was also included within the unit. Additionally, the literature is identifying the source of image as coming increasingly from the media and particularly the mass media.

Thus, it was concluded that image is a very important conceptual and managerial area of tourism, though this is increasingly being provided and determined by the media.

Additionally it was noted that in image formation that the organic and autonomous agents were perceived as the most credible. Nonetheless, there had instead been a predominate focus on real agents of destinations, and reference to induced agents within the literature. Due to the importance image and of the organic agent it was proposed that this was a crucial area, over and that of tourism or destination marketing for tourism managers to appreciate and understand. This was especially the case as pertinent to the destination manager was the management of destination image.

This had been noted as the increased competition not only for maintaining vibrant cities, but also to attract tourists in an increasingly competitive tourism environment. For destination managers an inclusive destination management strategy needs to be developed and implemented. Part of this strategy is the management of image. Also important in this process is the potential tourists' source of image, and the decreasing influence destinations have over these images. Overall, the breadth of importance of destination image in tourism is immense, though it has been identified that image's role in the decision making process was most important for destination managers.

In developing the unit there were a number of underpinnings in the relationship between image and the media. This needed to be contextualised within the much broader tourism conceptual foundation. Based on this foundation the pertinent conceptual aspects were identified as destination image, image formation, decision-making, the media and media tourism. Pertinent management aspects identified were image management, media management, promoting place with media, and media tourism management.

STRUCTURE

The unit was designed and delivered at Waiariki Institute of Technology, Rotorua, New Zealand. It was designed as an elective third year unit within the Tourism Management degree. Within this programme, all students had completed at least three tourism units, and thus had an introductory understanding to the study of tourism. At Waiariki semesters are 15 weeks.

Considering the points and the need for the inclusion of pertinent aspects, the following learning objectives were identified:

- Identify and discuss the relationship between tourism and image
- Identify and discuss the formation of destination image
- Discuss the role of the media in tourism
- Discuss the role of fictional media in tourism
- Analyse films' role in tourism

The following will briefly outline the main learning achievements of each lecture time. The specific content, learning objectives and tutorial exercises of each class. In the first lecture Morgan and Pritchard was the primary reading and was used to establish the role of image in culture. Within this context, and the foundation of students' previous tourism knowledge, connections were established between the three explicit elements of tourism, image and the media.

The main connection of concern identified was between the tourist and the destination and especially how tourists form images of destinations through the media; tourist's perception of a destination, positive or negative, is based on these images; tourists form motivations to visit place and expectations about that place through these images; image is the interface between the tourist and the destination; and the media provides this image. A film, A Passage to India, was watched for this week. The use of A Passage to India had two purposes. First the film was used to present examples of tourism and exemplify the role of media and image in tourism. Second, the film was used for students to consider the sources of images of place, how these may be modified through the media, and to exemplify the connections identified in the lecture. Students also noted their images of India prior to and after watching the film.

The second lecture was to further conceptualise destination image within the framework of previous investigation. Echtner and Ritchie was used as the primary reading and complemented with Jenkins and Gallarza, Gil

Saura and Garcý'a. Within this class the definition and modelling of destination image were presented as well as creating an appreciation of the role of image in tourism. Additionally considerations of previous methods to measure destination image were also presented, including what specifically was measured and how it was measured. In this class the lists of image attributes noted before and after watching A Passage to India were positioned on Echtner and Ritchie's model of destination image. The two modelled positions were then compared as discussed as the role of the film in changing the position of attributes and the holistic image. Week three looked more especially at the importance of destination image.

Woodside and Sherrell was used as the main reading, supplemented by Um and Crompton and stages in Nielsen. The role of destination image in decision making was especially the focus, though image management and building were also briefly covered. Within decision making the importance of the evaluative components. The Beach was watched in this class for two reasons. First, The Beach portrayed a range of tourists and tourism. Second, it presented an exotic tourism destination with existing images in students' minds. Students noted their images of Thailand before watching the film and they additionally noted the sources of these images. The students then noted their images of Thailand after watching the film. Destination image formation was the topic for the fourth week.

In this class Gartner was used as the primary reading and was supplemented with Baloglu, and McCleary, Croy and Kearsley, Fakeye and Crompton, and Mackay and Fesenmaier. Within this class emphasis was placed on the role of different sources or agents of images in creating a holistic destination image. This was especially to differentiate the role and credibility of different agents and also to note stages within image formation where different agents played roles. The images and sources of images of Thailand were then analysed to identify differing roles of agents in the creation of the holistic image and their perceived credibility. This was also compared to the post film images to identify the role of a film in changing this image. Image management in week five specifically assessed the development of image management, especially for cities, then the advantages and processes of including image management explicitly within destination management processes. In this Barich and Kotler was used as the primary reading, and French, Gregory and Wiechmann and Teleisman-Kosuta provided the additional readings. In this Barich and Kotler's implied image management model was presented and compared with tourism image changing practices During this week The Vertical Ray of the Sun, set and filmed in Vietnam was watched.

This film was selected because it showed an alternate view of Vietnam to most other media. It also depicted a location that was increasingly identified as a tourist destination. Again students noted their images of Vietnam and the sources of these images before watching the film and their images afterwards. The week six class focused on the media. This presented first definitions and description before reviewing the study of the media, and especially the role of media in culture. The role of this week was to contextualise media in everyday life and in this the importance of the media as a topic of study; as an industry; the interrelationship between culture and the media; and the role of the media in audience assimilation. Altheide was the primary reading for this week, supported by Grossberg, Wartella and Whitney, Nielsen and O'Shaughnessy.

The tutorial time analysed the previous week's images of Vietnam, noting the roles of different types of media, their roles in image creation and possible basic strategies that Vietnam could implement to manage image. Tourism and the Media was the topic of the next class. A stage from Nielsen was the primary reading and supplemented by Long and another stage from Nielsen. This week discussed the role of media in creating and enhancing place image and travel behaviour. It additionally discussed the media and tourism relationship and processes to provide for this increasingly important relationship at the destination and attraction level. In the tutorial national and regional tourism and media programmes were assessed and compared to image creation agent roles. The next three weeks looked especially at elements of fictional media tourism. Fictional media tourism is the re-building and re-imaging of associations with literary, television or film icons to promote destinations and to actively induce tourism. Film tourism was the first of the three discussed. Croy and Walker was used as the primary reading, and supported by Busby and Klug and Riley, Baker and Van Doren. The role of film as a tourism inducing force and its possible tourism promotion role were discussed. New Zealand was then discussed as a case study of film tourism and the promotion of a country with and through film. The Lord of the Rings: The Fellowship of the Ring was watched in this class.

This film was selected because it provided a local case, its recent use for destination promotion in New Zealand, and was also partially set at the location of the class fieldtrip, Hobbition. During viewing, students noted places in the film that they would most like to visit, and places they thought international tourists would most like to visit. The students also noted locations that they recognised in the film. The second of the fictional media topics was television tourism. Tooke and Baker was used as the primary reading and was supplemented by Hanna and Beeton. Within this week the role of television in tourism and its effects were compared to that of film tourism. Though further television specific issues were also discussed including potentially longer production and post production effects.

The tutorial was directed at Beeton's review of Sea Change and the identified effects of television production and tourism. Students then evaluated an invented application to produce a locally based television series for its potential impacts, positive and negative. The third fictional media tourism topic was that of literary tourism. The primary reading for this week was Fawcett and Cormack and was supported by Herbert, Muresan and Smith and Squire. This week discussed the role of literature, past to present, in enhancing tourism. Also discussed were the similarities to film and television tourism, including that books were the basis of many films and television programmes. Additionally noted were other avenues destinations had taken in promoting themselves as book towns or with book festivals. The tutorial was allocated to Anne of Green Gables and its creation a fictional place in a real setting. Especially focused on were the impacts on the community and tourists. Building upon and similar to the previous week, students evaluated the promotion of a destination based on a book. Week eleven was the fieldtrip to Hobbiton, Matamata. Hobbiton was used in The Lord of the Rings film trilogy depicting where the hobbits lived.

In Matamata, the manager of tourism marketing in the area gave a presentation giving a background to tourism in the area, though especially the development of the campaign based on Hobbiton and The Lord of the Rings. The class then went on a guided tour with the manager of Hobbiton, in which he provide the usual tourist trip as well as providing a lot of further background information on the site's development and use as a tourist attraction. Students also compared their expected to actual experience as a basis to critically review their process of destination image formation and to identify potential tourism impacts. Promoting place with film was the topic of week twelve. British Tourism Authority, Tourism New Zealand and Riley and Van Doren were used as primary resources for this topic, and were supplemented by Ashworth and Voogd.

The practice of destination promotion with the use of film was discussed and reviewed in previous as well as the contemporary cases of Britain and New Zealand. The Piano was the watched. It was selected as it was the first film used by Tourism New Zealand in international promotion and it provided again a local and realisable case. Students noted their images of Waitakere prior and post watching the film. Additionally students searched for further information of The Piano and The Lord of the Rings with explicit associations with New Zealand. This was to replicate a potential film tourist's search for the actual film location. Managing the impacts of film was the topic of week thirteen's class. Beeton and Croy and Walker were the primary readings, and supported by the review of film impacts of The Lord of the Rings production by NZ Institute of Economic Research. Within this class both enhancing and mitigating the impacts of film were discussed. Potentially impacted groups were identified and then the potential production and post production impacts were discussed. Discussion focused on different management techniques for the different effected groups and range of impacts. The tutorial assessed inducing agents of film and how these may be best managed.

The fourteenth week was on the future of tourism in film. Cetron was the primary reading, and with Muller and Todd presented perspectives of the future of tourism. Total Recall was selected as it portrayed a future of actual and virtual tourism and tourists. The film was watched and the different futures of tourism depicted in the readings and film were compared and discussed. This was very closely linked with the next week where The Fifth Element was watched. Again this was selected as it depicted another future of tourism and tourists. Again the different tourism futures were discussed. Also discussed was the role of film in the creation of these potential futures.

More importantly in these two classes was an ongoing review of the importance, measurement and management of destination image undertaken by Ivan Polunin, editor of Eclipse, a tourism marketing industry journal. Polunin had sent out a list of 23 questions regarding image in tourism covering definitions, sources, roles, managing and so on. These questions were passed onto the students to answer in discussion and as a review for the unit. The experts' responses were then compared to the students' and further discussed the similarities and differences.

ASSESSMENT

In this unit there were three internal assessment items, and no external assessment item. All assessment items were individual. The three items were awarded marks out of 20, 30 and 50 marks respectively making up 100 marks for the unit.

The first item was a review and media diary of New Zealand film and tourism. This had the objective to identify the significance of the film or television and tourism relationship in New Zealand, and to analyse the reported effects of this relationship. For this assessment item students collected and presented an annotated list of at least 10 objects about film and tourism in New Zealand in the previous twelve months. In addition the students, with reference Echtner and Ritchie, Gartner and Woodside and Sherrell wrote a 1,000 word review of the images that these films created to induce tourism as reported in the media. The second assessment item was an analysis of tourism, image and film.

This item had two objectives. The first was to identify the images a film presents to possible tourists and to analyse these in a critical manner. The second objective was to provide recommendations for destination management organisations as to how best use these images for marketing. Students had to base this assessment item explicitly on a film screened in class. From this they had to compare and contrast their images, the film's images and the destination's images identified in the literature. From this basis they then had to identify and discuss the formation of positive and negative tourism inducing images. They also had to provide recommendations regarding the film's effects on image management for that country's tourism authority.

The third assessment item was to identify a film tourism opportunity and develop it. In this students had to identify, explain and put into theoretical context a fictional media site, including a description of its operations and why it exists. From this they had to compare and contrast the chosen site to Hobbiton, Matamata. On the findings derived from the comparison students then proposed a new fictional media tourism attraction in New Zealand. The proposed new attraction was to be developed in consideration of destination image, image formation, decision making and fictional media-tourism literature. Additionally students also had to provide a brochure to summarise the entire report to attract local support and investors to the attraction.

REFLECTIONS

During and after the implementation of this unit the author undertook an explicit programme of reflections upon content, focus, assessment and student reaction. Overall the content covered the main conceptual areas, and covered them in sufficient detail and depth. This was also reflected in student feedback. The development and progression through the conceptual issues within the tourism, image and media relationship was well received.

The reflection on the importance of image at the beginning of many classes also linked the progressions into the overall context of the unit and tourism. The unit, whilst inclusive of other areas of media, was focused on film, this was particularly in the assessment. Though the students' feedback and evaluation was positive to this focus, reflecting, the author would suggest, the contemporary popularity of film.

In the future it would be recommended to broaden this focus to be more explicitly inclusive of other forms of media tourism, especially in the assessment. The focus in the actual classes, tutorials and readings was broader than the assessment. The fieldtrip was an excellent learning exercise, and a great promoter of the unit. The onsite learning and the inclusion of practitioners in student learning was very well received and applied. Most locations do have film, television or literary sets near by, though the numbers that have been developed for tourism may be limited.

In locations without fictional media tourism sites, the fieldtrip could focus more on potential development of locations and the issues that could arise. The first assessment item provided a good foundation of the conceptual issues and also explored a contextual understanding of the relationship between tourism, image and the media in New Zealand. This was quite contextual as New Zealand had had much media coverage of film production and its promotion for tourism during the previous twelve months. The second assessment item did provide a good conceptual application to a film in class. An extensive possible reading list was provided with the outline and was reflected in the submitted assignments.

The objective and how it was to be achieved created confusion, which the reading list helped with, nonetheless it would be recommended to simplify the item, or more explicitly identify the process that students may use in achieving the objective. The third assessment item, again, was laborious in creating clear expectations. This too could be simplified, though would suggest changing it to reflect other management issues within the relationships between tourism image and the media.

The assessment, whilst again positively received by students, could be changed to be more reflective of other tourism management issues in regards to image and the media. One tutorial exercise that worked very well and could easily be developed into an assessment item was the evaluation of impacts and development of criteria for the acceptance of film or television production in an area. A final consideration would be the shortening of the unit for inclusion in most universities 13 week semesters.

The introduction lecture and the destination image lecture could be combined. It must be noted that the introduction lecture was found to provide a great context for the unit within the student's prior learning and their knowledge about the relationship between tourism, image and the media. The final two weeks, the future of tourism in film and review could be omitted, though it would be important to include the review questions within prior weeks. It would also be necessary to allocate time to the discussion of responses of these review questions.

CONSIDERATIONS, IMPLICATIONS AND CONCLUSIONS

Destination and tourism business managers need to be aware of the importance of image and media's role in creating, enhancing and changing image. It is also an important conceptual area for tourism academics to appreciate considering its role within the industry, behaviour and impacts of tourism. The development of an appreciation and understanding of the concepts of tourism, image and the media was a proactive response to an important issue in the tourism industry. The conceptual foundation was sound, and linked well together. Pedagogically, students reacted well to the concepts, readings and exercises in class. In part this was due to the contemporary nature and popularity of the topic complemented with the recent coverage in the media, especially as related to tourism. A consideration for the provision of such a unit is the lack of a text, and therefore the necessity to develop a reading list. Implications for destination and business management are the increased awareness and understanding of the importance of image and the media in this by graduates entering the work force.

This will provide for the ability to manage a more sustainable industry. In conclusion, there is a very evident and important relationship between tourism, image and the media. These are very important conceptual and practical relationships. In response to this a unit was proposed and developed. In this development an appraisal of the pertinent concepts was undertaken, and these then formed the foundation of the unit's classes. The structure was further fleshed out with pertinent management aspects of these relationships.

Assessment items were provided, even though focused on the film component of the tourism, image and media relationship, still provided for the application of conceptual issues to contrived though practical situations. Overall, there was a positive reflection on the content, and focus of the unit. One point to consider was the further explicit inclusion of other forms of media in the assessment. Overall, this unit, it was felt, had very positive educational and practical outcomes and this was supported by positive feedback from students. This is a very important area that needs to be explicitly included in tourism management curriculum, and this thesis provides an indication of conceptual foundation, content, structure and assessment to do so.

4

Tragedy in the Adventure Playground

MOUNTAINEERING AND THE MEDIA

- People like to hear a bit of drama. And that is one part of climbing that is appealing too, is the stories to tell and the experiences and so on. But I guess the stuff that really pays, and pays in terms of stories to the, to the public is the real dramatic things about massive disasters on the big mountains. ... I guess from a non-climber's point of view it's hard to know anything about Everest other than this, this accident prone, environment.

One of the most frequently cited examples of the media's fascination with mountaineering disasters is the incident on Mount Everest in 1996, when eight climbers, including guides and their clients, died during one storm. Both the event and the aftermath were presented in the media with a commentary of triumph and tragedy -instantaneously through photos, films and radio dispatches filed on the World Wide Web, and in retrospect in numerous newspaper and magazine objects, books, documentaries and films.

Buchanan, this incident caused'adventure disaster' to suddenly become a'hot genre' in the mainstream media. It has been reported that news of the disaster, far from deterring aspiring Everest summiteers, actually intensified public interest in climbing the mountain and some mountaineers themselves have contributed to the media interest in Everest's reputation for fatalities. David Breashears, mountaineer and film-maker argues that in'a dark and mysterious way', the deadly nature of Everest has only strengthened its grip on the world's imagination, and that mountaineering is qualitatively different from other sports because this fatal attraction 'increases the psychic reward':

- Because the dangers are so obvious, Everest has come to symbolize for many people the ultimate in personal ambition and achievement. [It is]"a great metaphor for human striving". ... The risk of death is enticing, because it reminds you that you are alive.

Industry observers tend to agree that the media has played a role in creating greater public awareness of adventure pursuits. Advertising has provided a large degree of exposure, while the marketing value of risky sport illustrates their appeal to a youth-oriented popular culture. As Celsi, Rose and Leigh point out'high-risk sports have become a badge of our times. We are all admonished to"just do it," and"play hard," for"life is short."' In addition, they argue, high-risk activities are dramatic in form, and thus motivated to an extent by a dramatic worldview which is both reflected in and reinforced by the mass media.

Walter argues that mountaineering films and books provide'a peep into the reality, immediacy and humanness of death', something he suggests is otherwise denied to us in a culture which fears and represses an awareness of mortality. Manning, in his analysis of adventure narratives, identifies the pursuit of risky experience and the social construction of risk-particularly our appetite for the vicarious experience of risk through narrative-as distinctive features of postmodern cultures. Risks-both created and sought-are, he says,'windows into modern experience': they dominate institutional discourse and appear to shape modern consciousness and the content of mass media.

In such narratives, he argues, the tendency is to maximise and dramatise risks that can not be fully controlled, rather than those that can be anticipated and minimized in advance - 'Fortuna, chance and luck, inevitably interplay with strategy and skill'. In spite of these preoccupations, a number of theorists have suggested that risk, danger and death are not central to the subjective experiences of climbers and other adventurers. The findings from my study of the biographical narratives of New Zealand mountaineers correspond with these conclusions. During in-depth interviews my participants seldom, unless prompted, mentioned risk or danger, much less death. When asked how they felt the public perceived them, they expressed an almost unanimous feeling of being misunderstood.

Many felt the public perceived them as strange, irresponsible or self-centred, because mountaineering has a reputation for being extremely dangerous and scary, even a gamble with life. By contrast, they argued, mountaineering is a relatively safe activity in which the level of risk one takes is managed in a very calculated way. The misunderstandings, they felt, arise from the way in which it is portrayed in the media-emphasising drama and deadliness-as well as the fact that it is very hard to explain the enjoyment of mountaineering to people when it is completely outside of their experience.

Inspired by such comments, this thesis endeavours to explore more deeply the representation of mountaineering in the media, and the processes that drive it, through a case study which analyses the newspaper reporting of one fatal mountaineering accident-the Mount Tasman avalanche.

THE NEWSWORTHINESS OF THE MOUNT TASMAN ACCIDENT

On New Year's Day, twenty-four hours after the avalanche on Mount Tasman, New Zealand's three major metropolitan dailies-The Press, The Dominion Post and The New Zealand Herald-carried the story on their front pages. The Dominion Post led with the main headline"Killer Mountains" and three inter-related objects, illustrated with a photograph of Mount Tasman indicating the site of the accident, photographs of Paul Scaife and David Hiddleston and one of a survivor lying injured on a stretcher. In The New Zealand Herald the story covered most of page one, dominated by a photo of rescuers taking a body on a stretcher from a helicopter, and a further object on page three. The Press dedicated all of page one and two to the story. Objects about the accident were accompanied by similarly dramatic photographs-of survivors on stretchers, of the guides who died, their distressed colleagues, and Mount Tasman again, with its'killer slopes'. This degree of newspaper coverage for a mountaineering accident was quite exceptional, exceeding, for example, the attention given to a climbing accident leading to the deaths of four Latvians earlier in December on Aoraki-Mount Cook.

Contributing to this, undoubtedly, was the fact that New Year's Day is usually a'dead' day for news, and hence there was no serious competition for the front page headlines that day. However, objects related to the accident continued to appear in newspapers across New Zealand over the following seven months. Nine months after the avalanche the front cover of the October edition of the national magazine North and South read"Death in the Mountains" underneath a photograph of one of the survivors, and inside was a twelve page feature object on the accident and its aftermath.

The elements that made this story so newsworthy can be identified by applying Galtung and Ruge's categories of news values. These news values are what determine the selection, structure and presentation of news stories, and help to explain why this incident was so widely reported. Galtung and Ruge argue that the'more negative an event in its consequences, the more probable that it will become a news item.'

While both the Latvian and the Mount Tasman accidents could claim similar degrees of negativity and amplitude on account of resulting in the same number of fatalities, the Mount Tasman accident involved New Zealanders, and therefore this incident was, just as to Galtung and Ruge's theory, more meaningful to a New Zealand audience than the Latvian incident, in that they could identify more closely with those affected by it. In addition, the Mount Tasman accident had a good degree of consonance and relevance due to the cumulative effect of media reports of the earlier accidents, and a number of other high profile search and rescues occurring immediately prior to the New Year's Eve incident. Nine"foolish" Indonesian climbers, with no experience on ice or snow, were flown off Aoraki-Mount Cook on December 22, 2003, amid fears that they were placing themselves at serious risk. On December 29, two women were rescued in another part of the country after spending eight days stranded on a mountain side. It can be assumed that such reports over the past month had heightened public consciousness and concern regarding risk and responsibility in outdoor adventure activities-hence further accidents would be consonant with the public's'mental pre-image' of what could be expected when people go climbing.

Significantly in this case, Galtung and Ruge hypothesise that the newsworthiness of an event is enhanced if it involves'the unexpected within the meaningful and the consonant.' If the public were by now well aware that mountains are a potentially dangerous place in which to recreate, still, for the most part, these misadventures could be attributed to lack of experience, illpreparedness, or bad judgment. In the case of the Latvians, although the leader of the party was an experienced mountaineer who was a'hero' in his own country, the media reported that the party had all been roped together on a steep and icy slope, and that this was a mistake contributing to the tragedy-when one fell, they pulled the others off.

In the case of the Mount Tasman incident a number of factors combined to make it far more unexpected, and consequently more difficult to explain: the accident involved a professionally guided climbing party; two of the guides were among the most experienced and wellrespected in New Zealand's climbing community; and finally avalanches, though known to occur in summer, are far less common then than they are in winter.

The fact that two of the dead mountaineers were part of the elite of their profession, and that the deaths and their aftermath could be told in very personal terms, can also be said to have contributed to the news value of this story. Indeed, in the days and weeks and months following the original incident, these threads ensured the continuity of the story, another of Galtung and Ruge's criteria for news value. Personal stories are quite straight-forward to gather and present-an interview and a photo and you have a story-but in addition they satisfy a'need for meaning and consequently for identification ... through a combination of projection and empathy,' as well as a'cultural idealism just as to which man is the master of his own destiny and events can be seen as the outcome of an act of free will'.

WHAT REALLY HAPPENED

If what happened on Mount Tasman generated a large amount of newspaper coverage due to certain aspects of the accident that rendered it newsworthy, how accurate and balanced was the depiction of the event in the media, and how was mountaineering in general represented? As Lippmann observes, news, in the first instance, 'is not a mirror of social conditions, but the report of an aspect that has obtruded itself.' Bell, a linguist and journalist, goes further and argues that 'miscommunication is not only possible but inherent [in the news production process]. The news story is controlled by news values. It is not a neutral vehicle'.

The theory of news values, once an event has been selected as newsworthy, the news values that have deemed it newsworthy will be accentuated and thereby distorted. The further down the 'news chain' the item goes from event to reader, the higher the potential for selection and distortion. The 'news chain' refers to the multiple parties which handle a news story as it goes through the production process: typically from source to journalist, to chief reporter, to subeditor, then editor, and backwards and forwards amongst them throughout the process.

At any stage along the chain a story and its language may be modified and inputs or deletions made. In addition, most news which originates outside the region of a particular newspaper is reprocessed text from a news agency such as the New Zealand Press Association, even if it is bylined to a local reporter. Bell, miscommunication in the media is facilitated by the tendency towards over-assertion, which may be achieved by increasing 'the illocutionary' of words, phrases or sentences. Compare, for example, The Dominion Post headline "Killer Mountain", with The Press "Four climbers die after avalanche disaster" for the same story. Other forms of distorting a story include attribution deletion, that is, presenting an individual viewpoint as general information, and deleting or reordering information so that the balance or focus of the original text is altered. Clearly, these techniques can be utilised to exaggerate the negativity or drama of a particular incident, or to render it less ambiguous–another of Galtung and Ruge's news values.

While the New Zealand metropolitans differed subtly in style and the deletion or misreporting of certain minor details, a more extreme example of the cumulative effects of selection and distortion was the report of the Mount Tasman accident in The Courier Mail in Queensland on January 1. Not only is the language of this report of high assertive strength: the headline reads "Top climbers hurled 500m to icy death" and Aoraki-Mount Cook National Park is described as 'a treacherous meeting place for climbers'; but also the description of the event bears no resemblance to that reported in the New Zealand newspapers. The New Zealand thesiss all reported the details of the accident in similar terms to this description which appeared in The Otago Daily Times:

- The avalanche struck shortly after the party had completed one pitch of a steep part of the climb on the northern shoulder of Mt Tasman, and the guides had climbed ahead to set up belay points. Mr Hiddleston [a guide] was bringing Dr Platts up on the rope, with the two remaining clients waiting at the lower belay station, when the avalanche occurred. All six were swept off the slope, down the face and over several ice cliffs before coming to rest on the Grand Plateau 500m below.

The Courier-Mail, by contrast, tells the story as follows:

- The party was using an exposed rock bridge to cross a ravine, when the avalanche hit about 7am. One of

> the climbers tried to drive a steel peg into the ground to use as a hook when the bridge gave way. Three of the six climbers were killed instantly.

Thus, the way in which newspaper stories are selected and produced results in 'an image of the world different from "what really happened"'. Additionally, as Galtung and Ruge point out, while it can not be demonstrated here, it may be hypothesised that such processes have an impact on the ways in which the audience of such stories interpret and understand such events. Hence, we should perhaps not be surprised if some members of the public view mountaineering as an unjustifiably treacherous pursuit given the way in which news values drive the presentation of such stories, compounded by our tendency to better recall negative or spectacular events.

It has been argued that the only way to change this would be to completely overhaul the values which drive the selection, structure and presentation of news stories. In the case of the Mount Tasman avalanche accident, these processes resulted in an emphasis on certain factors —the drama and tragedy of the event, the personal competence and seeming invincibility of the guides, and the shock and devastation of the climbing community.

NARRATIVES OF RISK AND RESPONSIBILITY

While the processes of news production resulted in the Mount Tasman accident being portrayed in ways which differed from 'what really happened', the newspapers also tended to tell the story of the Mount Tasman accident in terms of certain narrative themes regarding risk and responsibility in outdoor adventure activities. Journalists report events in terms of stories with 'structure, direction, point, viewpoint'. In the case of the stories generated by the Mount Tasman accident, the narrative structures revolved around the nature and extent of the risks associated with climbing; the causes of the accident and hence who should be held responsible; and why, given the risks, people continue to climb mountains.

Conclusions about the narratives used in newspaper reports can be drawn from analysing the topics around which stories are focused, the structure of specific reports, as well as lexical and grammatical styles used. Newspaper stories are organised around topics or themes which represent certain 'macro-propositions' which are evident in the way in which the stories are structured. Bell argues that focussing a story is a 'prime preoccupation of a journalist', that is, determining the significance of a particular story and the way in which various elements of it can be evaluated.

This tendency also exists in personal narratives, but hard news stories differ from these in that they generally do not hold to a strict chronology–information is organised in terms of its newsworthiness rather than chronology —and the evaluation of the story comes at the beginning, rather than at the end as it tends to do in the personal stories we tell. Thus, the lead paragraph of a news story both summarises the narrative and focuses it, forming 'the lens through which the remainder of the story is viewed. The function is even more obvious for the headline, especially when it appears to pick up on a minor point of the story'.

A major topic of the Mount Tasman story was the overall number of climbing fatalities in Aoraki-Mount Cook National Park–in particular highlighting the fact that the toll for 2003 was one of the highest compared to other years. This background story provided the context and history for the incident, and tells the story in terms of a certain sequence of events–instances of people dying in the mountains. Thus, such stories represent the theme that mountaineering is a very risky and potentially deadly pursuit. The Press ran the following headline and lead in its story about mountain fatalities on page two of the same edition that broke the story of the avalanche:

- *Challenge Leads Many To Risk Lives*: The enduring challenge of climbing in the Mount Cook National Park has led many climbers to an early grave.

The object noted that the four fatalities on Mount Tasman brought the overall death toll in the National Park to 209–with ten people dying in 2003, including the four Latvians only weeks before. The 2003 accidents are outlined, and finally details are given of other multiple-fatality accidents in the park, as well as the worst ever climbing accident in New Zealand, fifty years ago, when six people fell and died on Taranaki/ Mount Egmont. The penultimate paragraph of this object, however, offers some perspective on this catalogue of deaths:

- Tragedies tend to overshadow the vast number of adventures in the park that end successfully and results in the reputation of the park spreading around the world.

Judgements about the relative importance of a particular topic or theme are subjective, and differ between journalists and newspapers. For example, The Dominion Post structured their reports in a way that emphasised even more intensely the theme of mountaineering being a deadly pastime. While the headline of The Press object suggested there was at least some reason behind the activities that result in these deaths, The Dominion Post ran the same object on the front page of their January 1 edition, with some interesting deletions.

Most notably they deleted the notion of challenge from the headline, and cut the paragraph which qualifies the fatalities to some extent. Hence their object reads much more like a bleak list of tragic deaths. A week later The Otago Daily Times ran a more personalised account of mountain deaths by their Wanaka-based journalist to coincide with reports of the guides' funerals on January 6. This story, like The Dominion Post headline "Killer mountains", emphasised the notion of the mountains as violent, even the agents of violence, through their personification: the headline read "Mountains are killing my friends', not 'My friends are dying in the mountains,' suggesting the climbers are passive victims at the hands of malevolent mountains. Similarly, a headline in The Press read: "At the mercy of nature."

The object told the story of the accident through the eyes of one of the rescue party, and the difficulty he faced in being called to recover the bodies of close friends, but the headline picked up on a comment attributed to the veteran alpine guide–that the guides were 'thorough professionals' and had been the victims of circumstance–establishing this as the most pertinent theme. In the same object two Swiss climbers, also knocked over by the avalanche, are described as having 'cheated death' because their rope caught on a piece of ice, arresting their fall. At the same time as a narrative is being told of mountaineers taking extreme risks in landscapes dominated by the whims of nature–and by extension that mountaineering is a form of life-gamble or surrender to fate–it is implied elsewhere that responsibility may lie in far more human hands. Thus the theme of responsibility is prevalent in some reports of the accident, pivoting around questions of the level of avalanche risk existing at the time, and the experience and competence of the guides, that is, was it bad luck or bad judgement?

Was the nature of the risk they faced calculable or incalculable, and thereby something they could not have foreseen? Again subjectivity comes into play, and there is some ambiguity in the picture that emerges from varying reports. The Press headline "Avalanche threat thought low" suggests bad luck, while The New Zealand Herald ran a story headlined "Victims may have set off avalanche".

Although this headline suggests a certain degree of culpability on the part of the climbers themselves, this is qualified in the final few paragraphs when Mountain Guide Association president Trevor Streat is attributed with the comment that the guides 'had undertaken the climb on an appropriate day' and that 'the accident may have been a combination of an error in judgement and bad luck.'

By mid-January a preliminary report into the deaths by the New Zealand Mountain Guides Association was released and reported as identifying a combination of bad luck and abnormal conditions as causing the accident. Significantly it was maintained that the guides had 'adopted standard mountainguiding techniques' and this incident should not be confused with other recent accidents 'where lack of experience and inappropriate technique would seem to be the most likely cause.

The NZMGA believes this has contributed to confusion in the public arena over the risks of mountaineering for experienced and suitably prepared parties'. This statement suggests some concern on the part of the NZMGA about public perceptions. Contributing to such perceptions may well have been an object in The Press on January 10–" 'She's right mate' attitude killing NZ holidaymakers by the dozen." The object attributes inexperience and underestimation of the dangers of the New Zealand environment with leading to the deaths of fifty domestic and foreign tourists over the preceding fifteen days. While the object does not specifically claim that such things led to the Mount Tasman accident, the accident is listed and pictures of the victims and the rescue prominently in the object.

But if the Mount Tasman accident did not fit the conventional narrative of foolhardy recklessness or a tragic lack of familiarity with local New Zealand conditions, the media required an alternative narrative to explain the course of events that led to the accident and position the way in which it is evaluated in terms of risks and responsibility in the outdoors.

This emerges in a number of stories that focus on the experience and competence of the guides, their personalities and the personalities of other mountaineers, and the reasons they climb. The picture that emerges from this narrative is one of "true" adventurers, highly skilled and aware of the risks involved in mountaineering, who nevertheless are driven by a passion and dedication to their chosen activity/profession, and accept the possibility of death, and thereby consciously take personal responsibility for whatever happens to them.

These themes are expressed in the headlines:

- Mates had the Mountains In their blood climbers will not stop climbing guide remembered for Single-minded Determination

Memorial services were held for the two New Zealand guides on 6 January and newspaper reports of the services described the men as:

- True adventurers, blessed with the spirit to push themselves and get the best from those around them, but also safety-conscious and constantly aware of the unforgiving environment they chose as their work

> place. ... the realities of his job, accepting that death was always a possibility in the mountains.

Editorials, much more explicitly than hard news stories, are not constrained by assumptions of 'objectivity.' Rather, they set out to explain and evaluate events–offering Conclusions and Moral sessions, as described by van Dijk in his analysis of news schemata. Hence this theme was expressed quite forcefully in a Dominion Post editorial on January 2 where it was explained that death was the price the climbers paid 'for a passion that drives them like an addiction':

- Even when trained, experienced and well-prepared well-equipped people have done everything properly, things will go wrong ... The possibility of death is something that climbers live with, a known risk they take into account and which, of course, they try to minimise. But in the end, their best endeavours may not be enough. ... The weather was good, the team was wellprepared and all signs point to there having been no warning that the avalanche risk was higher than usual. Families, friends and the mountaineering community will mourn the dead. Undeterred, other climbers will still have their eyes and hearts fixed firmly on reaching the top. That is the nature of the beast.

Two feature objects appearing in the second weekend of January picked up on this theme with more personalised accounts and evaluative comment. One of them, an object in The Press, is given weight by the journalist identifying himself as a mountaineer, and including a photo of himself on the summit of Mount Cook. He explains that when foreigners die in the New Zealand mountains, the question is always raised as to whether they underestimated the local conditions–as happened in the case of the Latvians. Fatal accidents involving professional New Zealand mountain guides, however, are far more rare, and force the conclusion that 'experience is no guarantee of survival': it may improve the odds against being 'in the wrong place at the wrong time', but 'sometimes survival relies on nothing more than dumb luck'. The Mount Tasman accident is compared with the rescue of the notoriously ill-prepared Indonesians, making it clear that those who have accidents in the mountains may be divided into the experienced who are unlucky. and thus the responsibility lies with the mountain which 'doesn't distinguish between the climbers on its slopes', and the inexperienced, who may either be lucky and survive as the Indonesians did, or unlucky, as the Latvians were.

Similarly, The New Zealand Herald ran a feature on the same weekend which profiled an amateur climber describing the rewards of climbing–challenge, satisfaction, breathtaking views, calm and contented feelings–and endeavouring to demonstrate that despite the high number of deaths in the previous months, there are 'hundreds who head into the Southern Alps each year, climb their intended route and go home without raising an eyebrow'.

The object also included an interview with Guy Cotter, a mountain guide identified as having the same level of experience and qualification as the two New Zealand guides that died. It is reported that Cotter 'knows the same fate could also take him', but he accepts it and does not see it as sufficient reason to stop climbing.

The object goes on to quote Cotter:

- "Some people assume we are in danger all the time, that we take enormous risks all the time and that just being in the mountains means we are in grave danger.
- It is not like that, it is the other way around... Every move and risk is meticulously assessed." That is not to say climbing mountains is completely safe.
- "Realistically, if you are not aware of the risks then you should not be in the business in the first place.
- The successful climber must learn patience, discipline and be able to take on responsibility for their actions.
- Sometimes the risks are just a lot greater than you realise, despite all the proper assessment and planning." This week Cotter rescheduled planned climbs to allow his guides to go to the funerals of

their colleagues. None of the clients was put off trying their own ascents.

- "Basically they paid their respects then said, 'But we're still going, aren't we?' To be doing this, you have to know the risks. We know, the clients know. You accept them and work hard to minimise them."

Differing shades of risk and responsibility appeared again with the reporting in July of the Coroner's interim decision on the Mount Tasman deaths, demonstrating again the difficulty of making a clear distinction between calculable and incalculable risks. This can be highlighted by comparing the reporting of the interim decision in The Press and The Dominion Post, and is perhaps summed up by the subtly different headlines they used for the same stories:

- Avalanche danger hidden from victims no avalanche risk seen on fatal day

While The Dominion Post story is a rewrite of what appeared in The Press, the headline chosen suggests that the climbers were passive victims, while The Press suggests more agency on the part of the mountain guides. Notably also, The Dominion Post version excludes parts of The Press object that suggest ambiguity and difference of opinion around the question of whether or not the guides should have been more cautious on the fatal day.

In particular, paragraphs were deleted recounting the opinion given by a Department of Conservation staff member at the inquest that the party was travelling in avalancheprone territory, that there were avalanche warning signs in the area, and that had the climbers been further apart at the time of the avalanche, they may not have all been swept away.

This demonstrates how difficult it can be to draw a definitive conclusion about the nature of risks and the assignment of responsibility in cases such as mountain accidents–particularly a case like the Mount Tasman avalanche where it can not be easily explained in terms of the standard scenarios of inexperience and/or bad judgement. To attempt to accurately represent such complexities in the media, which prefers unambiguous conclusions is even more fraught. It is further evident that the newspaper reporting of such incidents can paint pictures of events in differing ways–sometimes subtle and sometimes quite contradictory–through variations in the topics and themes they chose to report, the ways in which the reports are structured, and other variations in lexical and grammatical style. Such oversimplification and conflicting messages do little to assist a constructive debate about risk and responsibility in mountaineering in general, and more specifically for the tourism industry, about related issues of tourist safety and the marketing of adventure tourism.

IMPLICATIONS FOR ADVENTURE TOURISM

The Mount Tasman incident, and the varying narratives about risk and responsibility that it prompted in the news media, has certain implications in terms of broader concerns about tourist safety and the reputation of New Zealand as an adventure destination. An editorial in The Press on January 2 summed up a number of aspects of these concerns, namely, that despite the fact that the avalanche on Mount Tasman demonstrated that there are 'no absolute guarantees of safety', nevertheless there were too many foolhardy 'idiots' who were endangering lives, costing money and giving New Zealand an 'unwarranted international reputation' as a 'dangerous destination'. The editorial argues that education is not enough to stop such 'ill-considered outback ventures', which will only increase due to the 'images of alpine grandeur' promoted by The Lord of the Rings films. While no satisfactory means of stopping such accidents is offered, it is deemed 'essential' that they should be stopped, and that even though 'tragedies' such as the Mount Tasman avalanche will occur regardless, nevertheless 'the message to tourists must be that if they are well-prepared they will normally be perfectly safe'. When an Australian fell to his death on Aoraki-Mount Cook on March 30, these issues were raised again:

- Rings 'may add to mountain deaths' foreign climbers at risk

Both objects reported the New Zealand Mountain Safety Council as warning that more foreigners would die in New

Zealand mountains after being 'lured here by the Lord of the Rings films' and 'promotions marketing New Zealand as an adventure playground.' Towards the end of the objects it is reported that the Australian who died 'appeared to have done everything right'. Nevertheless, the report is structured in such a way as to connect with the idea that inexperienced foreigners are at particular risk, and that by attracting more international visitors to New Zealand as suggested, be adding to the sorts of problems identified in The Press editorial. It is an interesting irony that on the one hand there is concern about causing problems by attracting too many adventure tourists, and on the other hand, concern that the escalation of such problems will discourage tourists from placing New Zealand on their adventure itinerary.

A number of things seem evident from this discussion: that the reporting of the Mount Tasman accident demonstrates that determining the nature and extent of risk and responsibility in adventure tourism activities is complex, particularly through the medium of the news media which prefers unambiguous conclusions.

In this case, the narrative that emerged about "true" adventurers accepting the risks and taking personal responsibility for their safety, but sometimes falling victim to bad luck, sits somewhat uneasily with a simultaneous narrative about accidents happening only to the foolhardy and the inexperienced, and that by educating and encouraging people to take certain precautions, we can keep them safe.

It is worth noting that Johnston in her analysis of mountaineering accidents in New Zealand found no evidence to suggest any substantial difference in accident rates between international and domestic mountaineers in the New Zealand mountains, and concludes that the 'apportioning of blame for a high number of accidents is often based on misconceptions about the frequency of accidents involving particular groups.' The fact that this research was conducted more than fifteen years ago demonstrates that the perception that international visitors are at higher risk in the mountains than their local counterparts is an enduring one. Questions also arise regarding the acceptance of risk and responsibility in a client-mountain guide relationship. As noted earlier, a highly experienced guide was reported as saying that clients accepted the risks, thereby emphasising the notion that they control their own destiny. Gabriel Amador, one of the guided climbers who survived the avalanche is reported as saying 'I don't hold anyone or any country responsible, it was just a terrible accident not under anyone's control'.

However, he is also reported as saying, 'I don't ever want to climb another glaciated mountain again. Knowing someone could die changes everything'. Also of relevance here is the research by Carr on guided climbers in New Zealand. Her findings suggest that increased safety is one of the primary reasons for hiring a mountain guide.

CONCLUSIONS

Given the complexities surrounding subjective perceptions of the risks involved in mountaineering and other outdoor adventure activities, it is important that the adventure tourism industry develops a sophisticated understanding of these issues, beyond the simplistic and sometimes contradictory narratives told in the news media.

While an analysis of the current systems of news production explains the tendencies of newspapers to distort their reporting of mountaineering accidents in particular ways and to varying degrees, it also demonstrates that an informed debate about such events and related issues should be held beyond the confines of the media, in a realm where the discussion is not determined in relation to the news values described by Galtung and Ruge and is less influenced by the tendency to tell stories just as to conventional narratives of adventure.

As part of this debate it is also important to address the concerns of Palmer that in the marketing and promotion of adventure tourism 'the very real prospect of injury and death has been stripped from the activity itself.' Perhaps the most significant question raised by the Mount Tasman accident in this regard is whether it is perhaps unwise–if not irresponsible–to suggest that there can be such a thing as a completely 'safe' adventure tourism destination, if this means that tourists are thereby unprepared for the possibility that not all risks in adventure–as in life–can be calculated and mitigated, even by the most experienced and cautious among us. And this will likely always be the case, particularly if one accepts Simmel's argument that the genius of the adventurer is to fail to differentiate between their own ability and the vagaries of luck, thereby existing 'at the point where the course of the world and the individual fate have, so to speak, not yet been differentiated from one another.'

For Simmel a continuity runs through all the phenomena of life whereby they can be seen to rest somewhere on a scale 'on which every point is simultaneously determined by the effect of our strength and our abandonment to impenetrable things and powers.' It is this existential problem which allows us all in a sense to become adventurers. Whether we view the sum total of life as comprehensible and meaningful, or incalculable and insoluble, may depend, just as to Simmel, on the quantitative analysis of individual experiences falling into either category.

Having said this, Simmel adds that:

- None of us could live one day if we did not treat that which is really incalculable as if it were calculable, if we did not entrust our own strength with what it still cannot achieve by itself but only by its enigmatic co-operation with the powers of fate.

To consider the Indonesian, Latvian and Mount Tasman climbing parties and their fates in light of this argument suggests perhaps that we should not try to make radical distinctions between them, but rather consider that they exist on a continuum whereby we all attempt to convince ourselves that our skills and judgement can overcome the'accidents of the world.' This requires the acknowledgement that whatever our chosen'site of resistance', from which we derive'the illusion of controlling the seemingly uncontrollable' one day our fate will catch up with us. Mark Whetu, a New Zealand mountain guide, in a documentary about his struggle to come to terms with the death of a client and friend on Mount Everest, suggests that accepting this may be our saving grace:

- When you accept the fact that you are going to die-which, it's not a case of if, it's a case of when and where-once you accept that fact, you actually really start living.

5

Effects of Negative Media Events on Tourist's Decisions

INTRODUCTION

'Death toll climbs in Fiji cyclone','Visiting Great Britain? Beware of Foot And Mouth Disease!','Sars Warning over Taiwan','Colombia closes popular parks in yellow fever scare', and the headlines about negative events keep coming. What kind of influence do the mass media have on people, and is the tourist's decision-making process influenced by what the mass media are communicating? There are two major ways of [re]-creating a destination image in the minds of visitors after an event has occurred. The first one is through communication in the mass media, while the second one is through a real experience.

Even though Lombardi's theory seems logical, it can be criticised because there is no final definition of what he calls a'true' image. What this thesis queries is, if the mass media actually paints a true/factual picture of destinations after a crisis, or if they are more interested in boosting sales and thus creates a fictional image that is claimed to be true. However, the net result of a perceived and real image has more or less the same outcomes which, just as to Baloglu and McLeary are reduction in tourist arrivals and tourist receipts, and a change in visitor's perception of the destination. It has been suggested that the mass media also play an important role in the restoring phase after a crise that have led to negative media publicity and damage a destination's image. However, this thesis is limited to focus on the role the mass media plays in influencing tourists in their decision making process and the perception they generate about a destination. In conclusion, based on the models related to tourists' decision-making and the communication process, this thesis will aim to identify the role of the mass media and which factor it has in influencing tourists' decision-making.

METHODS

Although several researches have been conducted on tourists' decision-making process and destination images, the more complex relationship between tourism and the mass media is under-researched. The definition of a negative media event will be explained, followed by an example, which shows how negative media publicity can result in significant downturn in numbers of tourists visiting the destination. In addition to the role of the international mass media, the concept of freedom of press will be discussed. Many different theorists have discussed the role of the mass media in the tourist's decision-making process.

This thesis will present a model, which shows a simplified sequence on how the tourists reach the'defer','decline' or'decide' stage in the decision-making process. After having established the relationship between travellers and the mass media, this thesis raises the issue on how news can destroy a destination image. Examples are used to highlight how negative media events have resulted in consequences for the tourism industry in different parts of the world. For the purpose of this thesis, the term tourist destination region will be used, and can be defined as country, state, region or town that is marketed as a place for tourists to visit.

THE ROLE OF MASS MEDIA IN CRISES

Nielsen, a negative media event occurs when the mass media is communicating bad news, threats, irritations or other matters that can be seen as unfavourable by the audience. An important point is that the issues communicated by the mass media might or might not be the truth. However, the end result will not be of great difference whether or not the actual event has occurred. People feel shocked or afraid, and their degree of scepticism increases and reflects their decision-making. Sudden changes in the society can have remarkable consequences for individual TDRs, as well as for the global tourism industry in general. A human act or a nature catastrophe can transform the reputation, image and marketability of the most popular tourism destinations overnight.

Amongst incidents that have disrupted the global tourism industry were the terrorist attacks on New York City and Washington DC on September 11 in 2001, hereafter referred to simply as September 11. Beirman, these incidents generated a worldwide panic and fear, which especially had an effect on the tourism industry in form of economic downturns. The combination of SARS and the war in Iraq, which took place between March and June 2003, had severe impacts for the tourism industry and caused a steep reduction of tourism visitation globally, especially in the Asia Pacific region. The on-going unrest in the Middle East, after the initial war, continues to fuel global uncertainty.

Haalebos quotes the Co-Director of Curtin University of Technology's Sustainable Tourism Centre, Professor Jack Carlsen, who stated that'...at the World Tourism Organisation Conference in October 2001, it was estimated it would be two years before international tourism recovered. Since then we've had Bali, Sars and the latest events in Jakarta, Baghdad and Israel. Each event has set recovery back six to twelve months'. This is in line with what the Commonwealth of Australia announced in their White Tourism Thesis where it was identified that there has been a strong market decline in travel and tourism receipts within Australia after the incidents concerned with September 11, SARS and the war in Iraq.

In 2003 overseas arrivals to Australia decreased by 10 per cent in April and 21 per cent in May compared with the year before. At the same time the effects of SARS in China were even more dramatic. Zhou, Beijing Airport experienced a decrease of thirty per cent fall in passenger arrivals in April

2003, and an estimated loss of $US4.8 billion loss in the tourism industry. When events such as September 11 and the war in Iraq happens, the international media plays an important role both in publishing the actual catastrophe, as well as in reporting recovery and restoration programmes. However, the setback is that'negative' news sell better than'good' stories. Beirman, there are five different events or circumstances that media should cover which can create negative impacts on a TDR's image, and again can result in a significant downturn in tourism numbers.

Firstly, media should cover situations concerned with international wars or conflicts. Secondly, they should keep the public informed about specific acts of terrorism that is affecting tourists. The third type of events that the mass media should report are major criminal acts or crime waves, especially when tourists are targeted. The fourth area that the media has a duty to cover are natural disasters, such as earthquakes, storms or volcanos that are causing damage to urban areas or the natural environment and consequently impacting on the tourism infrastructure.

The fifth and last major type of event that the mass media are interested in is health concerns related to epidemics and diseases, which have an impact on humans directly, or diseases affecting animals. Based on what the media should cover, Beirman does not discuss the relationship between tourism and the effects of negative news reports. Silverstone on the other hand, argues that media has a role of sharing a meaning and provide a'taste of the everyday life'. By understanding the mass media's role, a link can be drawn to the issues concerned with tourists' motivation and how expectations are related to the tourists' decisions. Silverstone states that:

- Our stories, our conversations, are present both in the formal narrative of the media, in factual reporting and fictional representations, and in our everyday tales: the gossip, rumours and causal interactions in which we find ways of fixing ourselves in our relationships to each other, connecting and separating, sharing and denying, individually and

> collectively... it has been suggested that both the structure and the content of media narratives and the narratives of our everyday discourses are interdependent, that together they allow us to frame and measure the experience.

Especially noteworthy in the quote is the realisation that no narrative alone shapes a picture, rather the intertextual links between surface and content and between different sources of information forms the image. By focusing on media's role it may be easier to understand the nature of a tourist's decision making and the following travel experience. Silverstone argues further that an understanding of how the media works, will make travellers more critical to what the media presents. The relationship between the media and tourism is also commented on by Hall, who states'... in the age of global communication events can be played out live and unedited on television screens, and thereby potentially having a great impact on the viewing public'.

This statement supports the argument that it is important to understand media's response to events like September 11, which affects the tourism industry. Beirman the role of effective media communication is critical for tourist authorities in democratic countries where the mass media's role is to inform the general public. The concept of freedom of press in these countries means that the public relation management is an especially important tool for tourism operators because they have to'ensure that recovery and restoration efforts are reported'. Fall confirms Beirman's view and claims that advertising activities has decreased since September 11 in USA while public relation activities have increased.

In contrast, the government in non-democratic countries have far more control over what the mass media is publishing. Consequently, the media coverage tends to be managed in a staged process, and all information is filtered through the government. Although the nondemocratic counties try to'hide' destinations in crises, there are leakages. Medical epidemiologist and CSTC Professor Aileen Plant sympathised with the way the Chinese government handled the SARS crisis, and stated that'I could not criticise the Chinese for their closed-door attitude to the virus. They were simply doing what many other countries would have done to protect their travel and trade. We live in a new world-a globalised world. We cannot hide problems any longer'. This shows that when foreign tourists are the victims of a particular event, they are often subject to media attention, and consequently the media coverage can create a negative image for the TDR.

ANALYSIS

In order to determine the impact the mass media have on a tourists' decision-making process, it is necessary to ask the question whether there is a direct relationship between the information presented and the tourist's motivation. There are various decision-making stages by tourists, and theorists like Mansfeld have created different models for tourism planners and information providers. However, these models are complex and very theory based. Nielsen has simplified these models and created a model, which includes the effects of push-and-pull motivations, in addition to information on the tourists' decision-making process. Even though the model shows the major phases in the tourists' decision makingprocess, it can be criticised that it is generalising tourists' motivations to travel.

Morgan and Pritchard have established that there is a change in consumers' holiday needs, and that tourists are searching for greater variety of holiday activities and unique experiences than what Hall defines as'push' and'pull' factors. The trend also shows that there is no longer merely a need for relaxation, but also for recharging and rediscovery. This means that it is questionable how reliable Nielsen's model is. However, it gives a basic overview of tourists' decision-making process. The sequence in the starts with the tourists' motivation to travel. Motivations are dependent on a traveller's social status and background, their stage in the personal life cycle, education and family relationships. These factors will also play an important role when evaluating the issues that can influence the tourists' decisionmaking. The based on an assumed motivation to travel, or at least to gather information for possible trips. Hall states that factors like geographical proximity, ease of accessibility and availability, as well as a destination's social, political and economic stability, are the pull factors that support a tourist in the decision making process. Even though the promotion of TDR's have focused on the mentioned pull factors, recent motivational research has showed that the'push' factors,'which is the need to have a break from the daily routine', is of greater value for the tourists. Having established the basic travel motivation; it is possible to identify more specific motives to the selection process.

The next step is to search for travel alternatives through information providers. At this stage the tourists are heavily influenced by third parties' opinions. On the right hand side of Nielsen's model the tourists establish alternatives based on the'pull' factors that draw people's interest to investigate TDRs and then they collect information about the destination. However, the whole information-gathering phase can also be a combination of'pull' and'push' factors, but in both cases the person seeks further travel alternatives. Manfredo, there is a relationship between the information providers and the tourist's decision-making process, which leads to'defer'' decline', or'decide' upon the travel experience.

The stimulation might come from television advertisements, travel programmes on television or radio, a brochure, or any other source of information like travel agencies. This information gathering stage is the most critical stage when it comes to the tourist's decision making on to'go or not go'. This stage of the process is important for the tourism planners in order to know what the tourist's decision criteria are when they are reaching this point. Theorists have come up with diverse models on how the receiver of a message views the value of different kinds of information. The tourists are influenced by different factors before deciding whether or not to undertake the travel, and it can be concluded that the mass media plays an important role in the decision making process. Furthermore, the relationship between the media and the tourism operators can be discussed. Hall, tourism operators, on the one hand, are primarily engaging with the media when promoting the TDR. However, in these cases they are only focusing on the positive sides in order to motivate tourists to travel to that specific destination. The mass media, on the other hand have, just as to Silverstone, a duty to inform the general public about all types of major events affecting the tourism industry. The coupes in Fiji can be used to illustrate how media attention can have negative effects on tourist's decision-making process. Both in 1987 and 2000 Fiji experienced episodes of political instability.

These events had serious impacts on the tourism industry because of travel warnings published in the mass media. Coup leader Colonel Sitiveni Rabuka overthrew the elected multiracial government in the first coup in 1987. Even though, just as to King and Berno the coup was a'bloodless militarydominated takeover', it had an effect on the tourism industry in terms of decreased visitor numbers. The second coup took place in 2000 when a group of political dissidents took hostage over the members of the Cabinet for two months, but failed their attempt in overthrowing the elected multiracial government.

Berno the coups in 1987 and 2000 had severe impacts on the Fijian tourism industry, and especially the coup in 2000 became a global media event where images of unrest and violence where broadcast around the globe. As a result of this the visitor arrivals decreased with almost 70 per cent in year 2000. Findings by Beirman supports this, and both during and after these events the Fijian Ministry of Tourism and its marketing arm, the Fijian Visitors Bureau, carefully planned campaigns together with airlines and tour operators in order to restore Fiji's tourism industry.

Singh the major reason why tourists did not visit Fiji was because of travel warnings and images of unrest published in the media. During the crises both the Australian and New Zealand governments used the mass media as a communication tool and actively discouraged people to visit Fiji. These findings are strengthened by Brown and Junek who highlights the power government's travel advisories have over individual tourist's decision to travel after disastrous events have happened and the impact these advices have on effected TDRs. The Fijian case highlights the significance in the role of the media and of government tourism advisories as they are shaping tourism images. Beirman a negative media event can result in considerable economic crises, and for individuals it could result in loss of job and income. However, few tourists think about these consequences when they decide to go for holiday. Their major concern is their own well-being and security.

DISCUSSION

The idea that the mass media can influence tourists' in their choice of destination, as well as their perception on a certain TDR, is relatively new. The traditional way of collecting information has been through travel agencies or the tourism operators directly, and the tourists have made their decisions based on this information. However, just as to Seaton, the trend shows that more people are likely to search for supplementary information also from other sources, and the mass media are seen as credible. The question to argue is whether tourists are influenced by the mass media. A model created by Lombardi shows that tourists rely on an'abstract truth'.

It there are two major ways of creating a destination image. The first type of image is created through a specific event that the mass media is communicating to the general public. The image that the mass media is creating can be real or not, however, once it is prototyped to the tourists, it is up to the receiver of the message to recall the image when making a choice of holiday destination. The second way that an image can be created is just as to Lombardi through a person's experience. In this case the image is based on an event or experience that a person is a witness of.

The image is then supported by reality and truth. Lombardi's theory. Lombardi's model gives a picture that a TDR's image can be created through a real experience, which again leads to a true image. However, it can be argued what the truth is, because it can be perceived in different ways.

Understanding how a destination is perceived is fundamental to the image of a TDR. There are several studies that examine this theory of how a destination image is formed, and amongst the most important are those that discuss the relationship between the image and the tourist's motivation. However, Gunn supports Lombardi's theory by stating that there are two dimensions to a destination's image. The first one is based on the tourist's impression of a TDR without visiting, and in this case different communication channels have influenced the tourist. The second dimension is'included', which is formed by visiting the destination. In this case the image is created by the tourist's own perceptions.

This theory supports Lombardi's model of communication; however the created image is based on the tourist's perception, and not described as the'truth'. To sum up, travellers' perceptions are formed based on their knowledge about a destination from various sources. Images and the process of creating images can also be explained as a'mental picturing where pieces of information create individual features and attributes of stimuli'. This can be related back to the example from the coups in Fiji where images where projected around the world showing a shattered and burning TDR in strong contrast to TDR images of a relaxing and peaceful holiday destination.

Baloglu and McLeary have developed a model that includes the factors that influence a destination image and the relationship between the various factors. The model focuses on three main factors, which are personal, social and stimulation factors, which again are related to a perception a person have of a TDR, and these perceptual evaluations do have an affect on travel motivation. The criticised model of communication created by Lombardi can be used to illustrate how the Foot-and-Mouth disease has had an effect the tourism image in the United Kingdom. During the first half of year 2001 the outbreak of the Foot-and- Mouth disease had severe impacts on the British agricultural sector and caused significant harm to the UK's tourism industry. The British farm industry and rural regions had to face negative consequences for a previously wellmarketed tourism infrastructure. Reynolds and Balinbin, the intensity and degree of the mass media's coverage resulted in an image of Britain as a country that was damaged by this disease. Findings by Beirman support this, and explain further that the Foot-and-Mouth disease caused a major downturn in visitor demand, as foreign tourists cancelled trips to the UK. Mass media was contributing to the decrease in tourism, due to the graphic images of burning and slaughtered animals broadcast around the world. As a result of this the overall image of UK as a TDR was severely damaged.

However, the way the British Tourist Authority's reacted to the crises of the Foot-and-Mouth disease is interesting. Instead of only using communication channels like television, newspapers and radio that already had contributed in creating the less appealing tourism image of the country, the British Tourist Authority was one of the first in the world to use the Internet to change the image. With this tool the British Tourist Authority explained the'real' situation, and actually managed to create a truthful image without using other mass media as communicators. The Internetpages played an important role in the management of Britain's marketing during and after the tourism crisis. As in the example from the UK, it is evident that the use of mass media can create a'wrong' perception on a destination.

Lombardi people believe what they see, hear and read in the media. The general public view the media as an important authority on the same level as government warnings. When looking at this issue historically it is important to note that it is especially in recent years that the mass media has had a significantly increasing role as a communication tool. The mass media has given a new importance to the society because it is a source people tend to trust. Mansfeld points out that'one of the main problems facing destinations that were hit by tourism crises resulting from security turmoil is the evolving negative image.

Because tourists do not tend to thoroughly check the reality behind conveyed images, these images become highly biased and distorted'. Machin, the media gives popular representations of what is going on in the world. Seen in a historical perspective, this has undoubtedly had an impact on people in most developed cultures, as well as it has had an enormous influence on the TDR's images. Also illustrated in the examples from Fiji and UK, it is clear that some travellers are influenced by the mass media, and that they use it as an educational tool to learn about the wider society. This supports Beirman's argument that reported incidents, like the terrorist attacks on September 11, have had negative effects on the evolution of the global society, as well as tourism images. Depending on whom the news is affecting, one of the major advantages or disadvantages with mass media as a communication tool is that it is seen as credible.

This means that news written by a neutral third party is seen as reliable, while an advertisement or commercial presents an image from the advertiser's point of view.'Bad' news presented in the media is therefore seen by the audience as objective and factual. This publicity can bee seen as a hazard for tourism operators because it is only the editorial staff of the mass media that control it. In some cases the communicated message is presented in a vague and incomprehensible way, and this may confuse the audience and create problems for the tourism operators. In some cases, just as to Hsu and Powers the media also make a situation worse than it actually is. This happens when the editorial staffs chooses to humiliate a tourist operation or publish a story with negative attributes in some other way.

The paradox is that both the tourism operators and the mass media are dealing with the same target group, the general public. However, a clever tourism operator will learn how to deal with the mass media and use it as a part of their marketing strategy. One way to do this is to follow Fall's suggestion and put a greater focus on public relations activities rather than direct advertising. News that can have an effect on a TDR image has captured front-page headings during the last years, and tourists are not only motivated by stories from glossy brochures, but they are searching for a third party's opinion about the TDR. Hsu and Powers, the mass media is an effective communication tool because it reaches a wide and enthusiastic audience, and there is no doubt that tourism has achieved a special status in the news. However, many regions suffer from bad publicity, even if many years have passed since anything was last reported from the region. Few Australians would, for example, consider Belfast in North Ireland as a cheerful city full of character, with people that are warm and friendly. The coverage of unrest by the mass media has discouraged tourists to travel to North Ireland. The media has drawn a picture of Belfast as an unsafe place to travel to, and just as to Hall, it is human nature to prefer to travel to places that are perceived as safe.

Sonmez, Apostolopoulos, and Tarlow suggest that TDRs in areas affected by unrest should incorporate crisis management in their overall strategies in order to construct and protect the image of the destination. This should be done in order to have the capabilities needed to manage peoples opinions before during and after unrest has taken place in the TDR for the mass media. Richter furthers this point by stressing that:'rebuilding tourism requires more than repairs and promotion. A onesize- fits-all mentality will not do. Just as the sources of instability and their manifestations will differ, so too will the appropriate responses'. What she suggests is that managers in the tourist industry start to look more holistically at their practices and appreciate the fact that they are a part of an industry vulnerable to negative publicity. To manage a TDR effectively does not just mean that the product is enjoyable to visitors but also that it is secure.

CONCLUSIONS AND IMPLICATIONS

The aim of this thesis was to discuss the relationship between tourism and the effects of negative media events. Overall, the main objective of the mass media is to communicate news to the general public. The mass media has in this thesis been defined as a third party that tourists are likely to trust, and they are therefore influenced by the mass media in their decision-making process. Although tourists have different perceptions and motivational factors, it can be proven from this thesis that the mass media plays a paramount role in travel behaviour because it is affecting the tourist's decisions. However, further research is needed to establish the extent to which the tourism experience is shaped by the mass media. The popularity and desirability of a specific TDR is influenced by different'pull' and'push' factors as explained in the'Travel Motivations and Tourists' Decisions Making Model'. This model can be used as a basis for tourism operators to understand traveller's decision-making process and be able to meet future demands.

Operators are equally reminded of the fact that tourist's perception of destinations is formed through the dialectic of different narratives in the society. By learning how to use the mass media to the advantage of the destination, a positive perception is possible to create. This thesis was limited to discuss the role of the mass media, its effect on traveller's decisions and how a TDR image is created. Nevertheless, tourism operators can use the frameworks presented in this thesis to strategically prepare themselves for how to restore tourists' confidence in a destination after a major crises, and how to strengthen a positive image before negative events have occurred.

6

Films and Tourism

INTRODUCTION

The small town of Lone Pine in California is the site of one of the most audacious and unusual thefts in history. At the beginning of the twentieth century the Owens River flowing from the eastern Sierra Nevada was earmarked for a federal irrigation scheme. However, in 1904 a group of prominent business leaders, operating through the City of Los Angeles, began purchasing farms and the attached rights to irrigation water. This water was then pumped nearly 400 kilometres south to fuel the rapid suburban expansion of Los Angeles, leaving Lone Pine an arid wasteland. While Los Angeles stole Lone Pine's water and agricultural potential, it gave the small town Hollywood in return. From 1920 onwards films were made in the town and surrounding hills.

In his 1990 guidebook Dave Holland listed 152 films and eleven television series filmed on location around Lone Pine, but added that details of 1920s and 1930s films were incomplete. Further research has uncovered these earlier films, and at least 355 films are now known to have been made at Lone Pine. Such a number is double that made on the'Movie Railroad' at Jamestown, on the western side of the Sierra Nevada to Lone Pine but less than those made at'Movie Ranches' on the suburban fringe of Los Angeles. However, film-making in Lone Pine eventually declined. Whereas 56 films were made in the 1940s, 32 were made in the 1950s, 10 in the 1960s, two in the 1970s and three in the 1980s, before a small recovery with 18 in the 1990s and 13 since 2000. As film declined, Lone Pine turned towards tourism. On the major highway linking Los Angeles to Lake Tahoe and northern Nevada, Lone Pine is close to the natural attractions of Mount Whitney and Death Valley. Significantly, tourism promotion has now emphasised its heritage as a film location. However, rather than focussing on the wide range of films made at Lone Pine, its destination image has been based on the Western films made there. Indeed, reflecting upon these movies, Lone Pine has reshaped itself as a Western town.

FILM AND DESTINATION IMAGE

Discussions of the role of film in developing destination images have primarily focussed on single productions which have radically transformed tourism to destinations. For example, Riley demonstrated how Thelma and Louise increased visitation to Canyonlands and Arches National Park in Utah, Last of the Mohicans brought tourists to Chimney Rock Park in North Carolina and Field of Dreams created a successful tourist attraction out of an Iowa cornfield. Other studies primarily considering the impacts of individual films and television series include those by Beeton; Busby and Klug; Croy and Walker; Frost; Kim and Richardson; Tooke and Baker and Winter. Such revolutionary transformations often have significant economic benefits for rural communities suffering from declining traditional industries.

However, the film industry is not constructed on individual films, but on related groups of films. These groupings may be based on genre or theme, directors or star actors. The expectations of potential filmgoers will be guided by their prior knowledge, a like or dislike of, for example: science fiction films, the director Steven Spielberg or the actor John Wayne. Most importantly, many films are shot at a small number of established locations, either due to their scenic or cultural qualities, availability of infrastructure or cheaper costs. Often used locations include major cities such as New York, London and Paris. In recent years a number of cities such as Melbourne, Vancouver and Prague have specialised in runaway productions, taking advantage of their cheaper costs and ability to look like other locations. Such multiplefilms locations have hardly been considered in the literature linking film to the development of destination image and tourism. An important exception is Sargent's 1998 study of the Darcy Effect, that is, how multiple films and television series based on the works of Jane Austen and her contemporaries have been used to increase visitation to National Trust properties featured in these productions. This use of a location for multiple films increases the complexity of the process of destination image development and management.

A single film projects a single image, but multiple films project different attributes and views. Different visitors may be influenced by different films and expect to see their image. This potential for conflict may be greater if the location has been used to represent different places or in different types of films. Tourism operators within the destination may wish to shape the destination's image to fit that projected in films, though they may also have conflicting views as to which films and images should be focussed on.

This thesis considers Lone Pine as a case study of a multiple-film location which has successfully developed as a small-scale rural tourism destination. I argue that Lone Pine has been successful in selecting a destination image to project which is based on Western films. Even though Westerns were only one genre of films made at Lone Pine and the town is arguably not in the West, the image and heritage of the town has been reshaped as that of the Wild West.

WESTERN FILM AND THE WESTERN TRADITION

The period of the Wild West may be loosely defined as between 1860 and 1890. Even at this time, the media was providing hungry audiences in the east and Europe with a romanticised mythic image of the West. Buffalo Bill Cody was popularised through the dime novels of Ned Buntline, which ultimately led to the extensive touring of Buffalo Bill's Wild West Show. In that show Native Americans 'performed in New York and London while others fought their last battles in the deserts and mountains, or starved on their reservations'. The enduring legend of Jesse James was due to James' success in convincing contemporary newspaper correspondents that he was an heroic southern rebel rather than just a bank and train robber. In the twentieth century, film and television became the main shapers of the Western image, though novels, music, children's play and toys, events and tourism also contributed. The appeal of Western films and the West extends well-beyond its geographical area, being particularly strong in the eastern USA, South America, Europe, Japan and Australia. While the Western landscape may be attractive, it is the stories and personalities, the romance, the myth of the West which dominates both films and the image of the West.

This mythic image has three overlapping components. First, Westerns are 'America's unique contribution to that body of mythic lore familiar to most of the human race'. However, while unique, Westerns refer to, and are in the tradition of, widely known romantic myths and stories such as Greek epics and medieval knighthood. Furthermore, Westerns follow mythic conventions by portraying the battle between 'good' and 'evil'. As such, most Westerns are concerned about battles between human adversaries, with the environment as a setting rather than a protaganist. In adopting the patterns of such universal stories, Westerns extend their appeal both within and beyond America. Second, while Westerns are set in an historic period, historical accuracy is highly fluid.

As Rosenstone noted of historical romances in general, film-makers tend to concentrate on getting the historical image right, and 'as long as you get the look right, you may [then] freely invent characters and incidents and do whatever you want to the past to make it more interesting'. One of the most celebrated 'inventors' was John Ford, who in My Darling Clementine constructed a fictional story around the reallife personage of Wyatt Earp and then proceeded in Fort Apache to portray an accurate version of the Battle of Little Big Horn, but with fictional characters and setting. Nonetheless, even though such disregard for authenticity is widely known, it is accepted and enjoyed by audiences as part of the Western myth, and 'no amount of elucidation of the facts will destroy the myth'. Third, a significant motif in the Western is the 'good' bad man, the outcast or outlaw who rights wrongs, but can find no place in society. In many cases the spread of civilization, particularly the closing of the frontier, has displaced the hero and the Wild West values he represents. Such themes of alienation and the evils of modernity have a broad appeal, particularly in times of rapid change.

The universality of the outlaw myth extends the appeal of the Western and is reflected in a range of popular outlaw films and writings throughout the world. Western film has allowed the wide-scale consumption of the Western myth. As Hollywood churned out Westerns a range of places evolved as film locations. Indeed a pattern developed of filmmakers primarily using a limited range of familiar locations. Some of these locations and their characteristics. Lone Pine was but one of these competing locations.

LONE PINE AS A FILM LOCATION

The prime attraction of Lone Pine to Hollywood was the Alabama Hills. Arid and rocky, they provided a spectacular backdrop to many action films. In addition, other nearby mountains and desert plains were utilised. A generic arid landscape, Lone Pine could be used to represent a wide range of geographical settings. This diversity is demonstrated in the list of major films shot at Lone Pine. In particular, it is notable how Hollywood used this location to represent India. While Lone Pine was used for a variety of settings in major movies, most movies filmed there, perhaps 300, were B grade Westerns made between 1920 and 1950.

These included productions starring Tom Mix, Hoot Gibson, Ken Maynard, William Boyd, Gene Autry, Roy Rogers, Tim Holt and Randolph Scott. Cheaply produced and relying on stock characterisations and plots, few of these received any critical appreciation, the exception being the 1950s films directed by Budd Boetticher. However, many of these were immensely popular, both in first release and then later on television. In filming at Lone Pine, Hollywood took advantage of the support of the local community. With agriculture declining due to water shortages, local people saw films as an important source of income. Russ Spainhower, a local rancher, became the key supplier of livestock and western equipment to the film companies. Local authorities provided construction crews on request and town buildings were modified as required. Such established contacts drastically reduced the costs of filming and increased the attractiveness of filming at Lone Pine. Such co-operation was partially built on Los Angeles' control of the area, for example the key location man Spainhower came to Lone Pine as a foreman with the Los Angeles Department of Power and Water.

While the scenery at Lone Pine is dramatic, there were many arid and rocky locations much closer to Hollywood. Furthermore, some actors found the conditions on location primitive. Errol Flynn complained that the accommodation was poor, the weather freezing cold and the food gruesome. Why then was Lone Pine so popular? From the earliest days of film, Westerns were one of the few genres which were given freedom of location by studio executives. Filming on location allowed directors to escape financial and artistic control. Many stars enjoyed Lone Pine for its outdoor life, hunting and fishing and break from the city. Some found that the town offered less wholesome pursuits away from the prying eyes of Hollywood. During Prohibition Lone Pine was noted for its bootleggers and brothels catering for the film-makers.

HERITAGE AND TOURISM IN LONE PINE

Heritage and tourism in Lone Pine is projected primarily in terms of film. Its chief attraction is the Alabama Hills on the outskirts of town. Relatively undeveloped, it has no on-site interpretation or walking tracks, though guides and maps are freely available in town. It is in Lone Pine that tourism development is found. Since 1990 it has held the annual Lone Pine Film Festival in October, a community project organised by 500 local people. Its core event is a programme of films made in Lone Pine. Other activities in the festival include parades, concerts, barbecues, discussion panels and guided tours of locations. Much of the appeal is in the presence of actors and film-makers who worked at Lone Pine. For example, the 2004 festival includes panels of both stuntmen and children of the stars. The incorporation of film heritage into this small town's annual festival gives Lone Pine a distinctive destination image. None of the other twelve Western locations has developed a film festival, though Jamestown uses film as the background for its two events: the Movie Railroad Days and Gunfighters' Rendezvous. Revenue from the Film Festival is directed towards the establishment of a film museum. By 2001 $US230,000 had been raised and was used to purchase a site on the main highway.

Construction is scheduled to commence in 2004. Film memorabilia prominently inside a range of tourismrelated businesses, including restaurants, hotels, motels and bar. These restaurants and bars are used as venues for the Film Festival and for accommodation operators it provides an out-of-season peak. The State of California's Interagency Visitors Centre, while primarily concerned with nature-based tourism and recreation, features interpretation on film heritage. The close link between natural and cultural heritage is illustrated by the premier scenic drive–the Mt Whitney Portal Road, also being routed through the Alabama Hills and numerous film locations. A further feature of the area is that films are still being made and that the local county is active in seeking to attract films.

In developing tourism built on its film heritage, Lone Pine has chosen to reshape itself in terms of Westerns. While most major films made at Lone Pine were set in other areas, it is the B Westerns that have come to represent the town. As Rothel noted in visiting a local restaurant, their display of famous actors included only those from B Westerns and excluded those who made bigbudget films. The physical fabric of the town has been altered to portray a Western image. The Dow Hotel was built in 1923 in the then fashionable Spanish Mission style. However, now it has been clad in clapboards to present a frontier image. The local McDonalds is also clad in weathered clapboard rather than in the conventional corporate style. However, in reshaping itself as a Western town, Lone Pine may face problems in the long term. Many of its tourists are of the older generation, nostalgic for the B Westerns of their youth. Given that the popularity of Westerns has been in decline for over thirty years, it may be increasingly difficult to attract younger tourists. In adopting this Western image, other aspects of Lone Pine's history, such as the Gold Rushes and the battle with Los Angeles over the water from the Owens River, are marginalised. Hewison's conclusion that English heritage attractions promoted 'fantasies of a world that never was' could easily be applied to Lone Pine. In this respect, comparisons with the small town of Bodie, 260 kilometres north, are instructive.

Bodie is one of the world's remaining Gold Rush gems, with wellpreserved buildings and streetscapes in spectacular mountains at an altitude of 3,000 metres. Yet, like Lone Pine, Bodie is wrapped in a mythic blanket. It is promoted as a ghost town where time has stood still since it was abandoned. However, in truth it has inhabitants, some its houses have subtly disguised garages and gas cylinders and the buildings are managed, protected and repaired by California State Parks. Nevertheless it is the image of a 'real' ghost town which prevails, brings in tourists and benefits the nearby service centre of Bridgport.

Furthermore, Bodie is often described as having been used in movies, though this is not so. This confusion partially arises from Bodie looking like the town sets in movies such as Shane, The Good, the Bad and the Ugly and Pale Rider. De Lyser reports that it is common to hear visitors whistling the theme from The Good, the Bad and the Ugly and argues that 'many visitors and staff experience not Bodie's actual past, but filmic notions of the mythic West inspired by and projected onto Bodie's landscape'.

CONCLUSION

As a small rural town, Lone Pine needed to develop a destination image that would attract tourists and provide revenue for local businesses. Failure to attract tourists, as in many small rural towns, will lead to population loss and economic decline. In seeking its destination image, Lone Pine competes with scores of small towns across California. Many of these competitors share the same sort of attributes as Lone Pine, for example, a history as a Gold Rush town. To succeed Lone Pine requires a competitive advantage, a destination image that distinguishes it from the others and gives tourists a reason to visit. Lone Pine has achieved this through developing a twofold image. First, as a town which has a history of films being made.

That Lone Pine is surrounded by photogenic scenery reinforces the concept that filmmakers found something special there. Second, Lone Pine has adopted an image as a Western town, based on the majority of films made there. This choice of the West has allowed Lone Pine to take advantage of a vast and persuasive mythic image. This destination image has evolved over time, as the body of films shot at Lone Pine has continued to grow. No one film has had a revolutionary effect, dramatically transforming the town into a tourist destination. Nor has any one film become the key one associated with the town. Furthermore the town has not been a passive recipient of a film-induced tourism cargo dropped into their laps. The link between film and visitation has been developed by the local community, particularly through the running of an annual film festival. Such active effort has made the difference between a small town with an interesting history and a small destination with a vibrant, attractive and enduring image.

7

The Media and the Development of the Tourism Industry

INTRODUCTION

Although much has been written about the role of movies and film in the development of tourism attractions and destinations, little research has attempted to synthesise the role of the media in the development of the tourism sector on a broader level. The aim of this study is to gain an understanding of the influence of the media within the context of tourism on this level. In this thesis, the term 'media' refers to mass communication, specifically with regard to newspapers, magazines and broadcasting. The study explored the diverse role of the media in this process over an extended period, spanning from the early 20th century into the new millennium. It is important to gain a better understanding of the ways in which the media has interacted with the tourism sector, as this information can provide practitioners and academics with insights as to how the media can best be employed to benefit stakeholders of the tourism sector. Sessions can be learned from the past so that the experience gained from it can contribute to best practice in the future. In this way, strategies can be developed to cushion the tourism industry from damaging or erroneous portrayals of the tourism product.

RESEARCH APPROACH

- The study employed case study methodology which was appropriate given that case studies are '...

undertaken because one wants a better understanding of this case because in all its particularity and ordinariness, this case itself is of interest'.

In order, to highlight the variety of ways in which the media has had an impact on the development of the tourism industry, however, this thesis explores, analyses and reflects upon four individual cases within this context. This approach to analysis serves to reinforce and corroborate the findings and is referred to as a collective case study. Yin noted that this approach is particularly appropriate when the research to be conducted will focus on contemporary situations, does not require control over behavioural events and where the form of the research question is how or why.

Moreover, Strauss and Corbin assert that such inductive processes are particularly appropriate '...to uncover and understand what lies behind any phenomenon about which little yet is known'. In this study, tourism refers to the broad industry that encompasses travel and hospitality. Four specific cases studies were selected because they provide information on a crosssection of the tourism industry.

The cases were also selected because:

- They cover an extensive period of time;
- They highlight the diverse roles of the media with regard to the activities, and subsequent development, of the tourism industry. Each of the four case studies, which are presented in chronological order, are notable because they either highlight the consequences of media intervention or a perceived distortion of the event under investigation.

THE 1920'S WAITERS' STRIKE, SAN SEBASTIÁN, SPAIN

San Sebastián is a Spanish coastal town, located on the Basque border. Since the 12th century, the town has been victim to a number of sieges and, at times, was occupied by the French. During the 18th century, San Sebastián was burned to the ground, when Anglo-Portuguese seized the city from the French, but by the 1840's, Queen Isabel II of Spain resided in San Sebastián, during the summer, which was the catalyst for the city's rejuvenation. Indeed, the port city became a pioneer in the installation of trams, electric street lighting and telephones. By 1925, the city's population was 65,930, which was triple it population almost 40 years earlier. From the late 1880's, San Sebastián was one of Spain's two most popular seaside resorts.

San Sebastián directly competed with San Marco for domestic tourists from Madrid, and for international tourists from a number of countries, including France and South Africa. Considered to be a more elite destination than San Marco, San Sebastián drew upon its association with Spanish Royalty, and the Queen's residence was a major tourist attraction in itself.

In order to become an elite resort destination, San Sebastián experienced substantial socio-economic changes during the 1900-1930's, but this was set within the broader context of the corresponding changes in Spain's socio-economic transformation. There were a number of political factions in Spain during the 1900- 1930's, including socialist and anarchist groups, militant Catholics and Basque nationalists. In San Sebastián, these political factions were represented by a range of newspapers, that reported and commented on tourism development in the resort.

Walton notes that:

- The dominant discourse in the most visible San Sebastián media emphasized the resort as a vehicle for the civilising processes associated with sustaining a secure and comfortable environment for the wealthy visitors and with the introduction and assimilation of new standards of consumption and polite behaviour from the European high society.

Walton, however, also identified that there were contrary reports and opinions on the development of the tourism industry, and its impact on the San Sebastián community, in the local media, despite being less conspicuous than those positive views of the situation in the more popular press of that time. For example, La Constantia, a republican oriented newspaper, reported on the seedier side of tourism development in San Sebastián. These reports focussed on the levels of prostitution; the negative attitudes and behaviours of the local residents towards tourists; the dichotomy that was developing between the rich and the poor; and the impact of the casino, which was dubbed the 'Our Lady of the Roulette'. The government did not support this type of commentary, as it leant its support to the development of tourism in the port city. One major incident, or event, that took place in San Sebastián was the Waiters' Strike of 1920.

This strike, and the manner in which it was reported, provides insights into the potential of the local media in developing tourism in the resort. Before its economy was supported by tourism, San Sebastián was largely an industrial town, and the 'face' of the tourism industry for many of its residents were the camereros, or the waiters. The camereros were well-paid compared to many of the residents, hence the idea of them striking for better wages and conditions was viewed rather negatively by the local community. For the government, however, the issue was that the camereros were striking at the peak of the holiday season.

This was a concern in itself, not only because of the short-terms impacts, but also because of the long-terms negative impacts that the strike may have on the destination's image and, ultimately, the development of tourism. Walton and Walton and Smith, what transpired was a plethora of reports in a cross-section of the local media, specifically newspapers. The reports seem to reflect extreme views in that they either 1) support the waiters in their efforts; or 2) downplay their power and their impact on tourism in San Sebastián. Indeed, there seems to be an underlying national political agenda attached to the strike, which may have influenced its exposure in the media.

Walton and Smith analysed the strike in detail and their conclusion was that 'in the long run ... the events of August 1920, did not in themselves make much difference to the trajectory of the San Sebastián's development as a resort'. Although it is inconclusive, it appears that the power of the government in controlling the content and frequency of the media reports about the impact of the strike on tourism services in San Sebastián has obscured much of the 'voice' of the San Sebastián local community in relation to tourism development in this town.

SPECIAL EVENTS AND THE QUEST FOR MEDIA COVERAGE

Special events have been one way in which governments have promoted cities as tourist destinations. Using megaevents, in particular, as part of such a strategy is appealing because of the high levels of television coverage and viewer numbers that they command. The telecast of mega-events provides unique opportunities to portray host cities or nations as attractive tourist destinations. Indeed, Hall asserts that special events, particularly mega-events, can change how host destinations are perceived and that they can provide the new 'middle class tourist' with the impetus to visit the destination in the future.

Currently, mega-events are afforded a considerable amount of sustained media coverage, whilst the number of people viewing mega-events, particularly on the television, has grown substantially during the last decade. In 2003, for example, the telecast of the World Rugby Cup attracted an audience of more than four billion people worldwide. McDaniel, McDaniel and Chalip and Chalip, Green and Hill have conducted research on the relationships between mega-events, media consumption, tourism and consumers. McDaniel, for example, explored the role of consumer characteristics on viewing the network coverage of the 1996 Summer Olympics.

Chalip employed an experimental design approach; to capture the overall telecast of the Honda Indy 300 as well as to test its impact on a sample of students' by presenting them with images of the host destination. These studies have not only highlighted the comprehensive nature of television coverage, or the telecast, of mega-events, but have also reported on the levels and frequency of coverage of the host destination-its landscape, attractions, culture and people. It was found, for example, that as well as images of Sydney Harbour being catapulted into homes around the globe via the telecast of the 2000 Summer Olympic Games, many other aspects of Australia were conveyed to viewers, including other destinations and available tourist activities around the nation. This has led Chalip, Green and Vander Velden to argue that it may be the associated meanings of sports events that are the core of their product, rather than the sports themselves.

The use of special events in destination marketing strategies is underpinned by a range of marketing theories and concepts. Kim, Allen, and Kardes noted that in the case of television advertising, in particular, associating visual imagery with a brand [*i.e.* a destination] is an important component of eliciting affective responses in consumers with regard to that brand. Further, Priluck and Till suggested that much of the advertising on television, pairs products with pleasant stimuli such as agreeable images and enjoyable music aimed at evoking positive responses to the stimuli. It is further acknowledged that the growing use of the telecast of special events in sponsorship marketing campaigns has also influenced the overall use of this form of marketing communication in relation to destinations with regard to tourism.

Predating these important studies, but no doubt with a view to capitalising on some of the benefits, the German authorities commissioned a documentary based on the 1936 summer Olympic games in Berlin, "Olympia". Produced by Leni Riefenstahl, Germany's official documenter, "Olympia" is probably one of the most controversial films in relation to special events. Although, "Olympia" was not specifically commissioned to develop or enhance tourism to Berlin or Germany per se, it portrayed positive images of Berlin and Germany to manipulate viewers' perceptions of Germany and, no doubt, the Nazi regime.

Indeed some critics of the film have suggested that the documentary was part of the Nazi Party's propaganda campaign. A major criticism, for example, is that Berlin's image was 'sanitised' for the 1936 Games. Certainly, much of the commentary on the making of "Olympia" indicates that anti-Semitic signage around the city was removed shortly before both the staging of the Games and the filming of the documentary.

EPICUREAN MAGAZINES AND HOSPITALITY INDUSTRY MAGAZINES

A number of epicurean magazines have emerged in the past few decades, with the most notable of these being Vogue Entertaining and Gourmet. Although few studies have been conducted into the impact of these publications on the industry and its customers, Fattorini has found deep disparity in the content of the messages that are presented to consumers and industry employees. Asserting that consumers read epicurean publications, while industry employees rely on hospitality trade magazines, Fattorini contends that this has contributed to tensions between those who work in restaurants and those who dine in them.

His conclusion is based on an analysis of the content of these two different types of publications as well as the manner in which the content is presented to their audiences. Differences are immediately evident in the presentation of these publications. Hospitality trade journals, for example, generally conform to a standard layout, which Fattorini suggested is attributed to the fact that much of the copy is product advertising. Many of the products that are advertised, such as expensive cooking equipment, sophisticated point of purchase software or employee training courses, require the decision of management to purchase them.

Consequently, the target audience of trade magazines is generally decision-makers holding management positions within the industry and very little of the material in these publications is directed towards front-line employees. In contrast, Fattorini proposes that epicurean magazines are targeted at middle class audiences with relatively high disposable incomes. The information presented in epicurean magazines is designed to educate this audience to the latest trends in food and wine, often set within the context of better-quality restaurants. One of the major issues associated with Epicurean magazines is that they generally portray the hospitality industry as a glamorous environment in which to work. Concentrating more on photographic value rather than any sense of reality, chefs are regularly pictured, in their pristine uniforms, sitting leisurely with a glass of wine or a cup of coffee at a table in their restaurant. Indeed, some of the most recent images of chefs in epicurean magazines are quite artistic. Moreover, the magazines seem to be intent on presenting images of professional chefs who oversee well-managed businesses.

In contrast, within hospitality trade magazines, there is very little attention afforded to chefs, or waiters the main emphasis being on white-collared management personnel. Although both epicurean magazines and hospitality trade journals dedicate parts to recipes, the recipes published in epicurean magazines generally include expensive, or unusual, ingredients. This is an attempt to imbue a level of sophistication, based on the exotic nature of ingredients, to dishes that are often simplistic in terms of the preparation and cooking procedures so that novice cooks can recreate the dishes at home. In comparison, the layout and formatting of trade magazines is quite staid. Parts of these magazines are devoted to recipes, however, they are generally convenience or budget-oriented, rather than focussed on the uniqueness of the ingredients.

The resulting portrayals of the hospitality industry in these two forms of the one media are, at best, unrealistic. There are a number of negative impacts associated with these polarised portrayals of hospitality. Fattorini suggests, for example, that epicurean magazines have given rise to the 'psuedo-professional', who has a wide range of knowledge on food and wine, but has little, if any, experience of working in the hospitality industry. Another term for the pseudo-professional would be the 'foodie', coined by Barr and Levy. It is often at restaurant tables that the tension between those who work in restaurants, particularly those of the front-line, and those who dine in them is most evident. Pseudoprofessionals, as noted earlier, are likely to be from a different social class from the front-line employees serving them. Further, the knowledge that the pseudo- professional possesses about food, wine and its service, can far surpass that of the front-line employee. As a result, this can lead to different levels of understanding as to what represents quality food and service thus deepening the divide between expectations and perceptions of service quality.

THE DAWN OF THE NEW MILLENNIUM

In Melbourne in 2000, as the industry geared up for the New Year's eve celebrations Hede and O'Mahony report on the impact of, apparently, spurious media communications on the demand for hospitality provision. For most operators, hosting events on New Year's Eve would involve skilful financial management because expected increases in operating overheads would need to be recouped-invariably by way of increased charges to customers. It was also anticipated that customers would expect an extraordinary event and that additional staff may be required to meet customers' expectations.

Media reports during 1999, however, contended that hospitality providers would face a number of challenges because there would be an unprecedented demand for catering and accommodation from the public. The media predicted that this would result in exorbitantly high costs for food and beverages; and that employees would be able to command substantial loadings on their hourly rates. Indeed, Faroque reported that by mid-December, the price of food and beverages, had, and would continue to 'spiral', whilst Allen predicted that the loading on employees' normal rates would increase by as much as 400%.

The report concluded that hospitality employees would be earning up to AUS$50- AUS$70 per hour on New Years Eve. Given the need to develop a marketable product early in 2000, coupled with perceived increases in customer expectations many hospitality operators elected not to open on New Year's Eve. None of the hotels in the city in the three star category hosted events, for example, leaving the market open to four and five star properties. Of the hotels that did open, most were in the five star category and they elected to market the evening as a 'gala event' offering packages for food, drink and entertainment. However, prices had to be set in advance of negotiations with the unions about the rates of pay that employees would receive for their services.

Indeed, employee wage rates were not finalised until a short time before the event and early negotiations were hampered by media reports about the value and availability of hospitality employee labour. Consequently, event organisers were forced to predict grossly inflated wage costs which were built into the product price. Prices for celebratory events that were advertised at this time ranged from AUS$300 to AUS$500 per person which, in some instances, was up to three times higher than the usual price for a similar event. At these prices demand was weak and a number of other hotels chose to abandon their planned events.

In the Hede and O'Mahony study, hospitality managers attributed the high prices of their events to the media because they perceived that the media had increased employees expectations of the value of their labour. Although the official wage rates that were finally agreed were not inordinately high, managers explained that they had been forced to factor in substantial increases in labour before the official wage rates had been negotiated with employee representatives so that they could take advance bookings. Securing the appropriate staff for the evening was of paramount importance for them. Indeed, at one hotel, staff had been advised of their work schedules three months prior to New Year's Eve and asked to sign a contract committing to work on the night.

DISCUSSION

The aim of this thesis was to explore the role of the media within the context of the tourism sector, and specifically how the media has intervened with regard to its activities. Four case studies were explored for this purpose. The study has identified a number of ways in which the media has been influential or has been engaged to intervene in events within the context of tourism. The case of the 1920's Waiters' Strike in the resort town of San Sebastián, Spain, for example, shows how the media played an active role in the evolution of the strike and how the media was used, to a large extent by the government, to downplay the significance of negative industrial relations in the hospitality sector. Aligning itself with the local government, which was concerned that newspaper reports of the strike would negatively impact the image of the destination, the media downplayed the power of the camereros, in terms of their organisational skills and the impact that they would have on the service that San Sebastián would be able to provide their visiting tourists. In the second case study, it was noted that, within the context of special events, media coverage is largely exploited as a destination-marketing tool to project positive images of host destinations in order to enhance the destination to potential tourists.

It also clearly illustrated how in telecasts of mega-events, and particularly of the Olympic Games, governments use eventrelated media as part of their image-making strategies. This case also highlights how the media can be manipulated to present a particular image of a destination to potential tourists. The degree of authenticity in media communications is also important given that, although Olympia is considered to be a classical piece of film, the reaction to the documentary was, in the main, one of suspicion. In particular, the 'sanitisation' of Berlin in relation to the removal of any anti-Semitic communications around the city, whilst projecting a 'politically-correct' image, was, considered to be misrepresentative.

In the case of lifestyle magazines, specifically epicurean magazines, the study found that tensions are being developed between industry personnel and consumers of hospitality services. The increasing knowledge that the public has of culinary commodities and techniques, mostly gained through epicurean magazines, means that many of the lower-skilled front-of-house staff are often challenged by customers' expectations. The New Year's Eve case highlights the negative influence of media publications on hospitality provision. Tensions developed at this time were two-fold. In the first instance, tensions emerged between the industry and the media and in the second, tension emerged between the public and the industry. In this case, the media, was blamed for creating a number of unrealistic expectations for hoteliers, hotel employees and their customers. This resulted in financial loss for hospitality providers, whilst the public also missed out on the opportunity to celebrate a special event at a reasonable price. Industry employees were also disadvantaged because many employees lost the opportunity for increased earnings.

Collectively these case studies clearly show that the effects of negative media coverage can be detrimental to the tourism sector and to service provision within the industry. It emerged in this study, that within the context of the tourism industry, the media is a powerful tool that can be used to manipulate the public's perception of tourism-related concepts, including destinations and the industry itself. The study also highlights a political dimension, particularly in relation to tourism development.

This was especially evident in the San Sebastián waiters' strike, where the media was used to garner public support for the Government's position on the strike and its perceived impact on tourism development. A political dimension is also evident in relation to special events. Although the Berlin Olympics might be considered atypical, just as to Roche the power of internal politics is often manifest in the decision to host special events and the bidding process as well as the opportunities for urban development that is often associated with these events.

Given the consequences of negative media comment, it is suggested that destination managers and tourism organisations should be proactive in developing strategies and engaging the necessary expertise to manage the influences of the media on its operations. A coordinated approach by the industry and its relevant industry associations is recommended, including the provision of accurate information and the development of positive media releases in order to avoid media related losses in the future.

RESEARCH LIMITATIONS AND FURTHER RESEARCH

The study set out to gain an understanding of how the media influences tourism and tourism destination management based on the analysis of four case studies. This is clearly a limitation of the study in that it is selective rather than comprehensive or exhaustive. It is, therefore, acknowledged that generalisation of the results gained is tentative. This approach, however, was appropriate given the contemporary nature of the situation.

Further, research, encompassing a greater range of case studies, would be beneficial to uncover more ways in which the media is used, or intervenes, within the context of the tourism industry. The authors of this study would also propose that future research be directed towards developing appropriate strategies with regard to the media so that positive relationships can be developed between the consumers of tourism and the suppliers of tourism products and services.

8

Contribution of the Media to Expectations of Space Tourism

INTRODUCTION

Space travel, until a few years ago, was essentially restricted to professionals. The average individual visited space merely in their fantasies, or vicariously, through the influence of the media such as books, comics, television programmes and films. Those who watched Neil Armstrong set foot on the Moon for the first time in history in 1969 might have wished to have joined him, but the likelihood of this happening was practically non-existent until 2001, when Dennis Tito, the world's first space tourist, made space a potential new tourist destination for the super-wealthy. Recent developments would seem to indicate that space may be opened up to the general public this century, although the rate of this growth is hard to predict.

Individuals have thrilled to the exploits of space travellers through the pages of books, such as Jules Verne's From the Earth to the Moon, H. G. Wells' The First Men in the Moon and Kim Stanley Robinson's Red Mars and comics like Mystery in Space and Flash Gordon. In the 1950's, the Collier's magazine's series of illustrated objects on space reached a circulation of 4 million and Walt Disney included a space-themed segment in his Disneyland theme park at Anaheim known as 'Tomorrowland', which became a popular tourist destination. Space-related films include Rocketship the first 'Flash Gordon' escapade, Forbidden Planet, Barbarella, Star

Wars, Red Planet and Solaris. Television programmes based around space have been endlessly repeated to win new audiences, with well-known examples including Doctor Who, Star Trek, Lost in Space, Battlestar Galactica, and Buck Rogers in the 25th Century. Cartoons on space such as The Jetsons and Space Ghost and animated films like Disney's Ducktales: Space Invaders and Treasure Planet give children an introduction to space as a fantasy world, where the extraordinary is not only possible but probable, and individuals are generally actively involved in their environment, rather than passive bystanders. Destinations are often colourful, vegetated and populated by 'aliens,' friendly or otherwise. It is a far cry from the "magnificent desolation," noted by astronaut Buzz Aldrin as he became the second human being to walk on the moon.

This may be attributed in part to the fact that space movies are not filmed 'on location' and the intended audience's perception of what space is actually like is not generally coloured by experience, unlike films set in well-visited places on Earth such as Paris or the Grand Canyon. Film-makers are therefore free to invent fantasy space environments rather than representing or recreating its often bleak reality. Cinema and television are regarded as possibly the most influential forms of media in the 21st century. While novels on space-related themes may have a powerful effect on the imagination, it is arguably visual media that is most likely to shape popular views of space travel. As Morkham and Staiff state, "The ability for film to transport audiovisually other worlds into the present is unique ... bringing worlds to the spectator that may otherwise remain out of reach."

Most people in Western nations in the modern era have seen space depicted in at least some of the movies or television programmes that they have watched, and it is arguable that the images that they have seen have seeped into their consciousness and influenced their perceptions of space and space tourism experiences, even if it is purely on a subliminal level. Consumer behaviour with respect to space tourism is, as yet, under-researched and we know very little about tourist expectations about possible future space tourism experiences. The experiential aspects of space tourism are also yet to be studied, mainly due to the paucity of potential subjects at this present time and the difficulty of carrying out data collection in situ. One interesting area of future research is to consider the role the media might play in the space tourism experience. This thesis will consider how the cinema might colour the public's expectations surrounding space travel, including the amount of active participation in the experience, the type of activities likely to be engaged in while in space and the nature of the surroundings, as well as levels of satisfaction with the 'real' as opposed to the imaginary experience. It will also suggest areas for future research.

SPACE TOURISM: CURRENT AND FUTURE DEVELOPMENTS

Space tourism, while not yet a fully developed industry, is not merely a futuristic vision. It encompasses a number of different experiences, from terrestrial visits to space themed museums and exhibitions, and flights on a MiG fighter jet at more than twice the speed of sound, where the passenger can see the curvature of the Earth and the blackness of space, to orbital flights on a Russian Soyuz spacecraft to visit the International Space Station, such as those undertaken by Dennis Tito in 2001 and Mark Shuttleworth in 2002, and potentially by Greg Olsen in 2005. These latter flights are reputed to have cost $20 million each, a lofty price not within the budget of the average traveller.

Smith refers to this as "elite space tourism" but notes that costs are likely to decrease with technological innovation and increased volume of passengers carried. Research conducted to date, albeit limited, indicates that there is public interest in engaging in space tourism if not demonstrable market demand. The prevailing view seems to be that space travel for the masses is inevitable, but opinions on when it might occur and what form it might take are mixed. For example, a joint NASA/Space Transportation Association study "concluded that private, high priced 'adventure' trips to space with greater than today's commercial airline risk could become possible in the next few years. Much larger scale, lower priced, orbital operations, could commence in the decade thereafter." The former has occurred with the flights of Tito et al, and the latter might eventuate in the near future, depending on the outcome of recent developments, such as the Ansari X-Prize. This US$10 million prize was established in 1996, to be awarded to the first private team to launch a space vehicle capable of carrying at least three adults to an altitude of at least 100 kilometres, and repeating the feat within a period of two weeks. On October 4, 2004, Scaled Composites from the United States, with SpaceShipOne was successful in their quest to win the X-Prize and their technology is now being adopted by Sir Richard Branson for his newlyannounced Virgin Galactic space tourism venture.

There has been some consideration of the factors that are likely to shape development of space tourism in the 21st century. Aside from the outcome of initiatives such as the Ansari XPrize, its progress is likely to be driven by factors such as the rate of technological development, which makes cheaper and safer reusable vehicles possible, and the nature of future legal and regulatory requirements for the industry, which are not inimical to viable businesses and commercial investment, as well as public support and confidence in a fledgling space tourism industry. Due to cost and safety considerations, most early space tourism experiences are likely to be sub-orbital flights, which might only last for a short duration, allowing the participant to view space for a few minutes and maybe experience some brief moments of 'weightlessness' if they are not required to be strapped in for the entire journey.

Even if space hotels are constructed as potential holiday destinations, they will probably be sparsely furnished and utilitarian, as the cost of transporting construction materials into space will be high based on current technology. Smith paints a picture of future 'frontier' accommodation in space which is less than salubrious and designed to maximise efficiency and functionality. "Of necessity space hotels are new 'techno tourist bubbles' and small in size. Crowding and the regimen of space utilization can be taxing. Sleeping rooms are available to guests on an 8-hour shift basis. Food will be provided from vending-type machines, in packaged solid form. Leisure space will include recreation room for reading, movies and the Internet, earth watching, and exercise." The first space tourists, Tito and Shuttleworth, found themselves wedged in the cramped Russian Soyuz spacecraft, shoulder-to-shoulder with their crew-mates. Privacy was impossible in such a vehicle, and the ride was uncomfortable. 'Space walks' were not available to them, and they spent much of their time gazing on Earth and taking photographs. This is not travel which is likely to satisfy those who like comfort and luxury, nor is it likely to appeal to individuals who like to actively control their travel experiences, at least in the early years of the fledgling industry.

CONSUMER EXPECTATIONS AND SATISFACTION

The anticipation stage of tourist behaviour and tourist expectations have been the subject of much research and discussion, not least because it would appear that "...expectations play a crucial role in framing satisfaction evaluations". There is still scope however for further research in this area. For example sees the potential for new research on expectations to focus on consumer reactions to technological advances and products "and the psychology of responding to those changes." Space tourism arguably falls within this category, and there is thus scope to examine space tourist expectations as an example of consumer response to new and innovative technological developments.

Lovelock, Patterson and Walker define 'consumer expectations' as "prepurchase beliefs about service provision that act as a standard reference point for judging post-purchase performance ..." Consumer expectations can be formed through such means as past experience, word of mouth, external communications by providers and consumers' general attitudes towards a brand. Data on expectations is generally gathered by a researcher before an event or purchase takes place, although it has been argued that expectations about future purchases or events can be gathered after a product use experience. Potential space tourists are unlikely to have their expectations pre-flight shaped by either direct prior experience or the feedback from others, due to the small numbers of people who are likely to have actually engaged in sub-orbital or orbital space tourism in the early days of the industry. Promotional literature might be important in helping to frame expectations, but might fail to take into account attitudes to this new emerging form of tourism which have been influenced by popular culture such as cinema.

TRAVEL AND THE MEDIA

The media can have an important influence on consumption, and travel behaviour, through stimulating the imagination or shaping or influencing tastes and ideas. "Daydreaming is not a purely individual activity; it is socially organised, particularly through television, advertising, literature, cinema, photography and so on". In fact, it has been said that to read a book, watch a film, gaze at a painting or pour over a map is to travel. Celsi, Rose and Leigh acknowledge in their ethnographic study of skydivers that the dramatic worldview presented by the modern media was an important factor motivating participation in this high-risk activity. "In the twentieth-century mass media, the musings of individuals, which were once largely abstract and imaginative fantasy, are concretely instantiated.

Thus, possibilities that might never have been previously considered, including high-risk sports, become tangible behavioural alternatives". Cinema can also be characterised as 'pull factors' for tourism. Many of our films are in turn based on literary works, and literature plays an important role in influencing culture and inspiring visits to places associated with literary works, or literary characters. Hennig highlights the fantasy aspects of travel and its links with the arts, with tourism described as "part of the great and bounteous realm of the imagination," and notes this link between films and literary texts and their influence on "tourists' expectations and experiences". Riley, Baker and Van Doren comment on the cinema's ability to "construct anticipation and allure that induces people to travel" by creating "exotic worlds that do not exist in reality but can be recreated through a visit to the location where they were filmed." There have been a number of studies considering the influence of movies or television as inducements to tourism, such as Tooke and Baker; Riley, Baker and Van Doren; and Busby and Klug but none to date has explored how movies might help to shape our pre-travel expectations in the context of an emerging tourism niche, where there are few other influences to guide or frame tourist expectations.

SPACE TRAVEL IN FILM

Space travellers in the movies fly their own vehicles, visit extraordinary destinations, and battle aliens, in surroundings that are a mixture of the familiar and the unfamiliar. Life on the frontier of space is seemingly never tranquil nor dull. Even though we have yet to find evidence of life in other parts of the solar system, extra-terrestrials are a common feature of space-related literature and film. As Wright notes, "In countless movies and stories space warriors suited with fish bowl helmets [have] focused their ray guns on creatures from outer space." Films such as ET the Extra-terrestrial, Contact, and Independence Day feature aliens interacting with human beings.

A few are benign but most threaten the continuation of the human race and some are depicted as possessing intelligence beyond that found on Earth. The irony is that science is now looking at the most likely signs of life in our immediate solar system as Close Encounters of a microbial kind, which mirrors some of the cinematic depictions of aliens in typical horror flicks such as The Andromeda Strain, The Alpha Incident and Toxic Spawn. Most of the likely destinations for future long-duration space tourism are effectively barren wastelands. At present, we know Mars to be a frozen place with a largely sterile surface regolith, subject to violent dust storms and possessing an atmosphere largely composed of carbon dioxide, with some nitrogen and only trace amounts of oxygen and water. The Moon, as a result of the Apollo flights of the 1960's and early 1970's, was found to be "a desolate, lifeless world", hostile to life, even in its most primitive forms. Will a generation brought up with ET and the Daleks find travel to uninhabited places in our universe a little uninspiring and even boring, let alone being confined to a vehicle or hotel in space with their fellow travellers, rather than roaming the stars like the crew of Star Trek's Enterprise? The narrative of the 'fantastic journey' runs through many of the most popular spacethemed films and television programmes, such as the Lost in Space TV series and movie, Star Trek, the movies Journey to the Far Side of the Sun and Star Quest and the TV series Space 1999.

Star Trek in particular often uses the imagery of exploring "strange new worlds". Adler, story lines or 'tropes' can often form the foundation of travel experiences, and transcend travel styles. One example is the narrative of the "discovery of new territory," or "voyages of discovery" which Adler describes as "a cultural epic that set the [mould] for many later travel postures." Zurick also refers to these voyages of discovery, grounded in literary works and permeating our consciousness like a half-forgotten dream, propelling "people into the world's remote lands." The level of influence this trope has on the future space tourist and their pre and post travel experiences is yet to be studied but it would seem likely that the level of restrictions and lack of active involvement in early space tourism experiences might frustrate those used to the active experiences depicted onscreen.

Other common narratives in space- themed movies are the rescue of Earth and human beings from some calamity or disaster from space, whether from aliens, the impact of a comet or meteor or impending nuclear doom. These are again active rather than passive experiences. Very few films with space-related themes depict space travel as it really is, complete with space sickness, cramped conditions, isolation and reliance to a degree on others back on Earth, perhaps because the fantasy is more appealing. Examples of more 'realistic' movies are generally based on real-life events such as Apollo 13 and the

From the Earth to the Moon TV series. Their applicability to a modern-day space tourism experience is likely to be limited, given they represent experiences which took place over thirty years ago, by professionals rather than tourists, and had the cachet of 'exploration' or pioneer travel about them, involving the first human beings to visit the Moon. Recent documentaries showing astronauts in space, such as Mission to Mir and Space Station 3D are the most accurate representations of current space travel, as opposed to space tourism, we have on film.

THE CINEMATIC EXPERIENCE

While there have been numerous movies with space-related plots since the first credited science-fiction movie, Le Voyage dans la Lune none so far has utilised space tourism as a major theme. Space Future, "While there are plenty of movies from far in the past about space travel, we are unaware of any in which space tourism is a major business activity, or in which realistically portrayed orbiting hotels play a major role. Nevertheless the concept of tourism turns up here and there-just enough to show how the coming reality of space tourism has not been foreseen at all clearly in the movie industry." The movies highlighted in this thesis incorporate a space tourism experience which is possibly more faithful to the 'real thing' than space travel is generally portrayed on screen, but still falls short of the likely reality.

In 2001: A Space Odyssey, passengers are shown flying in Pan Am shuttle spacecraft to space stations, where they wait to catch connecting flights to the Moon. The sole passenger in one scene watches movies screened on the back of the chair in front, just like passengers do today on a typical international flight, although the movie version shows a pen floating around in the zero-g environment, and the flight attendants are forced to wear velcro-based shoes to grip to the 'floor.' Food is served in trays, but has to be taken in liquid form through straws. The atmosphere is quiet, efficient and businesslike, far removed from the fantasy elements of some of the space-themed movies discussed in this thesis. The flight is a mixture of the familiar and the novel to audiences, even in the 1960's but less so today, but there are enough of the unique touches to make it seem innovative and 'new' in comparison to a more commonplace aeroplane flight. The revolving space station on the other hand creates its own artificial gravity, so the guests don't have to contend with items floating around or the potential risk of space sickness. There is little of the hustle and bustle of a hotel on Earth. All is calm and relaxed, with an almost eerie hush.

Space is a pure, almost spiritual experience. A Hilton Hotel sign can be seen on the space station, which is furnished in sterile, minimalist style and mainly in neutrals, other than touches of bold colour. This adds to the feeling of zenlike tranquillity. Moon Two Zero was billed as the first Moon 'western' and features a futuristic tourist industry which handles regular flights to the Moon and Mars in vehicles such as the 'Pan Am Moon Express,' where cabins are strangely just as empty as those depicted in 2001: A Space Odyssey, and a permanent presence on the Moon, complete with saloon bar. Artificial gravity inside the structures gives life in space an appearance of normality, although there is still the need to wear a pressurised spacesuit when going outside.

Tourists can visit the site where Neil Armstrong landed in 1969, to become the first person to set foot on the Moon, in a portent of future visits to historical space sites and places of interest are pointed out as being sights "no tourist should miss." Space travel is mainly commercial in focus, with one character noting that "passengers [are] where the money is." The Moon is shown as an alien environment, and the tourist as a 'foreigner' is a theme running through the movie, even extending to the local population as distinct from visitors. "We are all foreigners here.

Perhaps we should never have come," says Captain Kent. "I suppose bleak is as good a way as any to describe it [the Moon]." Space tourism in The Fifth Element, which is set two hundred and fifty years in the future, is more like today's luxury travel. Some of the action takes place on an orbiting space hotel the mythical planet Fhloston, which is described as a "hotel of a thousand and one follies." To get there, one travels by spacecraft which is fitted with individual cubicles like a Japanese hotel, complete with 'sleep regulators' to allow the passenger the opportunity to sleep for the duration of the flight. We are told that the hotel has twelve swimming pools, including one on the "rooftop" and floats in a higher orbit after 5:00 pm "for the view." Guests watch an opera singer perform in a replica of one of the grand opera-houses on Earth. This extravagant space-equivalent of a modern cruise-ship is not the sort of accommodation which is likely to be built for the first space tourists to enjoy.

The space hotel portrayed in The Fifth Element is certainly vastly different to the utilitarian surroundings of the International Space Station, visited by space tourists Dennis Tito and Mark Shuttleworth, as is the spacecraft in which they travelled there from Earth. "Whilst aboard the ISS space, [Mark] Shuttleworth will not have all the luxury-extras he might be accustomed to in a room on the French Riviera, with day to day life in [space] being sparse given the restrictive environment". Movies from the in-house space station library, rather than live opera performances, are available to the highpaying guests on the ISS, and even a humble shower has yet to be installed for the use of 'guests.'

The space tourism experience, as envisaged by the creators of the movies, clearly has yet to become reality. As the former space policy analyst for the Federation of America Scientists, John Pike, noted in 2001 in relation to the movie 2001: A Space Odyssey, "Pan Am went bust, there are no bases on the Moon, and the Space Station doesn't have a Hilton". Tourists such as Dennis Tito are essentially passive spectators, lacking a large degree of control over their surroundings and their experience and forced to submit to the authority of others. Neither luxury nor privacy appears to be an element of the space tourism experience, at least for the foreseeable future.

FUTURE AREAS OF RESEARCH

Future research may demonstrate that space tourism in the early years of its development disappoints rather than excites participants, based on pre-flight expectations which may have been fostered by cinematic images viewed since childhood. There is scope for examining these early space tourism experiences to see what types of expectations exist during the 'anticipation stage' and what factors have influenced the development of these expectations. Further phases of the research could then look at whether expectations have been met or exceeded, and the reasons for this, with attention paid to the possible role of the media in framing pre-flight expectations and post-travel satisfaction levels. Multiple item scales could be used to measure expectations, and then post-travel satisfaction ratings could be provided for the same items.

Factor analysis could then be used to examine the underlying dimensions of both expectations and satisfaction. A qualitative study of space tourists, concentrating on expectations and satisfaction, might also assist in uncovering some of the more subtle, unconscious influences, such as movies and literature. Other useful avenues of research could involve comparing the results of the study to consumer expectations and levels of satisfaction levels with respect to other examples of new technological developments. Understanding the factors which influence expectations and hence satisfaction with these 'new to world' developments may help providers to 'fill in the gaps,' by focusing on providing information, including promotional literature, which corrects potential stereotypes or myths created or fostered by the media.

CONCLUSION

Tourism research with respect to a new and emerging field such as space tourism is clearly still in its infancy and there remain a great variety of research challenges ahead. Space tourism can be viewed as the outcome of technological change, with scope to consider consumer behaviour towards these new 'futuristic' products and services. The degree to which the media can and does influence expectations of and satisfaction with space tourism experiences, or indeed other examples of technological advances, has yet to be determined, but it may have great implications for future marketing of these new developments. Where there are few other 'reference points' or avenues of information for the consumer to frame prepurchase expectations, such as word of mouth or prior experience, the media may have a powerful influence as a way of filling the void. The subtle effect of the space fantasies created on screen on the minds of potential consumers may need to be counteracted by pre-travel information which provides a more realistic basis for expectations, and thus potentially leads to greater levels of satisfaction post-travel.

9

Understanding the Film-Induced Tourist

INTRODUCTION

Major motion picture films can provide the places, objects and subjects for the gaze of many people, and for some, films may induce them to travel specifically to the locations where they were filmed. Although most motion picture films are not produced with the prime intent of inducing people to visit locations, it has been stated that this medium can enhance the awareness, appeal and profitability of locations through the power of imagery and the fantasy of the story.

These cinematic images may influence consumer decision making processes in terms of motivating visitation to film locations, however, this relationship is complex and little understood. Understanding the relationship between tourism behaviour and popular media, such as film, is becoming more crucial as destinations strive to differentiate themselves in a crowded marketplace.

While there have been several studies examining the relationship between film and tourism, they have tended to focus on:

- Defining the film tourist activity and product;
- Analysing specific manifestations of film tourism;
- Investigating the impacts of film tourism on host communities; and
- Exploring the connections between destination image formation and management.

However, an understanding of the consumer and the

consumer experience is limited. Therefore, further research is warranted to identify, characterise and understand both the potential and actual motivations of the film tourist. In particular, research is needed from the consumer perspective to specifically examine the effects of film on tourist behaviour. That is, does film actually induce tourism? To what extent can film encourage or entice the viewer to become a tourist to the destination depicted or seen in a film? If so, what factors in film prompt site-specific tourism? Is it attributes of place such as the scenery, or is it personality based attributes displayed in the film through characterisation or is it performance oriented storylines that motivate the viewer?

The purpose of this thesis is to contribute to the literature by introducing a new conceptual approach to understanding the potential and actual motivations of the filminduced tourist. For this approach, the Push and Pull Factor theory of motivation presents an appropriate theoretical framework in which to examine film induced tourism. It is proposed that a distinction will be made between the three concepts of Place, Personality and Performance, and whether different or distinct motivations drive or induce travel behaviour.

There may be a wide range of consumer drivers which would allow for plotting tourist types on a continuum, ranging from the specific film-induced tourist to the general film-induced tourist (those who are not specifically drawn to a film location but who participate in film tourism activities while at a destination) to the serendipitous film tourist (those who just happen to be in a destination portrayed in a film. Their presence is not related to film or media portrayal, and they may or may not participate in film tourism activities). This thesis will provide examples, sourced from previous literature on filminduced tourism, to illustrate these three concepts.

It will also review some of the literature as it relates to the nature of the film tourism experience. Through the proposed categorisation approach of media portrayal of Place, Personality and Performance, it might indeed be possible to introduce to the literature a film tourist typology based on push and pull motivation factors. In doing this, a continuum of film created motivation will provide an analysis and breakdown of specific film tourists compared to general film tourists, based on specifically identified motivations. As the model is introduced here in its simplest linear form, it suggests that there is an increasing interest in film as the individual becomes a more specifically motivated film-induced tourist. This model shall be further developed and discussed throughout this thesis.

DEFINING FILM-INDUCED TOURISM

A range of useful definitions has been provided in previous studies, and there also appears to be a variety of ways to refer to this phenomenon, including: Media Induced Tourism; Movie Induced Tourism; Filminduced Tourism; the Cinematographic Tourist; and the Media Pilgrim on a Media Pilgrimage. One universal theme, however, suggests that this newly defined tourism niche refers to a post-modern experience of a place that has been depicted in some form of media representation. That is, an experience that is highly personalised and unique to each individual based on their own interpretation and consumption of media images. It seems that there are different contexts or perspectives from which to define this term.

In its most straightforward and logical context, film-induced tourism has been defined as "tourist visits to a destination or attraction as a result of the destination featured on the cinema screen, video or television". Iwashita furthers this by stating that film, television and literature can influence the travel preferences and destination choices of individuals by exposing them to the attributes and attractions of destinations. Following this type of supply or production driven approach, film-induced tourism has also been discussed in a cultural, heritage and historical framework.

Feature films are often made at significant and identifiable historic or heritage sites and gain increased popularity as tourism destinations after the film has been released. In fact, it has been suggested that some of these special sites actually only become popular tourist attractions because of the film produced on site. It is also important to note that film-induced tourism does not simply occur at identifiable film locations; that is, the sites where feature films have been made, but it also exists in purpose built, commercialised sites such as Movie World, QLD, Australia; Universal Studios, Los Angeles, USA; or Granada Studio Tours, Manchester, UK. Other researchers have defined this tourism niche from the consumer perspective highlighting the behavioural aspects of the film tourist. This approach is usually set within Urry's framework of the 'tourist gaze' in terms of film constructing a gaze for an individual to observe. In this case, people may be induced to visit the places they have gazed upon the cinema screen.

Riley, et al state that it is when "people seek the sights/ sites they have seen on the silver screen, it is then that they, indeed, become movie induced tourists". Major feature films have also been referred to as 'hallmark events' in terms of the potential impact they might have on a destination or special tourism events or as tourism promotion. In fact, it was Riley and Van Doren who characterised movies as a nonmarketer controlled category of hallmark event. Although it is recognised that films are not produced with the purpose of inducing tourism visitation, it is commonly accepted that feature films, seen by mass audiences, can indeed enhance the awareness of the locations in the film, as well as the appeal of these tourist destinations.

MOTIVATION

The study of motivation in consumer research involves two fundamental challenges including understanding the interrelationships between motives and specific behaviour; and developing a list of motives comprehensive enough to capture the diverse range of motivating forces that stimulate and shape behaviour. Having said that, motivation has been defined as the driving force within an individual that impels them to action. It is also recognised as but one of many variables which may contribute to explaining tourism behaviour. Motivations may not be easily formulated or expressed, however, individuals are usually aware or conscious of their plans. The importance of motivation in tourism is obvious. It acts as a trigger that sets off all the events involved in travel. Tourism motivation can be defined as "a meaningful state of mind which adequately disposes an actor [individual] to travel, and which is subsequently interpretable by others as a valid explanation for such a decision". Dann suggests that there are basically two factors or stages in a decision to travel: 'push factors' and 'pull factors'.

Dann, "pull factors are those which attract a tourist to a given resort or destination and whose value is seen to reside in the object of travel; and push factors refer to the tourist as subject and deals with the factors predisposing him to travel. Consequently, Dann hypothesised that the motivation for travel is based on these twin concepts, although, push motivations are generally accepted as the dominant factors. Crompton advances the 'push' and 'pull' framework of motivation and builds on it to include nine specific motives which include:

- Escape from a perceived mundane environment;
- Exploration and evaluation of self;
- Relaxation;
- Prestige;
- Regression;
- Enhancement of kinship relations;
- Social interaction;
- Novelty; and
- Education.

Further, Crompton argued that push factors may be useful not only in examining the initial arousal or 'push' to go on a holiday, but may also have "directive potential to direct the tourist towards a particular destination". Iso-Ahola also identifies two main types of 'push' and 'pull' factors including: personal and interpersonal factors. In his escape–seeking dichotomy, he argues that people are motivated to seek leisure activities in order to leave behind personal and interpersonal problems of everyday life and obtain personal and interpersonal rewards from participation in these leisure activities. Escaping is "the desire to leave the everyday environment behind and oneself", while seeking is "the desire to obtain intrinsic rewards through travel in a contrasting environment". Although Iso- Ahola notes that in relation to other leisure behaviours, tourism is more likely to be triggered by the escape motive. Crompton and McKay, these dimensions are similar generic categories to the push and pull forces proposed by Dann. These motivations are similar to those identified as fulfilling the needs that movie-going fulfills in consumers.

Specifically in relation to film-induced tourism, it is argued that this push and pull theory of motivation is the most appropriate framework in which to investigate film tourism motivation. Indeed, Riley and Van Doren have examined film tourism as a form of promotion and motivation through push and pull factors. Pull factors in tourism motivation theory attract the tourist to a destination while push factors, on the other hand, refer to the tourist and the internal drive leading to action. Thus, it is considered possible to track film's role as an information source, or pull factor, and its influence on tourist motivation and the decision to travel to a destination. The approach suggested in this thesis also hopes to discover which intrinsic motivational factors prompt film sitespecific travel behaviour.

It is anticipated that there are a diverse range of push factors associated with visiting film sites including: fantasy; escape; status and prestige; search for self concept or identity; ego enhancement; as well as a sense of partaking in a vicarious experience. Some of these types of motivations may be more prevalent at different points on the continuum. For instance, as an individual becomes a more specifically motivated filminduced tourist, who actively seeks out places seen in film, it is proposed that there could be an increase in self-actualisation motivations, as these tourists place greater significance on visiting film sites for personal reward.

Whereas a 'general film tourist' is perhaps more strongly motivated by the novelty of visiting a film tourism site or participating in a film tourism destination and a 'serendipitous film tourist' may simply be visiting a film tourism site or participating in a film tourism activity in the course of social interaction with family or friends. Therefore, it is argued that the push and pull framework provides a simple and intuitive approach for explaining the motivations underlying film tourist behaviour. Although the two factors have been viewed as relating to two distinct decisions, it has been suggested that they should not be viewed as operating entirely independent of each other.

For instance, people may travel because they are pushed by their own internal forces and simultaneously pulled by the external forces of the destination attributes. The discussion will now turn to examine the possible range of push and pull factors in film-induced tourism.

PUSH AND PULL FACTORS IN FILM- INDUCED TOURISM

Pull Factors have generally been characterised in terms of the features, attractions or attributes of a destination, such as sunshine or scenery, that lead or pull an individual to choose one destination over another, once the decision to travel has been made. It must be realised that the pull of a particular destination attribute can be driven by multiple motivational forces.

For example, going to a beach holiday destination may be motivated by various internal push factors such as:

- To fulfill socialisation needs with family and friends;
- To satisfy escape needs with rest and recreation; or
- To fulfill sunlust desires to get a suntan.

Recognising that there are likely to be a range of motivations among individual tourists visiting a specific film site, it is proposed that a distinction will be made between the three concepts of Place, Performance and Personality, and whether different or distinct motivations drive or induce travel behaviour.

These three concepts can be categorised this way:

1. *Place*: location, scenery, destination attributes;
2. *Performance*: storylines or plot, themes, genres; and
3. *Personality*: cast, celebrity, characters.

This could prove a useful categorisation for investigating film tourism motivations as it will highlight the specific media representations and attributes that are important to film tourists. That is, what is the tourist experience as it relates to a motivation to visit a site-specific destination? What do these tourists want to do when they arrive at a film location? What is important to tourists in fulfilling a given motivation?

For example, is it the spectacular destination attributes of Place that inspires or contributes to travel to a famous site seen on film or is it the romantic love storyline attributes of Performance that induces travel to fulfil a motivation of escape and romance through vicarious experience? For others, it may be the pilgrimage motivating factor to visit a film location that has showcased their favourite film star or Personality. Thus, this "3 P" categorisation will set a framework for investigating the specific attributes of film tourism motivation.

PLACE

Let us first examine Place as a possible pull factor in film-induced tourism assuming that it involves film location attributes, such as spectacular scenery or unique landscapes that are immediately identifiable and attractive to a viewer. There is no doubt that the development and promotion of a place can be dramatically influenced by film and other popular forms of media. Iwashita has defined popular media-induced tourism, as involving "places which have been popularised or signified as a tourist destination by those popular cultural products which are widely distributed by the ordinary majority". The concept of place relates to an area that has a distinctive internal structure, to which meaning is attributed and evokes certain responses from individuals.

It is through film that such place meaning can be created, altered and reinforced. Santos suggests that the messages and representations created by movies, magazines, television and books cross over to provide an ongoing sociocultural discussion of destinations that serves to construct a dominant frame. The development of such promotional collateral as Movie Maps, which identify film sites and locations, is testament to the pulling power that films have on destinations. Many studies have demonstrated that films are effective as motivational pull factors and can successfully induce film place specific visitation. Many of these destinations have transformed their film sites into tourism attractions, which are then considered worthwhile places to visit. Taking a somewhat different perspective, Croy and Walker examine the use of fictional media in rural areas to assist in the development of a positive tourism destination identity, or sense of place.

Their research demonstrates a growing recognition and appreciation by regional tourism organisations in New Zealand of the role of fictional media in diversifying and developing their regional economic base. For example, images of the Waitakere region of Auckland where the film The Piano was shot, have been used for tourism promotional purposes such as Tourism New Zealand's 100% Pure New Zealand campaign. As a result, the Karekare Beach site still receives visitors from around the world because of the sites seen in the film, and the ongoing use of this imagery. In this example, it could be argued that it is this physical place of the moving image that has pulled the tourist to it.

PERFORMANCE

Next, we shall examine Performance as a pull factor based on storyline, plot or thematic content of film which may, for example, induce travel to fulfill a motivation of escape and romance through vicarious experience. In the case of film induced tourism, Riley and Van Doren provide two examples of films which pull the visitor based on the thematic content of the film rather than any specific physical environmental attractions of place. These include the successful 1989 feature films Field of Dreams and Steel Magnolias.

The first telling a moving story of historic and heroic baseball lore, the other captured the drama of a group of women living in a picturesque southern community. Visitation to the farm where this baseball movie was filmed increased significantly from 7500 visitors in 1989, to 35,000 visitors in 1991. Similarly, there were reports of up to 40 per cent increased tourism to the site of filming Steel Magnolias in Natchitoches, LA. People are not only drawn to the places that form the settings and landscapes for feature films, but they may also be drawn to particular stories and genres, that is the drama of the plot, the elements of the theme and the experiences of the people in the film. It may be that some people make very strong connections with the performance aspects of film and are determined to put themselves in the physical place that has formed the backdrop to the drama. This can be illustrated especially well by the popular Australian television series, Seachange, which first screened in 1998.

The storyline of this series revolved around an overworked city lawyer who decides to give up the fast life for the slower and quieter lifestyle of a small seaside town. This concept or storyline proved extremely relevant, intriguing and popular with audiences, and sparked an increase in visitation to Barwon Heads where the series was filmed. Clearly, tourists were pulled to this destination because they could relate to the situation of the characters in the show. In this case, tourists were drawn to this destination via the concept of making a 'seachange' rather than the destination itself. Another aspect of the performance based attribute in film-induced tourism can be seen in action or adventure films where the adventurous and dangerous storylines are the main attracting feature.

For instance, there are accounts of increases in adventure tourism in non-specific locations after film releases such as Deliverance, Vertical Limit, All the Rivers Run Wild, Cliffhanger. This phenomenon could be attributed to the power of these film genres and storylines. In his examination of historic films, Frost, states that the touristic interest generated from films such as High Noon and Ned Kelly is the strong historical story-based attributes rather than being visually based. He suggests that while films such as these may be set in attractive locations, this is not the prime pull factor for tourists, rather they are pulled by the performance aspects of historic storylines. Riley and Van Doren also provide a television example with Dallas which was the long running

American drama located at the fictitious 'Southfork Ranch'. Riley and Van Doren state that international visitors, in particular, visit this site to relive the expectation of the American Dream of "wealth, cowboys and western lifestyles". Thus, it is not so much the physical site of the 'Ranch' as the place motivator, but the performance motivations to vicariously experience the lifestyles and values of the characters depicted in the series.

PERSONALITY

Finally, another possible Pull Factor in filminduced tourism may be a pilgrimage motivating factor to visit a film location that has showcased a favourite film star or Personality. In this discussion of personality attributes of film, it is film characters as well as the actors/stars who portray them that is of interest. There is no denying the pulling power of Hollywood, the star system and celebrities. These facets of the entertainment industry are all profoundly cultural enterprises and our fascination with these aspects of media reflect our involvement in the meaning transfer they set out to accomplish. Film stars, actors and celebrities are very powerful ingredients of mass media and they are able to draw powerful meanings from the roles they assume in their movie or television characterisations.

Indeed, this is recognised in the public relations, advertising and celebrity endorsement literature. Till and Shimp state that"feelings towards a celebrity are expected to transfer to any endorsed brand through their power status and the recurring association". This is precisely why tourism destination marketing organisations put so many resources into utilising celebrities to promote their regions. Therefore, it could be assumed that if a fan associates Monte Carlo with a famous film character such as James Bond, they may indeed be'pulled' or enticed to put that destination on their holiday list. Moreover, can this explain why many North American fans of the character Mick Dundee in Crocodile Dundee sought out the Australian outback as a tourism destination? Or was it equally because the actor Paul Hogan, with his celebrity status, appealed so much? An example of how popular culture or media may influence tourism behaviour, via the attributes of a personality, is discussed by Pearce, Morrison and Moscardo in relation to the role of famous individuals or celebrities who have become famous in their fields, as the basis for marketing tourism destinations.

They examine the use of famous icons or celebrities such as the 1950s rock legend Buddy Holly in Texas; the legendary pioneer Buffalo Bill in Wyoming; outlaw Ned Kelly in Victoria; and the revered Scottish poet Robert Burns in Scotland, as tourism attracting products. They argue that, without appropriate marketing, the appeal in visiting sites, shrines or museums dedicated to such heroes may be limited to people with active literary, artistic or musical tastes and motivations, or those who are absolute fans. In other words, appealing only to the specifically media induced tourist niche market rather than the incidental tourist travelling on a general itinerary.

AUTHENTICITY

Hall states that authenticity is one of the key motivational factors for tourists, and film tourism, for instance, is one medium that allows people to live out their fantasies of their favourite movies or actors in sometimes mythical places. If visitors seek an imaginary place and its association with fictional characters, questions of authenticity arise in an unfamiliar form.

That is to say that visitors"attach personal meanings to such places and authenticity thus becomes a subjective experience, a combination of the developers' intentions, the consumers' interpretations and the interactions among them". He goes on to suggest that individual motivations vary and that authenticity is not necessarily the major concern of tourists, with affective qualities of place often being more important.

In examining the influence place, personality and performance, as pull factors and issues of authenticity, the concept of literary tourism provides useful examples of destinations that have featured in famous historical and contemporary novels or poetry. Literary tourism is defined as visitation to"places celebrated for associations with books or authors". Squire argues that literary tourism is premised upon a desire to experience a version of the past and to make connections between past and present, fact and fiction. She states that literary tourism trades in images and expectations of people, places and particular historic periods. In a sense, this special interest niche of literary tourism has been a precursor to film induced tourism, with many similar, and indeed identical, product characteristics as well as consumer traits. For example, in relation to place, tourists are drawn to the places or sites that have a connection with famous authors, such as their homes and surrounds.

There is much evidence of this occurring, for example: Bronte Country or Hardy's Country where a region has become characterised by a famous author. In such cases, and in the absence of visual portrayal, it is not so much the destination itself that are important pull factors, but the association with authors and their fictional worlds. The interesting aspect to draw from these types of classifications is that they can be broadly identified as'real life' versus'imaginary' places and often this distinction not clear cut. Herbert suggests that visitors to literary sites probably do not make any distinction between the two worlds. Squire's research revealed that tourists visiting Hill Top Farm of Beatrix Potter's Peter Rabbit fame, experienced great levels of nostalgia for childhood, as well as experiencing notions of a sense of place or English rurality.

This raises issues of authenticity and the fantasy/reality spectrum which are particularly relevant to film-induced tourism. With specific reference to film tourism, Couldrey says that film and television locations are examples of Baudrillard's theory of'hyperreality' in the sense that'hyperreality' represents"simulacra in which'model' and'reality' are confused in a world where access to unmediated reality is impossible". Couldrey further argues that such locations are significant as more than just'simulacra', and that one can assume that visitors to these sites know they are based in fiction. He says the basis for the Coronation Street set's significance is that it is the place where the programme is filmed, and therefore the actual place that one has seen on television, and thus one of the main motivations in going there. Conversely to this, visitors to Nottingham's Sherwood Forest have an image of place derived largely from Robin Hood feature films. This combined with the doubtful historical basis of the legend, may be thought to detract from the visitor experience at the site.

However, it seems that visitors to Nottingham either do not care whether the legend was authentic or expect Robin Hood to be a myth. In his work on Granada Studio Tours, home of the external set of the long running British television soap, Coronation Street, Couldrey refers to the set as a'ritual place' and that the visitors are in fact"media pilgrims fulfilling a motivation to gaze" and experience this site.

He believes that visiting the Coronation Street set is a type of pilgrimage in that it is a journey to a central site which focuses on underlying values. Moreover, when visitors enter the set, an intrinsically significant connection is made between the media world and the real world. As such, it would seem that authenticity is another important consideration in conceptualising a film tourist continuum. It might be argued that the need for an authentic tourism experience, in the traditional sense, is not as important for the specific film tourist as it might be for the general tourist. While authenticity tends to be an important consideration for the traditional tourism experience, the specific film tourist could be said to accept hyper-real experiences in which model and reality are confused.

INTERNAL DRIVERS

In terms of investigating push factors or internal drivers of film-induced tourism, it is anticipated that there are a range of possible motivations that come into play. Such push factors might include; ego-enhancement; fantasy or escape; status/ prestige; search for self-identity; or vicarious experience. These push factors can often be strongly related to the previously discussed pull factors. For example, search for self-identity by acting out the experiences of a favourite actor in a specific location or circumstance. Tourists may be drawn to film sites for more personal motivations such as reliving nostalgic memories from childhood, for example, as in the generational favourite, The Sound of Music, which then becomes a sentimental journey, or visiting Notting Hill for romantic notions. A critical internal driver, or push motivation, in film-induced tourism is the'tourist gaze' in terms of film constructing a gaze for an individual to observe.

The character of the gaze is central to tourism and there are distinct objects to be gazed upon because they are famous for being famous. Sites made famous from film or celebrity tourism could be avenues for pilgrimage to visit the site to gaze. In terms of the gaze, Riley and Van Doren also suggest that film tourists may be motivated by vicarious involvement and identification with locations through movie storylines which allow greater personal meaning to the beholders of the gaze. This notion of'vicarious experience' can be understood through the concept of empathy.

This suggests a visceral feeling about someone else's life which allows an individual to participate in the'posture, motions and sensations' of someone or something else. In certain types of place-oriented films, audiences can learn about the destination by participating in the place related experiences of the characters. They state that it is not unreasonable to consider vicarious experiences with a destination featured in a film as another type of destination experience.

Although just as to Griffin, tourism, in essence, is sensual, emotive and driven by a desire to experience a place and that the sights, sounds, ambience and people are integral to that experience, therefore vicarious experiences can simulate some aspects, but not the totality. Couldry also suggests a push motivation of pilgrimage to ritual sites and labels film tourists as'media pilgrims' who are fulfilling the motivation to'gaze' on sites they have seen on screen. Beeton also suggests that film tourism is about tourists looking for the sites, people, experiences and even the fantasies portrayed by films. This introduces the intangible elements of the individual tourist experience based on individual motivating factors, such as fantasy. Indeed, Riley and Van Doren emphasised that the attractions seen in films"are not only associated with the allure of picturesque physical environments, but also for reasons of pilgrimage, escape and nostalgia". As the Continuum of Film-Induced Motivation is further developed, the internal drivers or the push factors demonstrate their increasing importance as the tourist moves along the continuum. It is at the most specific film tourist end of the continuum that the push factors are at their most significant, in terms of fulfilling a range of self-actualisation type of motivations including ego-enhancement, self-identity, status and prestige and the crucial element of the vicarious experience.

Having suggested this, as Klenosky has pointed out, push and pull factors should not be viewed as operating entirely independently of each other. That is to say, people may travel because they are pushed by their own internal forces and simultaneously pulled by the external forces of the destination attributes. In the case of the specific film tourist, it could be assumed that pull factors are also becoming more important as the tourist moves along the continuum.

It is at this end of the continuum that these absolute film-induced tourists must physically be at the sites of their favourite films, to stand in the footsteps of their movie heroes and relive the special film moments. The proposed approach aims to advance prior work by suggesting that the nature of the Film Tourism experience will influence any such classification scheme, in that some film-induced tourists may be motivated by the externally driven pull factors derived from the screen, while others may be motivated by internal drivers.

Thus, it is proposed that a Continuum of Film-Induced Motivation is an appropriate way to examine the role of film in the travel decision process. More speculatively, the present research suggests a holistic picture of complex motives for film-induced tourist behaviour. It is evident that the moving image has great power to alter, create and reinforce specific destination images, and there is no doubt that film has become a dominant source of information and images. Film also has the power to influence consumer behaviour by creating motivations within individuals which can induce them to act in certain ways. This thesis has contributed to the literature by introducing a new conceptual approach to understanding the potential and actual motivations of the film-induced tourist.

For this approach, it has been argued that the Push and Pull Factors of motivation present an appropriate theoretical framework in which to examine film-induced tourism. The three concepts of Place, Personality and Performance have been introduced as a framework for investigating whether different or distinct motivations drive or induce travel behaviour.

Furthering this approach in investigating the potential and actual motivations of the filminduced tourist, through a motivation-based research design, will provide a new dimension in understanding the film-induced tourist. There may be a wide range of consumer drivers which would allow for plotting tourist types on a continuum of film-induced motivation, ranging from the specific film-induced tourist to the general film-induced tourist to the serendipitous film tourist. It will ultimately bring to light some clarity of the role of film as a contributor to the motivation to travel to a destination.

MOTIVATIONS OF VISITORS

Film-induced tourism has received increasing attention from tourism operators due to its ability to provide benefits to screened locations. Busby and Klug contend that movie production creates visitor number increases at film sites. An investigation into visitor motivations to the Hobbiton Movie Set could outline drawcard features of the destination and general preferences of the travellers, thus allowing tourism planners to focus marketing efforts on these areas of interest. Findings would also assist film site management as they competitively map out attraction differentiation to target their product more specifically for appropriate interpretation.

AIM AND OBJECTIVES

The aim of this study is to determine the motivations and demographic characteristics of visitors to the Hobbiton Movie Set.

The research encompasses the following six objectives:

1. To identify the visitors' point of initial knowledge of the LOTR story, such as the viewing of LOTR or the reading of Tolkien's novel
2. To indicate whether the visitors are aware of other LOTR screened locations
3. To gain an understanding of the motivations of visitors to the Hobbiton Movie Set
4. To determine whether the visitors' motivations incline towards iconic attractions within LOTR rather than other factors such as learning or novelty
5. To specify whether the visitors' motivations include an interest in Tolkien's novel
6. To ascertain demographic characteristics of the visitors to the Hobbiton Movie Set

STUDY SITE

Matamata is situated within the Waikato region of New Zealand's North Island. Located approximately fifteen minutes from Matamata, the Hobbiton Movie Set was created on the property of the Alexander family farm for the production of LOTR in 1999. In October 2002, the Alexanders were given permission by LOTR's production company and legal owners of only the created set, New Line Cinema, to allow visitors to the screened location. This facilitated the Alexander's formation of Rings Scenic Tours and the subsequent launch of Hobbiton Movie Set tours on December 1, 2002. This study was conducted at the Matamata Visitor Information Centre, currently managed by staff from the Matamata Public Relations Association. The Visitor Information Centre is the start and end point of the two-hour, fully guided Hobbiton Movie Set tours.

CONSUMER BEHAVIOUR

Within tourism research, emphasis has been placed on

consumer behaviour analysis. Consumer behaviour within tourism is "...the study of why people buy the product they do, and how they make their decision". This why and how emphasises that needs as well as consumer values, perceptions, motivations and decision-making are critical to the expansion of travel behaviour knowledge. Consumer behaviour also involves perspectives from psychology, anthropology, sociology and economics. The psychological aspect of consumer behaviour examines consumer motivations, perceptions and attitudes. The paucity of research pertaining to the sociopsychological aspects of film-induced tourists has signified that this subset of consumer behaviour justifies investigation.

MOTIVATION THEORY

Motivation just as to Fridgen is: "...a force within an individual which causes him/her to do something to fulfil a biological need or psychological desire". This relates to Crompton's proposal that individuals live in a socialpsychological equilibrium that may become unbalanced over time, resulting in a state of tension, imbalance or disequilibrium, triggering need arousal within an individual. The recognition of a need causes an individual to choose a course of action in an attempt to re-establish equilibrium. For an individual to satisfy a need and return to a state of equilibrium, an objective must be present. The next part will discuss travel as the objective and the notions of 'being away to' and 'being away from' as motivations for travel.

TRAVEL MOTIVATION

No single theory can possibly encompass all individual travel motivations. This, alongside the heterogenous nature of tourism behaviour and the belief that multiple motivations can be experienced simultaneously, makes it a challenging area to investigate.

THE SEEKING AND ESCAPING DIMENSIONS OF TOURISM MOTIVATION

McCabe acknowledged that a major contribution to travel

motivation theory is Iso-Ahola's social psychological model of tourism motivation. Mannell and Iso-Ahola identified two motivational forces or dimensions of escaping and seeking that operate simultaneously to stimulate and result in tourist behaviour. An individual's travel behaviour is influenced by the desire to escape from one's routine personal and/or interpersonal environment while seeking rewarding personal and/or interpersonal experiences. The personal and/or interpersonal escaping dimensions refer, respectively, to an individual leaving behind personal troubles and/or co-workers or family members.

Conversely, the personal and/or interpersonal seeking dimensions consist of learning, exploration and relaxation for the individual, while social interaction is the focus of his/her external reward. Dann, Argyle and Goossens support Iso-Ahola indicating that the personal dimensions of escaping and seeking are frequently expressed intrinsic needs which accurately reflect a person's basic motivational force. Concomitantly, Ingham contends that there is a clear distinction of extrinsic motivation or the drive behind activities to which obvious external rewards are associated.

This belief is directly proportional to Iso-Ahola's interpersonal seeking dimension. In addition, the intellectual factor component of Beard and Ragheb's empirical results include individual motivations such as exploring and learning which clearly exemplify a link with the personal seeking dimension of Iso-Ahola's model. The ambiguity regarding the dominance of one motivational dimension over the other under a given condition constitutes a theoretical gap. This relates to this investigation as it is anticipated that the findings will establish the relevance of each dimension to the social phenomenon of filminduced tourism.

FILM-INDUCED TOURISM

The relationship between tourism and feature films is a relatively new field of academic study. Filminduced tourism has been defined as "...tourist visits to a destination or attraction as a result of the destination being featured on television, video or the cinema screen". Hottola contends that popular movies have the propensity to cause certain things to happen within the everyday scene of tourism. They can impact extensively on a screened location not just during production but also after the film has been released. For example, in Australia, a new tourism industry has emerged following the production of George Miller's The Man from Snowy River and its sequel. Through her research, Beeton found that Mansfield in Victoria, the screened location for the movie, experienced a surge of movierelated businesses after its release.

To date, the influence of film on tourism has been evident at film sites globally mainly through referring to changes in visitor numbers following a movies' release. However, this has only been established anecdotally and has yet to be empirically measured. This study will address the lack of empirical evidence in film tourism literature by analysing responses from face-to-face structured interviews conducted with tourists who visited the Hobbiton Movie Set as featured in LOTR.

THE FILM-INDUCED TOURIST

Literature pertaining to the concept of a film-induced tourist is scarce. Urry, however, proposes that as an individual chooses to gaze upon a place, anticipation is sustained through a variety of non-tourist practices, such as film, which construct and reinforce the gaze. Riley, Baker and Van Doren contend that the 'sight/site' properties of a film location qualify as icons for tourists to gaze upon. In this respect, the film-induced tourist is defined as "...a person who seeks a 'sight/site' that is seen on the silver screen".

In terms of this research, a visitor to the Hobbiton Movie Set may be a film-induced tourist who has also read Tolkien's novel, on which Peter Jackson's LOTR is based. Nevertheless, this visitor cannot be classified as a literary tourist as they are described as "...people who are drawn to places that an individual author has wrote about or was associated with". Tolkien's novel was not written about specific places, and nor was Tolkien associated with New Zealand. Thus, the definition of a literary tourist is acknowledged but will not apply to this study. However, it is anticipated that the experiential gaze of a visitor may not only be reinforced through scenes in the film, but also by impressions created through reading Tolkien's novel.

MOTIVATIONS FOR TRAVEL TO SCREENED LOCATIONS

Fictional and non-fictional films are powerful motivators especially when storyline and film site are closely related. Movies have essentially become 'pull' factors, enhanced by viewer involvement in the story and the film maker's ability to captivate. Riley et al. contend that the attractive qualities or 'sight/site' properties of a screened location that induce people to travel to it are as diverse as the movies in which they are depicted.

In linking the notion of a film-induced tourist to iconic film attractions and motivational theory, Ross and Iso-Ahola's empirical conclusion that the seeking dimension of Iso-Ahola's model is the main motivational force for sightseeing tourists may be valid. Visitors to screened locations seek 'sights/sites' portrayed in films and may also be seeking personal rewards such as novelty or knowledge.

METHOD

Given the exploratory nature of the investigation and its research objectives, a triangulation method was selected as the most appropriate. Hussey and Hussey indicate that triangulation is where both qualitative and quantitative methods are used in varying ways and degrees. The utilisation of triangulation can also assist a researcher in the choice of a suitable research instrument. For this research, interviewer-completed questionnaires were selected to obtain the data required for analysis.

INTERVIEWER-COMPLETED QUESTIONNAIRES

Interviewer-completed questionnaires involve the researcher narrating structured questions to respondents, face-to-face, recording short notes on the questionnaire and tape recording if required. During this type of questionnaire procedure, the research instrument is not visible or provided to the respondents. This method is most suitable as it is associated with qualitative and quantitative methodologies. This technique also provides instant feedback and clarity, allowing the researcher to elicit extremely rich information. Further, this form of questionnaire delivery achieves higher response rates and more accurate answers compared to respondent-completed questionnaires.

RESEARCH INSTRUMENT DESIGN

The interviewer-completed questionnaire comprised 17 questions in total and was structured into three forms of questioning: screening, objective-related and transitionary. The pair of initial screening questions aimed to filter respondent relevance through two basic criteria. The respondents were required to be at least 18 years of age and have travelled at least 30 kilometres to the Matamata Visitor Information Centre. The second criterion allowed for the respondents to clarify their place of origin, whether a town within New Zealand or another country.

The 11 objective-related questions focussed on eliciting data relevant to the research objectives, while the four transitionary questions assisted in balancing the intensity of the procedure. The use of interviewercompleted questionnaires suggests that close-ended questions are paralleled with the positivist paradigm and open-ended questions with the interpretive paradigm of any research method. Therefore, the objective-related questions were sub-divided into open-ended, allowing respondents to speak for themselves, and close-ended questions, designed to elicit 'yes/no' replies.

RECORDING DATA

The interviewer-completed questionnaires were administered to respondents after they purchased their tickets but before they embarked on the Hobbiton Movie Set tour to ensure that motivations and not satisfactions were measured. For each open-ended question, several anticipated response categories were prenoted on the questionnaire with numeric codes attached to facilitate efficient grouping for subsequent analysis. The responses to the majority of the close-ended questions were similarly recorded. As the research process was interviewercompleted, two 'show cards' were prepared for the demographic questions relating to each respondent's age group and average level of personal annual income. Tape recording was utilised during the data collection phase with the consent of individual respondents. Each interviewer completed questionnaire process was recorded on a separate audio tape, ensuring a systematic approach. During the data collection period, openended responses on each recording were transcribed, and each completed questionnaire was also cross-checked with its respective recording.

POPULATION AND SAMPLE

The population is defined by Veal as "...the total category of subjects, which is the focus of attention in a particular research project". The sampling method utilised was the 'next to pass' or convenience sampling technique, allowing a focus on the elaboration of issues in microsocial contexts in this case the phenomenon of film-induced tourism. This sampling method involved the researcher approaching the next individual who entered the Matamata Visitor Information Centre after his/her ticket purchase for the Hobbiton Movie Set tour, in non-random manner. Recruitment and data collection were conducted until a sample size of 40 respondents was reached. This non-probability sampling method was selected due to the inherent exploratory nature of this study of traveller motivations, and reduction of bias that can occur in a personal selection process.

DATA ANALYSIS

The data collected was analysed in two ways, dealing with its qualitative and quantitative responses respectively. During the transcription phase, important elements within the open-ended responses became clear and connections between them were formed. These elements were restricted to the initial response by the respondent and while some responses may have had multiple elements, only the first mentioned element was taken into consideration. This is because the initial response is the most immediate and is the primary focus of this research. The responses were then arranged and evaluated in relation to the research. Lazarfeld's notion of complementary grouping was applied, giving rise to several common theme categories, trends and patterns within the open-ended responses.

Frequency distributions were also generated for these common themes and categories, ensuring that the relevant research objectives were met and indicating the importance of identified motivational factors. Second, a univariate method was selected for the analysis of the close-ended responses. The numeric codes attached to pre-noted responses of the close-ended questions were arranged and displayed through a frequency distribution for each variable. As for the income variable, the mid-point of each income bracket selected by a respondent was taken as an average singular reference for conversion to the equivalent Australian currency.

For respondents who earned more than 100,000, 100,000 was taken as the reference. The responses to the two demographic questions were manually arranged into common categories. Response categories concerning the respondents' highest level of education were developed, however the Australian Standard Classification of Occupations was used for categorising the respondents' current occupation to ensure accurate socioeconomic analysis. Subsequently, these categorised responses were assigned numeric codes and frequencies.

LIMITATIONS

The primary limitation is that the study was conducted at an overseas location thus creating time and budget constraints, and resulting in a restricted sample size.

DELIMITATIONS

A delimitation exists within this research that restricts the results to a specific but focussed discussion. Poynter identified delimitations to be "...restrictions placed on the study to make it doable". This investigation was conducted at only one location, that is, the Hobbiton Movie Set, where participation in film-induced tourism was apparent.

RESULTS AND DISCUSSION

Results from the interviewer-completed questionnaires will be discussed in two parts. First, the demographic details of the respondents are presented. Following this, information elicited from the close-ended and open-ended questions within the research instrument are revealed in tandem with the non-demographic research objectives outlined in the Introduction.

DEMOGRAPHIC PROFILE OF RESPONDENTS

During the data collection phase, 46 individuals were approached and asked to participate in the interviewer-completed questionnaire. Of these, six were either deemed ineligible based on the screening questions or declined to contribute. Hence, 40 visitors qualified and participated in the study, conferring a valid response rate of 86.9 per cent.

SOCIO-ECONOMIC DATA

In line with the Method discussion, all average income levels of respondents are represented in Australian currency. The range of occupations held by respondents, of which 27 were full-time positions. The respondents' marital status was essentially divided into the 'single' and 'married with children' categories. Also, most respondents had attained a completed Bachelor Degree or higher, with respondents' average level of personal annual income being quite varied.

GEOGRAPHIC DATA

It is apparent from that respondents originated mainly from the USA and the UK. As it was the Northern Hemisphere's summer during the data collection period, it is contended that the practice of embarking on international travel during summer in these countries, especially the USA, contributed to the extent of their presence. This can be supported by the fact that respondents from other European countries and Canada were also present but scarcely and evenly spread. In addition, the sample consisted of only one Australian respondent suggesting that Australia's proximity to New Zealand did not outweigh the fact for potential travellers that both countries were experiencing winter.

10

The Role of Media Communications in Developing Tourism

INTRODUCTION

Media communications technologies are imperative for frontline investments for sustainable globalised tourism development indicators. The powerful effects of media communications technologies can dawn on the African continent with sweeping changes of attitudes and behaviour among the key actors in local, national and global tourism for peace, security and sustainable development. The social, cultural, economic, political and environmental benefits of tourism would usher in monumental and historic changes in the African Union. As the verdict goes, the media has a social responsibility to enhance the blending of local, national and international cultural values for enriched politics, society and economy in Africa.

Public communications strategy based on access to quality information and knowledge will drive the new global tourism partnership for Africa to heal the current North-South widening gaps through partnership initiatives such as: peace and security, conflict resolutions for eco-tourism, quality tourism, joint ventures, technology transfer, exchange bids, subject-to-subject attitude, being explicit about values, transparency in interests, clear standards, sticking to mutual agreements, capacity building and development, institutional building and observance of tourism ethical standards. Development communication is one of the best ways to go in developing eco-tourism in Africa. This strategy involves the planned communication component of programmes designed to change the attitudes and behaviour of specific groups of people in specific ways through person-to-person communication, mass media, traditional media or community communication. It is aims at the delivery of services and the interface between service deliverers and beneficiaries where people are empowered to by informed choice, education, motivation and facilitation effecting the expected changes.

This can be done by media advocacy targeting all key stakeholders involved in the tourism industry. Effective use of communication techniques can barriers and promote better uses participatory message design which combines both traditional and modern media. Participatory communication strategy design methodology is used to build on the results of the participatory rural communication appraisal. It involves a systematic process for participatory communication strategy design, and the principles for communication planning, message development, multimedia material production and the implementation of communication activities in the field.

BRITISH WAR-TIME PREMIER SIR CHURCHILL SAW THE "PEARL OF AFRICA"

Some of the basic concepts and principles of ecotourism rotate on catchwords like: environmentally and culturally-oriented tourism; conservation of natural resource enhancement tourism; local community based socio-economic welfare tourism; participatory community development of tourism. Uganda is emerging from years of political instability and entrenched poverty. Soon after 1971 military coup which ousted President Milton Obote from office, Uganda's flourishing tourism industry was dealt a death blow by a series of political upheavals and social turbulence which ravaged tourism industry in the country. Tourism is now waking up once more in Uganda, a country which was once described as the "Pearl of Africa", by the British war-time Premier, Sir

Winston Churchill. Uganda's unique rich biodiversity makes it a natural candidate for ecotourism industry because tourism is currently the best product and service which Uganda can market globally with increasing competitiveness.

Some of the key principles of sustainable tourism development include the following:

- Tourism should be initiated with the help of broad-based community-inputs and the community should maintain control of tourism development;
- Tourism should provide quality employment to its community residents and a linkage between the local businesses and tourism should be established;
- A code of practice should be established for tourism at all levels-national, regional, and local-based on internationally accepted standards.

Eco-tourism seeks to provide yardsticks for tourism activities, environment impact assessment and auditing. Sustainable tourism guarantees the optimal use of environmental and natural resources for sustainable development among government, the private sector and communities. Ecotourism is sustainable tourism that caters for the ecological conservation of both human and natural ecology.

THE CHALLENGES AND ISSUES IN DEVELOPING ECO-TOURISM POLICY

There are some basic challenges and issues affecting the development of sustainable tourism policy in Uganda and the rest of Africa. A glance at the current Uganda's Tourism, Trade and Industry policy and working documents, depicts the country more or less as a plausible "work-in-progress". The ministry has a policy desk. The role of ministry is to formulate and support strategies, plans and programmes that promote and ensure expansion and diversification of tourism, trade, cooperatives, environmentally sustainable industrialization, appropriate technology, conservation and preservation of other tradable national products, to generate wealth for poverty eradication and benefit the country socially and economically. Since 1990, the World Bank and Global

Environmental Facility have stepped up investment development for conservation potentials of ecotourism. In 1995, GEF initiated a US$4 million ecotourism project in Uganda, and a similar initiative was planned for Zimbabwe. Ugandan law protects national parks and reserves for the highest conservation standards. The main snag here is inadequate resources to monitor legal and policy compliance, although a project component was launched to provide effective patrols and economic incentives to the local communities.

The media would be instrumental in communications campaigns and better coverage. Media campaigns could be an effective check on the unscrupulous activities of eco-tourist agents or agencies including the public sector actors. Although the Ugandan National Environmental Action Plan covers the whole country, its implementation has been ignored in some parts of the country due to poverty. There is a huge uncertainty about the sustainability of the current ecotourism initiatives in the county on the grounds that the current formula for revenue sharing among the stakeholders cheats the operators.

The national tourism policy was formulated to promote economy and livelihood of people, especially poverty reduction development of sustainable and quality tourism. Though the number of tourists has significantly increased by about 68.18% between 2003 and 2004, the visitors' numbers to protected areas is relatively lower due to inadequate security situation in some protected areas, and lack of implementation of a sound marketing strategy and the new tourism safety plan. Tourism plays a major role in Uganda's economic development. But over the years, the industry has suffered bad publicity which has contributed to its slow progress.

For example, the protracted civil strife in Northern and Western parts of Uganda has affected tourism development in the country for peace and security reasons. Uganda has registered low figures from its major tourists' sources like UK and USA. Urgent challenges facing tourism sector in Uganda are: institutional weakness; lack of appropriate legislations and legal framework; pressure on the protected areas; local conversion of land for alternative uses; and lack of funding to run the industry. Greening tourism industry is a multidisciplinary approach aimed at: better dispersion of tourism in time and space; promotion of environmental friendly forms of tourism; reduction of private car use in favour of public transportation; better management of mass tourism; and eco-awareness of tourists. A lot of local initiatives to prevent gross pollution by waste- soft drink-cans, plastic bags, mineral water bottles.

EU tourism development issues are: public and industry awareness of the dangers of mass tourism; development of eco-tourism; more responsible management of tourism at member-states level; the exponential development of tourism sector; development of environmentally friendly tourist activities; the undermining of environmental policies in sensitive areas by tourist activities; lack of clear regional strategy for promoting a more environmentally friendly tourism; and the fact that tourism sector's environmental impact can't be fully evaluated because of the fragmentary nature of information available.

PEACE AND SECURITY ISSUES IN UGANDA'S TOURISM ECO-INDUSTRY

Gorilla tourism in Uganda was suspended for several years in order to avoid the risks of very frequent gorillas-human interactions for a while. Uganda's tourism industry is quite small owing to the emerging ecosystems investment development in the country. There is cause to fear that some of the ecosystem elements may be affected by local people who are less informed about the current eco-conservation guidelines. There are several environmental problems in and around the biodiversity rich conservation zones in Uganda. In some cases many people found themselves in these areas as a result of civil wars, abject poverty in their villages, and poor social service delivery by both the local and central governments.

Rapid deforestation in Uganda is nationwide in both urban and rural local communities mainly as a result of eco-suicidal government investment projects and the overwhelming national dependence on biomass fuel for cooking, boiling, lighting, drying and space heating. Increasing numbers of visitors also increase damand for fuel. Rich biodiversity are being abused by eco-illiterate tourists who roam their natural habitats. The lands within the Bwindi and Mgahinga parks are part of the threatened Afro-montane forest. The only remaining population of the highly endangered mountain gorilla lives in Uganda. In August 1989, the Ugandan game department stopped gorilla tourism on the advice of biologists.

Deaths of gorillas as a result of human contact and infection had been reported in neighbouring countries. There was also a notable lack of professional supervision over Ugandan gorilla habitats. After the ban, steps to be taken to implement governmental policies for the integration of conservation into tourism were defined. More generally, tourists, even ecotourists, may not be so utterly conscious as to not litter along their way. Uganda's Bwindi Impenetrable Forest is home to not less than 300 mountain gorillas, which stand for about half of the world's species' population.

PROSPECTS AND PROBLEMS OF ECO-TOURISM DEVELOPMENT ACTIVITIES IN UGANDA

In 1991, the local farmers living near Bwindi Rainforest Park in Uganda were legally prevented from accessing the traditional areas where they used to harvest firewood and herbs as a result of a new conservation project set up by an NGO. The alienation of the poor farmers caused a stir but it was rectified by involving the local farmers in environmental, economic and community development activities. Their interests were met when some of the US$4 million GEF project money was used to build health clinics, schools, fund the park management and eco-research. The European Development fund is also funding Uganda sustainable tourism development programme to strengthen tourism industry to benefit the rural communities in the protected areas and to develop the current community tourism projects there. Due to the current slow performance of the industry in Uganda, there are still very few new investment development initiatives so far. The ministry is under funded and there is little wonder that the result has been minimal development. Uganda's national tourism industry's has some of the most enthusiastic private sector actors. Unfortunately they are less professionally equipped to perform their perceived role in the industry.

The current legislations guiding the development of tourism in Uganda are under review and the proposed human resources development programmes have not yet got off the ground. The tourism sector in Uganda is still underutilized, under capitalized, underdeveloped, and the private sector is paying a high price due to low profit margins from their reinvestment. There is a loud cry for a big improvement in the quality and standards of services, products and operations in the business. There is evidence of poor performance and slow investments in the enterprise. There is weak capacity in both the public and private sectors as the single most difficult challenge.

At the same time the lack of capacity in the private sector cannot be ignored. If the overall Government policy of a private sector driven industry is to be achieved, continuing work will be required to achieve success. The EU has funded the private sector foundation of Uganda to implement the institutional strengthening of private sector groups. Uganda's eco-friendliness is attested to by the creation of six more new national parks and many community-based ecotourism projects with components to curb the spread of HIV/AIDS while promoting women's rights.

While the local climate is very fine, Uganda has experienced intermittent armed clashes and civil strife in the eastern Democratic Republic of Congo and the influx of refugees into the country's national parks. Media reports indicate that the UWA is collaborating with the security agencies to monitor the security situation along Uganda's common international border with DRC. Several security measures are being implemented to ensure the safety of the tourists visiting our national parks and all the other tourist areas and the regular influx of refugees into the country is part of the national peace, security and tourism conflict situations to be handled by the government. The three neighbouring countries of Uganda, Rwanda and the DRC have planned to run a single pricing system for gorilla tourism. Each of the three Great Lakes countries provides gorilla trekking services by various tour companies. All the three have decided to unify the procedures for booking gorilla permits, making payment refunds, providing business incentives to the private tour operators.

Until recently, persistent civil and political conflicts, poaching, illegal trade and ecological degradation resulted in the decline of biodiversity loss in many parts of the country. Biodiversity poaching has plagued Uganda's tourism industry at alarming rate countrywide. It is only recently that tens of poachers have decided to either resign or retire from the poaching business in Uganda. The new found hope cuts across many African countries including the Cameroon in West Africa. The "dark days" of poaching are predictably coming to a sobre end as scores of illegal hunters have started to down their tools in response to an open amnesty by the Uganda Wildlife Authority.

Until recently, Uganda was dogged by a "loud absence" of the White Rhino species from among its national biodiversity bank. The apparent climb-down by many Ugandan poachers was attributed to a national education and awareness campaigns for behavioural change in Uganda. Uganda now has six more rhinos at Ziwa Rhino sanctuary and this is projected reach 20 in the coming years. The country still has to come to terms with the following bottlenecks: low incomes; low public awareness at national and international levels of the potential of tourism, weak collaboration and coordination in the tourism development process and a lax commitment by private actors in the country.

Some of the key issues which put in doubt, the sustainability of Uganda's wildlife management survival are: persistent land use conflicts; cancerous poaching; illegal settlements within protected areas; eco-hostile tourists' behaviour; conflicting national laws and policies. The main objectives of the national wildlife policy 1995 are to: ensure in perpetuity for Ugandans and the global community, the wildlife resources within and outside protected areas and to enable the people of Uganda to derive ecological, economic, aesthetic, scientific and educational benefits from wildlife. The crux of the matter is to include the rural people who share much of the land with wildlife in the new business. Uganda is known for its rich wildlife species some of which are endemic in the country.

Uganda's biodiversity is ranked among the top 10 countries in the world specifically the mammalian species. The country hosts 11% of the global birds and over 50% of the world's mountain gorillas. The major national constraints facing the country's wildlife resources include: land use conflicts, illegal resource harvesting, policy failures, instability and civil strife, and financial constraints. The forest department in Uganda has started pilot activities in ecotourism as a viable option for non-consumptive use of forests. Infrastructure has been development in Mabira, Budongo, and Mpanga forest reserves and both sites are already registering unprecedented of the local and foreign eco-visitors, the current trends show.

ICTS PUBLIC CAMPAIGNS AND POLICY STRATEGIES FOR SUSTAINABLE TOURISM

African countries should promote the use of effective information and communication technology public campaigns and policy strategies for widespread adoption of sustainable tourism, peace and conflict resolution, cultural competence and mutual inter-cultural communications in the continent. The audience access to the intended information is the main determinant of the choice of media strategy to adopt for effective tourism campaign strategy. A combined mass media and interpersonal communication approaches would achieve maximum audience exposure to the intended media messages. ICT innovations should allow users to find and use relevant information and give a feedback in a similar fashion. Institutional capacity building project for protected areas management in Uganda in the ministry of tourism, trade and industry and the national tourist board of Uganda has begun. The funding covers a national information communication and policy strategy for the country. Appropriate use of information communication technologies can increase the credibility and effectiveness of projects to improve access to quality information, transparency in public sector decision-making, capacity building in both the private and public sectors. The policy objectives of the ICTs project are to: develop a national information and communication strategy; establish a national ICT policy; promote the use of ICTs for development; implement an integrated public sector information management system; improve transparency in fiscal accountability oversights; and set up a national web-site. Developing public communications campaigns for sustainable tourism in Africa is the bedrock for achieving sustainable development for poverty reduction in the African Union.

One of the main reasons is that sustainable tourism is the basis for the attainment of sustainable peace on the continent. Tourism in Africa is synonymous with environment and natural resources. Indiscriminative destruction of our natural resources is a sure recipe for the current mass poverty in Africa. It is a living reality which deserves global approach. Awareness campaigns are critical for effective policy, constitutional and legal implementation of sustainable tourism principles, plan, goals and projects in Africa and globally. Effective information and communications strategies are crucial for policy and decision makers themselves who are often the divers of natural resources destructions on the continent.

THE EFFECTS OF MASS MEDIA ON THE CONTEMPORARY CULTURE AND SOCIETY

The media are agencies of mediation in that in reporting events they propose certain frameworks for the interpretations of those events. They mould or restructure our consciousness in socially and politically consequential manner. It can be said that the media is a part of social reality which shape our perception. A case in point is the "reality TV" programming.

The reality-defining role of the TV programming is a propaganda function of the press in that each media tends to recruit public support for the political or social philosophy it favours, seeks to sell a particular political or social definition of the events it reports. Analysts like Evans argue that the invasion of reality TV has begun and the craze is set to grow in United States and its effect will overlap to Africa due to its popularity with young audiences. Media programmes such as Survivor and Big Brother have proved to be big winners for the network. Reality TV programming format meets both local and international needs because of its sensationalism and trivializations based on real situation and involving the real people. The internet transcends the censorship and regulation imposed on radio and television.

The internet granted the freedom enjoyed by print media and common carriers such as letters, mails, and cable to the public media. Through audio streaming it is possible to enhance the reach of radio signals to any part of the world. The internet's vast capacity enables each media house to exhaustively investigate and publish in-depth analyses. Internet radio is not limited to audio as pictures,images, digital files and graphics are accesible to the users. Advertisers and their audiences can easily interact via the internet radio broadcasts. The internet technology provides interactivity with the trainer or educator and other information for business and advocacy services, internet radio could charge for listening or viewing, offer a music or video clip for free, but charge for the full song, album, or video.

Chibita in Nassanga, argues that appropriate media content arises if one considers what it takes for the media in a country like Uganda, under the wave of globalization and commercialization to provide citizens with information, advice and analysis to enable them to know and pursue their rights as well as providing them with a decent range of information, the relevance of content determines the extent to which they can participate meaningfully and access vital information of public opinion, make meaningful choices and be culturally competent. Uganda and most African countries have adopted trade liberalisation policies which have freed the airwaves in the early 1990s. Radio talk shows facilitate political competition through offering opportunities for government leaders, political groups, and civil society organizations to speak directly with and mobilize public support. The government articulates its agenda on the talk shows. At the same time, opposition politicians and civil society groups have an opportunity to challenge the government over the same issues, articulate alternative political agendas, and demand for accountability.

At another level, talk radio has turned into a civic forum through which citizens acquire information about public affairs, attempt to exert influence upward on political leaders, question, challenge, and demand accountability from official power holders, engage in public discourse and debate on collective public problems and policy, or simply let off steam. Broadcasting ranks top high as the most universal means of public communication, conveying information, entertainment, education, and persuasion. Today the broadcasting industry has evolved into an influx of radio and television networks. In Uganda for instance the number of radio stations has grown from one in the early 1990s to more than 150 to date.

Television stations have also increased from one in the same period to six to date. In the United States there are more than 12,000 radio stations, more than 3,500 TV stations, almost 11,000 cable systems and satellitedelivered programming. Frequency modulation has expanded the number of frequencies through which both radio and television broadcasts can be relayed. Television's VHF channels have also helped to improved visibility and picture quality. The new developments in the media industry has increased the quality and variety of programmes from commercial, entertainment, educational, and infotainment formats.New developments in the broadcasting technology have made it possible to link media access toTV, radio, music, internet, services for information, shopping, games, banking and development services.There are a variety of media contents can be digitally retained, retransmitted and transported, enabling an interaction by the user, exactly at the moment that is convenient to the user. The new media technologies have influenced most local cultures through the increased access to allien cultures. The radio has today become one of the admirable piece of work as it sells itself as a medium that reaches listeners while they drive, work, shop and jog. Advertisers like radio's ability to reach targeted audiences. The new innovations in the broadcasting industry have led to an increase in internationally syndicated programming on local radio and television in Africa.

Most of the music aired by F.M radio stations in Uganda and several African countries come from foreign productions led by U.S.A. This also applies to TV broadcasts where the bulk of the programmes are foreign content due to the cultural effects of globalisation in Africa.Media industry convergence is an emerging phenomenon in broadcasting sector on the continent. It influences the technology, media content, market shares of the revenues and public broadcasting in Africa. One of the impacts of technology convergence is the development of innovative broadcasting products and services being launched more rapidly in the market.

MEDIA COMMUNICATIONS ISSUES, CULTURE, ECO-TOURISM AND ENVIRONMENT

The media industry in Africa is instrumental in exerting its influence on the society. Rogers argues that awareness and knowledge of an innovation can be best disseminated by the mass media and that there are five stages of adoption process: awareness, interest, evaluation, trial, and adoption of the decision. During awareness stage, an individual is exposed to a new innovation without prior knowledge of it. In the next stage, one gets interested in the new idea and looks on the issue. The eco-tourism industry can do no worse than adopt as its policy, the development of partnership with the media industry as its secret weapon for surviving global tourism competition. Likewise, the application of priming theory by the media would help the public to follow the political behaviour of the policy and decisionmakers on the continent.

Priming refers to the impact of news coverage on the weight assigned to specific issues in making political judgments. The issues that are highlighted in the priming theory are: responsibility, political knowledge and media trust by the audience. Interpersonal communication can mean the ability to relate to people in written or verbal communication in the context of either both a one-on-one, face-to-face and a group contacts. This requires ability to comfortably deal with all kinds of people we meet in different settings. It is body language which is seen through our behaviour or actions such as: gestures, eye contacts, body movement, dressing, appearances or presentations.

Interpersonal communication is crucial during listening, talking, counselling, dressing, and conflict resolution. The African Union should adopt new innovation communications strategy where the media plays a key role to advance eco-tourism industry-led innovation in public policies at all levels for poverty reduction on the continent. Africa should exploit the new media technology to develop the concept and practice of "lead markets" where public authorities, facilitate industry-led innovation by creating conditions for a successful market uptake of focused innovative products, processes and services for global competitiveness. Prime targets should focus on areas that respond to societal demand-driven areas such as local jobs, accommodation facilities, transport or health, peace/security and new eco-innovations.

Media communications campaign must consider at least four key challenges: partnership, resources, leadership and duration. Communications have to be opportunistic about new events, messengers, and allies. Although the campaign use many tactics to deliver its story, mass media over time play a major role in reaching decision makers and other key audiences. Some of the most serious challenges to be addressed in the development of African ecotourism industry communications environment are: media support, developing media professional skills, ensuring public broadcasting programming that meets the audiences' priorities, cultures and languages, and promoting professional ethics among the media communicators. Media communication should be based on a multi-media approach particularly in implementing major campaigns, in working out campaigns and programmes; there should be a deliberate effort to understand the communication environment, including target groups, appropriate media platforms, messages and forms of interaction. The main measures of impacts should include: the amount of media exposure or media the campaign has gained for example from: television, radio, print, billboard, and internet. The Uganda national environment management authority has been conducting public awareness campaigns on FM radio stations and a weekly interactive TV programme in the country. Media broadcasts can be effectively used to disseminate key eco-tourism media messages across Africa.

Media research is crucial because it examines the specific communication medium, the user and use of medium, the effects of the medium, how the medium can be improved, content, and the communicator. Communication inputs and audience responses reflect on the following message design factors: production related factors, content related factors, media related factors, and audience-related factors. The latter may examine the application of the "uses and gratifications" theory which is based on the idea that media don't do things to people; but people do things with media.

Media communications should be well planned and targeted for maximum audience exposure to the messages. Communicators, who wish to inform, persuade or simply hold the attention of their auditors must adapt more closely than in the past to what ordinary people find interesting, relevant and accessible. Berlo argues that there is a need to know the receiver's attitudes, level of knowledge, listening and comprehension abilities, social and cultural background to communicate more effectively. Public service agencies which commission media campaigns in support of their goals should know that the use of several media channels and multiple presentations in a variety of eye and ear-catching formats is recommended. Slade and Weitz observed that various media such as newspapers, television and radio should be used to promote environmental values and awareness. The use of appropriate theory or model is crucial for any successful media campaigns aimed at creating, raising and sustaining public awareness for behaviour change. Coffman asserts that more theory development and theory integration for public will campaign are needed because part of the problem with the communication campaign is lack of awareness among the campaign practitioners, evaluators and their sponsors about what outcomes and methods are appropriate and available. Hubley contends that communication strategy decisions should involve surveys to determine communication systems in a community; audience familiarity with and exposure to different media; characteristics of target groups; effectiveness of different media; opinion leaders that can be engaged in the project.

Through priming theory, the media can create, raise, and sustain public awareness for sustainable tourism and "eco-guard" behaviour change. The Priming theory which in media is related to the Agenda Setting theory; is the process by which certain portions of media content are 'brought to the forefront' and other portions are relegated to the background for maximum effect. This process allows the media to exercise control over public opinion. Priming is most important when issues are new and information is scarce. By applying The Frame Theory the media can "frame" new innovations and ecotourism policies, international conventions and best practices, community projects and regional success stories as well as sessions learned for informed public debates and awareness education in Africa.

Framing is a process of selective control over media content or public communication. Framing defines how a certain piece of media content or rhetoric is packaged to allow only the desirable interpretations at the expense of others. Ugandan President Yoweri Museveni recently accused the local press of being irresponsible and irrational agents of saboteurs of Africa's future. The Ugandan media had set the agenda which sparked off a fiery nationwide eco-debate against the current government plan to supplant the biggest

Uganda's natural forest by a sugarcane plantation, a move which the president himself defended, as a struggle to industrialise the pre-industrial backward African state. Uganda, with a population of over 25 million inhabitants, now has 140 radio stations and 20 TV stations. In their efforts to inform, educate and entertain the public, the media industry in Uganda triggered off a nationwide and international public debates against the anticipated wanton destruction of about 8000 hectares of ecologically diverse Mabira natural forest which is also the host of Eco-Tourism Centre run by the National Forestry Agency of Uganda.

The media just as to the public sphere model are defined as central elements of a healthy public sphere-the "space" within which ideas, opinions, and views freely circulate, Croteau and Hoynes. Mwesige found that open-air talk shows provide more opportunities for citizen participation by allowing at least three minutes of talking time to an average of 15 people per show. Members of the public are also able to participate as equals in these debates, which also attract political elites. McQuail argues that just as to this principle, truth triumphs over error in the end and leads to free market place of ideas; which seems to bless private ownership and the free enterprise system.

Uganda like many other African countries adopted the free enterprise system and liberalized the airwaves in the early 1990s. Chibita in Nassanga under the wave of globalization and commercialization to provide citizens with information, advice and analysis to enable them to know and pursue their rights as well as providing them with a decent range of information, the relevance of content determines the extent to which they can participate meaningfully and access vital information of public opinion, make meaningful choices and be culturally enriched. The media imposes a range of effects which range from insignificant, medium to great or powerful effects on the audiences in the society. Media communications across cultures include: speaking, writing, editing, information gathering, dissemination and community participation in public campaigns. There are three main components to any communication: subject matter, medium of delivery, and cultural considerations. They are hard to define even for our own culture because we take them in with our mother's languagc. Global communication, transportation, and changes in living styles have begun to blur many of the surface distinctions between different cultures. There are common denominators in every cross-cultural communications which require cultural competence by tourists and their hosts. Cultural competence refers to the ability to work effectively with individuals from different cultural and ethnic backgrounds, or in settings where several cultures coexist.

It includes the ability to understand the language, culture, and behaviours of other individuals and groups, and to make appropriate recommendations. Cultural competence exists on a continuum from incompetence to proficiency. Cultural sensitivity is a necessary component of cultural competence. Effective communication between providers and clients may be even more challenging when linguistic barriers exist. Cultural competence is a developmental process that requires a long-term commitment. It is not a specific end product that occurs after a two-hour workshop, but it is an active process of learning and practicing over time.

People who work among different ethnic and cultures may become culturally competent by developing awareness, acquiring knowledge, and maintaining cross-cultural skills. Developing cultural awareness involve: admitting personal biases, stereotypes, and prejudices; becoming aware of cultural norms, attitudes, and beliefs; valuing diversity;willingness to extend oneself psychologically and physically to the client population; recognizing comfort level in different situations; acquiring knowledge; knowing how your culture is viewed by others;attending classes, workshops, and seminars about other cultures; reading about other cultures; watching movies and documentaries about other cultures;attending cultural events and festivals;sharing knowledge and experiences with others; visiting other countries -making friends with people of different cultures; establishing professional and working relationships with people of different cultures; learning another language; learning verbal and nonverbal cues of other cultures; becoming more comfortable in cross-cultural situations; assessing what works and what does not; assessing how the beliefs and behaviours of the cultural group affect the client or family; learning to negotiate between the person's beliefs and practices and the culture of your profession; being more flexible;attending continuing education seminars and workshops; learning to develop culturally relevant and appropriate programmes, materials, and interventions; learning to evaluate culturally relevant and appropriate programmes, materials, and interventions; ongoing evaluation of personal feelings and reactions;overcoming fears, personal biases, stereotypes, and prejudices.

In order to achieve better communication skills, competitive tourism industry; the tour operators are encouraged to develop and implement a strategy to: recruit, retain, and promote qualified, diverse, and culturally competent administrative staff, clinical, and support staff; promoting and supporting the necessary attitudes, behaviours, knowledge, and skills for staff to work respectfully and effectively with clients and each other in a culturally diverse work environment; developing a comprehensive strategy to address culturally and linguistically appropriate services, including strategic goals, plans, policies, and procedures; hiring and training interpreters and bilingual staff; providing a bilingual staff or free interpretation services to clients with limited English skills; translating and making available sign and commonly used educational materials in different languages; developing structures and procedures to address cross-cultural ethical and legal conflicts, complaints, or grievances by patients and staff; preparing and distributing an annual progress report documenting the organizations' progress in implementing these standards, including information on programmes, staffing, and resources.

While cultural competence has increased significantly, there is still much to be done on the personal, organizational, and societal levels. Education and training to enhance the provision of culturally effective health care must be integrated into lifelong learning. As intercultural contact increases, norms from one culture may appear strange or shocking to people from another culture, but the key to improving cross-cultural dialogue is to develop what is known as cultural competence or the ability to recognize cultural differences, rather than judging another culture by the norms of your own. Cultural competence allows educators and communicators to work effectively in cross-cultural situations. Becoming culturally competent means not only learning about other cultures, but also learning which of our own traits and don't have to travel to find different cultures.

All environmental educators and communicators should be culturally competent to reach diverse audiences both at home and abroad. People who work in foreign lands should learn the cultures of their hosts. There are many major world cultures with common patterns of behaviour including common thought, communication styles, actions, customs, arts, beliefs, and values that are all framed by a worldview. Environmental communicators must be aware of how culture, along with gender and other factors, influences how people interpret our messages.

Culturally sensitive and appropriate messages are very effective. Effective communication leads to greater homophily between the communicators. Nonverbal communication methods vary among cultures as such understanding cultural components of nonverbal communication including body language, gestures, and concepts of space and time, are essential to effective cross-cultural communication. The media is the major source of information followed by schools. Effective environmental communicators should consider culture at the first stage of the audience research, followed by pre-testing messages and materials as the message may be interpreted differently across-cultures.

The media has drawn the attention of the public on sensitive ecological issues and trends. Uganda media recently locked-horns with the government when it gave extensive coverage on the impending government plan to replace the country's legally gazetted natural forest with a sugarcane plantation. The streets of Kampala capital city soon overflowed with eco-demonstrators with fatal consequences when the police force opened fire on the protesting crowds. Media communications raised awareness and political impact on public opinion prompted a fresh political rethinking by the government. It is well known that human-induced climate change and the loss of biodiversity are the key global environmental issues today.

The media should intensify campaigns to raise awareness and shift public opinion. Conservation communicators must make the issues relevant for a highly confused public. In UK, government targets concerning the quality of protected areas are now embedded in policy. Recent proposals for major infrastructure projects which were expected to impinge on protected sites like the Hastings Bypasses and the Dibden Bay port development were rejected despite a strong economic argument aggressively made in their support. Sustainable tourism plays a pivotal role in the conservation of natural and cultural heritage.

It caters for the welfare of the local and indigenous communities in its development and operation, contributing to their well-being; interprets the natural and cultural heritage of the destination to visitors; and lends itself better to independent travellers, as well as to organized tours for small size groups. Developing public communications campaigns for sustainable tourism in Africa is the bedrock for achieving sustainable development for poverty reduction in the African Union. One of the main reasons is that sustainable tourism is the basis for the attainment of sustainable peace on the continent. Tourism in Africa is synonymous with environment and natural resources.

Indiscriminative destruction of our natural resources is a sure recipe for the current mass poverty in Africa. It is a living reality which deserves global approach. Awareness campaigns are critical for effective policy, constitutional and legal implementation of sustainable tourism principles, plan, goals and projects in Africa and globally. Effective media communications strategies are crucial for policy and decision makers themselves who are often the drivers of natural resources destructions on the continent. Public awareness communications campaigns provide vital information and knowledge for community empowerment for active participation in eco-tourism project planning and management in Africa. An effective media campaign fosters national, regional and international collaboration among the eco-tourism development partners: the private sector investors, the civil society, the policy makers, and the local communities in the industry.

Media practitioners, project monitors and evaluators benefit from the awareness campaigns for better insights for improved campaigns strategies. The campaigns help to speed up the implementation of the legal and policy instruments. They provide the energy for the vital attitudinal and behaviour change as they accord respect and transparency to the whole campaign process. Media campaigns are human rights issues which should be enshrined in the legal provisions for access to public information. Media campaigns, as a strategy, are crucial for objective verification and analyses of key eco-tourism promotional and investment issues on the continent of Africa.

Sustainable tourism awareness campaigns could be rapidly created, raised and sustained throughout Africa, Americas, Australia, Europe, Asia and globally. Many media practitioners and professionals agree that media campaigns would result in effective eco-tourism policy and project implementation in Africa. Public service agencies which commission media campaigns in support of their goals should know that the use of several media channels and multiple presentations in a variety of eye and ear-catching formats is recommended.

Media campaigns should be guided by informed ethical, theoretical and sustainable tourism factors. The campaigns should be systematic from inputs to outputs. The process should be evaluated. Public communications campaigns are varied, multifaceted, highly planned, and strategically assembled media symphonies designed to increase awareness, inform, or change behaviour in the target audiences. The goal of environmental communications campaigns is to instil in learners the knowledge about the environment, positive attitudes towards the environment, and competency in communities in environment and natural resources management skills and gender-equity empowerment. Communications campaign models act as road-maps as they guide the campaign managers how to proceed.

The measures of effect that come about in the target populations or communities as a result of the campaign include: knowledge and awareness, saliency, attitudes, norms, self-efficacy, behaviour intentions, behaviour, skills, environmental constraints, media frames, policy change and impacts. Media research examines the medium, user and use of medium, effects of the medium, how the medium can be improved, content, and the communicator as many media scholars have argued. Communication inputs and audience responses reflect on the following message design factors: production related factors, content related factors, media related factors, and audience-related factors.

The media can also apply the "uses and gratifications" theory, the idea that media don't do things to people; but people do things with media. Communicators, who wish to inform, persuade or simply hold the attention of their auditors must adapt more closely than in the past to what ordinary people find interesting, relevant and accessible. We need to know the receiver's attitudes, level of knowledge, listening and comprehension abilities, social and cultural background to communicate more effectively. Public service agencies which commission media campaigns in support of their goals should know that the use of several media channels and multiple presentations in a variety of eye and ear-catching formats is recommended.

Multi-media channels like: newspapers, television and radio are vital for promoting environmental values and awareness in Uganda with a focus on community participation in creating awareness among individuals. There is a need for more theory development and theory integration, particularly for public will campaign because part of the problem with the communication campaign is lack of awareness among the campaign practitioners, evaluators, and sponsors about what outcomes and methods are appropriate and available. Media communication strategy decisions should involve surveys to determine communication systems in community; familiarity with and exposure to different media; characteristics of target groups; effectiveness of different media; opinion leaders that can be used in the programme. Through priming theory, the media can raise awareness about this new gender based convention.

Priming theory in media is related to the agenda setting theory. Priming is the processes by which certain portions of media content are "brought to the forefront" while other portions are relegated to the background. This allows the media to exercise control over public opinion. Priming is most effective when issues are new and information is scarce. The media should focus on practical community and gender needs for ecotourism policy. The media can "frame" some of the most important ecotourism issues in Africa for public debates and awareness education. Framing is a process of selective control over media content or public communication.

Framing defines how a certain piece of media content or rhetoric is packaged to expose only the desirable frames at the expense of others. The first and foremost main ingredients of successful public communication campaigns that are designed to change behaviour is increasing knowledge and awareness as the starting point. Communications campaigns are one of the policy areas for non-formal environmental education in Uganda where the key programme areas identified include: networking and co-ordination, development of EE training materials, development of environmental resource and information centres, public awareness media campaigns, research, development of training manuals, strengthening the role of indigenous knowledge and practice in EE and integrating gender issues into environmental policy planning, and implementation. Most "eco-suicidal" decisions made in Uganda and the rest of Africa are motivated by official corruption involving the state actors under the pretext of foreign investments. Corruption is a formidable poverty driver which shows no signs of abetting in most African Union states. Uganda government defines corruption as the use of public office for private gain. This covers: embezzlement, nepotism, favouritism, selfdealing, insider trading, influence peddling, or the use of public office or assets for political advantage. Official surveys regularly conducted in the country by the national "Ombudsman" show that most Ugandans believe that state corruption by the government is cancerous. Uganda government says it hopes to: strengthen the law enforcement capacity for investigation, prosecution and judgments, procurement system; public sector reform; public financial accountability; coordination of anticorruption agencies; codes of conduct, corruption laws, and "allow" the civil society to monitor official corruption in the country. It is only an informed public that can contribute to the reduction of state corruption in Africa. Media campaigners can frame some of the key eco-tourism issues in Africa for public awareness education.

CONCLUSION

The media can spur the current prospects for the African countries to actively collaborate in a wide range of eco-tourism enhancement activities which include: joint product or service development, research, human resource development and management, exchange of tourism experts and tourism information within the existing economic and trading regional blocks like: the Common Market for Eastern and Southern Africa, Preferential Trade Area, Southern African Development Area Coordination Conference, East Africa Community, Economic Community for the Organisation of West African Countries and the African Union. There is a huge virgin market for Africa's ecotourism investment which should be developed and strengthened. Sustainable tourism cannot survive without a working environment management system and regular environment impact assessment. Legislations and codes should be developed to ensure balanced development of tourism in African tourist destinations to facilitate access to information about African tourism and ecological conservation. A case in point is Kenya where tourism is a major employer accounting for almost 11% of the total national labour force there. The Kenyan ecotourism society aims to market eco-tourism as a tool for the conservation of the natural environment for sustainable community livelihoods in the protected areas. It plans to develop eco-management standards for better tourism and hopes to publish eco-tourism regulations and codes of conduct as well as to develop public awareness campaign strategy to mitigate potential negative ecological, cultural, social and economic impact of tourism in the country. Sustainable tourism will materialise in Africa if we integrate tourism into the overall policy for sustainable development, development of sustainable tourism, and management of tourism.

11

International Tourism and Media Conference

MAPPING GEOGRAPHIES OF DESIRE AND INCIDENTAL TOURISM

Some essential dichotomies of Australia are the known and unknown, the local and other, and the here and there. Australia's short history as an outpost of European culture is primarily understood as that of a young culture in an ancient land(scape). Driving through the Australian landscape is often as much about necessity as it is about dreams. It is so often the latter that stimulate the road trip, the elements of which both locate and characterise, as well as serving the dual function of being a means to an end and an opportunity to experience new locations, as well offering the possibility of dis-location. Three recent Australian films, however, presented a distinctively different perspective on location and dislocation, that being to introduce Japanese characters–played by Japanese actors–into Australian narrative settings and explore the results.

All three films-Clara Law's The Goddess of 1967, Sue Brooks' Japanese Story and Rachel Lucas' Bondi Tsunami — have narratives of dislocation, both personal and physical and of diverse desire set in iconic landscapes at once both alluring and alienating. The three narratives share the road as a metaphor of both departure and arrival, as well as that of a journey offering not only deeper self–knowledge but also an experience of journeying through the Australian landscape.

Here, then, is where the personal landscape meets that of tourism, as each of the journeys is a personal search of sorts. Whilst the touristic nature of the imagery may be incidental to the narrative action it is, nevertheless, emphasising how the elemental qualities of the landscape may echo the inner personal landscapes and journeys of the characters. Two studies of tourism that explore destination image-Wang and Urry —will be utilised to provide a framework of sorts for the discussion.

TOURISM, CITIZENSHIP AND THE REGULATION OF HUMAN MOBILITY

Tourism is a high profile subject that appears regularly in the media. Broadly speaking it is possible to identify two types of tourism features in print, radio, television and web media: 'tourism stories' and 'stories pertaining to tourism'. Where the former record tourism directly, the latter detail happenings with connections to, or implications for, tourism. Clearly, the media has a powerful role to play in the social constructions of place and hence the practices of tourism. The findings from this thesis raise a series of methodological observations worthy of further reflection.

As historical sources, tourism stories are empirically useful in documenting, charting and benchmarking the development of tourism production and consumption. They signal and simultaneously shape how tourism is perceived by individuals and groups within society, as do stories pertaining to tourism. One obvious but often unarticulated view is that the location of the story will affect the nature and form of texts and how the discourse may unfold. While we are often prepared to examine the content delivered in the attention economy, we sometimes lose sight of the role and importance of production processes.

CONTESTED AND MEDIATED RURALITY

Rural areas have gone through dramatic changes in the developed world. The forces of globalisation, industrialisation and the consequential economic restructuring of rural and, more relevantly, urban economies have had dramatic and far reaching effects on rural areas. The changes have increased importance of new business units to diversify the regional economic base. As rural areas have changed tourism has been identified as means to maintain, diversify and enhance its abilities in the new economy. These changes to rural areas and national populations have also induced changes to national psyche, where largely urban countries personify themselves as rural. The imagery of rurality has established demand for the rural tourism product, though there is often a lack of development of tourism or functional relationships needed for the industry in rural areas.

This thesis assesses images promoted in the media and how these images have enlivened the contests of rurality and tourism. First it assesses historic demand for and impacts of tourism éxperiences in New Zealand's South Island High Country to identify recreation contests in this rural environment. The thesis then assesses 'new' media images of the South Island High Country and identifies new rural/reel contests that may occur, especially with the increased interaction with a much broader and international audience. This new contest and discussion is based on the trilogy of The Lord of the Rings films.

An introduction to the South Island High Country is presented, before summarising research into High Country tourism. This is followed by the new media images that may present further contests for rurality. Conclusions drawn provide insights into the issues for the sustainability of the visitor experience, the local community and rurality in this now increasing popular and contested environment.

FILM-INDUCED TOURISM CUTS BOTH WAYS

This study explores the linkages between the film and tourism industries, and the potential for the tourist industry to provide support for film production. The aim was to produce recommendations of benefit to both industries, concerning methods of strategic development of tourism marketing, linked with independent film production, creating alliances between these industries. Previous studies have investigated the phenomenon of film-induced tourism, however, a gap exists in that investigation is after the event and from the point of view of examining existent events, and their effect on tourists or on tourism. The study explores linkages between the industries by utilising a case study of the NRS group, an independent film production company based in Canberra. The data obtained revealed that tourism bodies can render practical assistance to film production and benefit in return from the exposure gained, particularly from planned publicity.

FILMS AND TOURISM

The present thesis is part of a wider research project focused on the synergy and all the possible connections between film productions and territories. In particular, it deals with the influence of films on tourism motivations as well as their impact on destination images and the role in affecting tourist purchasing behaviour. Two different research methods were used: a web survey and an on-site interview in two Italian regions. The results reveal that the cause-effect relationship between film viewing and travel experiences shows varying intensity degrees along the subsequent phases into which the choosing and purchasing process of tourism products can be divided. More precisely, the influence of film viewing on travel choices gradually weakens as such process goes on, showing decreasing percentages from the first phase to the following ones up to the final purchasing act.

THE INFLUENCE OF DISASTER MEDIA REPORTS ON THE YOUTH TRAVEL MARKET

Few studies of the youth market have considered the influence of negative disaster media reports on their propensity to travel to the affected destination. This study considers the effect of news reports, travel advisories and the Internet on young people's intention to travel to Phuket following the 2004 Asian tsunami. It was found that this market is relatively resilient, however many expressed concerns about travelling to Phuket, preferring to substitute it for another destination. It recommends that destination marketers adopt a positive re-marketing exercise to counter media misrepresentations as soon as possible in order to retain this market.

FESTIVAL IMAGE CREATION: THE ROLE OF THE PRINT MEDIA

The aim of the thesis is to consider the images created of a performing arts festival by Australian national and state newspapers. To achieve this, a content analysis of newspaper coverage of the Melbourne International Comedy Festival was conducted before the commencement of the festival, during the festival and immediately following the close of the festival. The Melbourne based thesis covered the festival extensively, with previews and reviews of shows, profiles of artists and objects on comedy as an art form.

However, there was surprisingly scant coverage by the national and non-Victorian newspapers of the festival, despite the Melbourne International Comedy Festival being the largest cultural event in Australia in terms of ticket sales. The descriptor words used in the non-Victorian newspaper objects were noted and the related newspaper photographs and illustrations were examined. The images created of the festival by the non-Victorian newspapers appear to be light-heartedness and fun, where the comedians are depicted as experienced, professional performers skilled in the art of making their audience laugh. Opportunities for future research are identified.

EXPLORING LOCATION AND AUTHENTICITY IN FILM-INDUCED TOURISM

Films may represent a place, but be made at another. In the early years of film-making, quite elaborate sets were constructed on studio backlots. In recent years, runaway productions have represented the USA while being shot in other countries. The dissonance between film setting and film location raises the question of which is more likely to attract tourists. It also suggests that tourists may have difficulties with authenticity. This thesis seeks to examine these issues by taking an historical approach to the changing ways in which location has been used by film-makers over time.

UNDERSTANDING POPULAR MEDIA PRODUCTION AND POTENTIAL TOURIST CONSUMPTION

Research on the tourism implications of television-induced tourism generally remains limited, with no single agreed approach to its study. In particular, there are methodological difficulties in understanding this phenomenon and a subsequent lack of empirical research into the relationships between films and TV programmes and tourism. Furthermore, there has been limited attention to the underlying mechanisms and structures in the relationships between the production and consumption of films or TV programmes, audiences and potential tourists, particularly in non-Western contexts.

Considering these limitations in this subject, the thesis aims to provide insights into the complicated inter-communication processes between TV programmes from the production side and audiences/tourists as consumers. Based on a triangulated approach, this thesis delineates an empirical study to investigate theoretical positions and research methodologies that may be used to explore the production end of popular TV programming and the ways in which particular production values may appeal to tourists in diverse settings Based on a case study of the 'Hallyu' phenomenon, five major elements of the production of popular TV dramas are proposed by this thesis and verified by the interviews with professional producers.

Quantitative research supports examining causal relationships between the highlighted major elements of TV drama production and patterns of consumption associated with audience involvement, its sequential loyalty, and destination choice in the context of Hallyu drama tourism. This thesis will, therefore, draw attention to uniquely transnational and interdisciplinary approach which will enable the researcher to develop new ideas and perspectives on the relationship and mediation between production and consumption of popular texts and associated tourism.

THE ROLE OF THE MEDIA IN SHAPING MOTIVATIONS BEHIND TRAVEL EXPERIENCES

This thesis aims to explore the role of the media in shaping tourism experiences, using examples drawn from a qualitative study of frontier travellers, being those individuals who travel to places which currently lie at the fringes or extremes of our world or experiences, both geographically and socially/ culturally. In the first phase, long interviews were conducted with participants and the data analysed using grounded theory. A content analysis of additional data collected from autobiographies and diaries written by frontier travellers formed the second phase.

Many participants referred to seminal experiences, often occurring during childhood, which were considered to be the genesis of their future frontier travel experiences and these often involved image formation agents such as literature, both fiction and non-fiction, cinema, television and pictures or photographs. Findings of this study indicate that literature has had a greater impact on future motivations behind frontier travel than more modern forms of media such as film and television, and that there is a strong mythical element of these travel experiences, which can be particularly linked back to childhood literature. Future marketing of frontier travel experiences might use some of these findings in developing travel products or promotions, including media selection.

DEVELOPING A PLAUSIBLE CONTEXT FOR ESTABLISHING MUTUAL E-COMMERCE MEDIA IN THE TOURISM INDUSTRY

This research applies the 'Scenario Analysis Instrument' adopted by the Stanford Research Institute to simulate the analogic context to establish an E-commerce platform for Taiwan's tourism industry. This research subject is one of three decisive issues voted by the panelists in a Four-year Project of the Institute for Information Industry and sponsored by the Ministry of Economic Affairs. The representative experts are invited from divergent industries, public sectors, academic institutions and R&D units to draw up and decide upon essential issues for upgrading Taiwan's tourism industry. By adopting the Delphi method, three crucial decisive issues dominate over others and this research focuses on one of them: item L emphasizes how to develop a mutual E-commerce platform for effective connection of an information network. Eventually, we propose two critical findings.

Firstly, when establishing mutual E-commerce platforms which transcend across various sub-industries, the coordination and integration of an existing resource commitment is the most critical mission for advanced preparation. Simultaneously, the fulfilment and perfection of law-making for online consumption including the scope of B2B and B2C must be accomplished promptly.

Secondly, establishing mutual E-commerce platforms for different sub-industries respectively, distinguishing boundaries among various businesses from different scopes of sub-industries causes a controversial and preceding problem. This thesis reports on research that was conducted to discover how film viewing might be related to tourism activities and whether motivations drive people to become film specific tourists or whether visitation to film locations is simply an incidental tourism experience.

A survey was designed to collect data relating to film tourism motivation, film viewing behaviour, general travel behaviour and demographic profiles. The questionnaire contained a range of information including 29 motivational statements drawn from the literature and previously conducted in-depth interviews. Based on empirical evidence, it appears that these respondents were most interested in the novelty, prestige and fantasy elements associated with film-induced tourism. Factor analysis was applied in order to reduce the 29 statements into themes of motivations which were labelled Novelty, Prestige,and Fantasy. A model, using logistic regression, was then developed to predict likely future film tourist behaviour. It can be concluded that membership of the 'likely to take a film tourism holiday in future' group was most probable amongst those respondents who had taken a film based holiday in the past, had high Novelty motivations and had high Fantasy motivations. The findings of the research also suggest that most tourists are more likely to be incidental film tourists.

TO BE AUTHENTICALLY FREE AND FREE AUTHENTICALLY

In contemporary society, youth travel is understood and represented, by travellers and media alike, as a contemporary rite of passage or significant, transitional moment. It is argued that the rapid accumulation of experience, an inherent component of travel, influences processes of identity construction and reconstruction.

Central to these conceptualisations are concerns with authenticity and freedom, discourses that ultimately serve to structure the travel space and influence interactions between travellers and the travel media and industries. Based on semi-structured, in-depth interviews with young Australian travellers and discourse, image and content analysis of key travel publications and advertisements, this thesis will examine the interplay between discourses of authenticity and freedom in traveller narratives and travel media.

It will examine how travel media imagine backpackers and the backpacking community and how backpackers' own self and travel-narratives correspond with or contest such representations. Central to this examination is the centrality of discourses of authenticity and freedom, and the tensions that emerge between the two, as they arise in traveller narratives and media and industry representations of travel. Ultimately, I will argue, following Wang that travellers reconcile some of these tensions with reference to existential authenticity, and that this intersubjective awareness, along with heightened reflexivity, gives rise to a concern with 'authentic freedom'.

MEDIA IN THE ANTICIPATION PHASE OF A RECREATION EXPERIENCE

Natural areas around the world have been used as sites of recreation, leisure and tourism for centuries. A key facet of this increased usage of natural and protected areas and a key tool for management is the role of image. Though the significance of image has been asserted, little study has been undertaken in Australia as related to images of natural and protected areas. Importantly it is the role of the media in promoting and providing expectations that can also be used as a tool to manage potential impacts.

Within this context research was undertaken at Port Campbell National Park, Victoria, Australia. This research was implemented during the park's tourist off-season to assess satisfaction, crowding and park issues to provide management indications. Around half of the respondents obtained information from the past experiences of family and friends. Tourism-specific media such as information centres, travel agents and the internet were also popular.

This thesis performs analysis to identify the role of the media in shaping adequate expectations of the facilities and service provisions at PCNP. In this context relationships between media and expectations matched and unmatched are ascertained. This not only creates awareness of the varied information sources visitor decisions are based on, it also provides valuable insights into the role of the media in shaping expectations of the facilities and services in protected areas. This has practical marketing implications for protected area management groups as a means for enhancing and managing visitor satisfaction.

A STAKEHOLDERS PERSPECTIVE

This thesis identifies the impact of movie induced tourism locations that have become popular due to their featuring in a well liked television series. The researcher's hypothesis is that television induced tourism has a significant impact on the development of a destination. The aim of this research is to identify the benefits of such tourism; therefore this thesis will investigate the current literature on television induced tourism. The study area for this thesis is Yorkshire, U.K., which has been the film location for a number of popular English television series' and is already the subject of much research in the tourism discipline; Mordue and Tooke and Baker. The hypothesis was initially tested on a survey of visitors to Yorkshire in 2003.

The main aim of the survey was to assess the linkages between movie induced tourism and destination branding. The review of the existing literature identifies a gap in previous research, which indicates that there has been little research on the impacts of a television series on the general tourist perceptions of a destination. The survey undertaken by the researcher was an initial attempt to fill this gap.

The findings of this survey and the issues from the literature review highlighted a number of implications for the future development of destinations. To proceed to the next stage of the research, strategic conversations were held with the key stakeholders involved in the development of Yorkshire as a tourist destination. This is an ongoing piece of research but for the purpose of this thesis, the impact of television induced tourism from the stakeholder perspective will form the basis of the discussion.

CASTLES MADE OF SAND

Until 1992 a handful of scientific researchers and allocentric backpackers were the only foreigners to visit the Indonesia's Mentawai islands-a remote and impoverished regency of West Sumatra plagued by epidemics of preventable disease and infant mortality rates as high as sixty per cent. Within five years the global surf media transformed this depressed region into a surfer's nirvana, the most filmed, photographed, written about and desired surfing tourism destination on earth. Despite this local communities are yet to benefit from surfing tourism. This thesis provides a brief history of surfing tourism and presents empirical research demonstrating that the surf media has been instrumental in socially constructing mythical surfing tourist space based upon four symbolic elements: perfect surf, uncrowded conditions, cushioned adventure and an exotic tropical environment. The generic nature of these elements has led to a disembedding of nirvana from its local context and the'writing out' of local communities. The Mentawai nirvana is a castle made of sand under threatened by a rising tide of surfing tourism development and disgruntled destination communities. A re-embedding of nirvana in the local is advocated to secure the future of local communities in the management of their surf resources.

TRAVELLING COMPANIONS

Guidebooks play an influential role as mediator between the independent traveller, the travel experience and the travelled destination, providing a lens through which travellers come to see and know their travelled and untravelled world. Guidebooks advise their readers of where to go, what to do and what to see at particular destinations, and many aspects of the backpacker travel experience are shaped and framed by these texts. Despite the centrality of guidebooks in the independent travel experience, the question of how travellers use, engage with, and negotiate these texts has received little attention in tourism research. This thesis explores the influence of guidebook texts on backpacker experiences with, and interpretations of, Aboriginal Australia. The empirical data are drawn from interviews with a sample of 28 international backpackers travelling in Australia.

The research reveals that guidebooks are negotiated through the lived and imagined experiences of their readers at various times throughout the travel experience. Backpacker engagement with guidebook information at any given destination is interpreted in light of prior knowledge and experiences. Significantly, the interplay between the backpacker travel experience and the guidebook text is dynamic and primarily situational. The findings highlight the role that the text plays as mediator between the traveller and the travelled culture, and the tensions that exist between texts and lived experiences.

12

E-Tourism

INTRODUCTION

The Internet is the most important innovation since the development of the printing press. There have been significant innovations, such as the railroad, electricity, the telephone, the automobile, the airplane, radio and television, which had widespread impact on both business and everyday life. However, the Internet combines many of the features of existing media with new capabilities of interactivity and addressability; thus, it transforms not only the way individuals conduct their business with each other, but also the very essence of what it means to be a human being in society. Nowadays, millions of people worldwide rely on the Internet for working, learning, socializing, entertainment, leisure and shopping.

In 2009, worldwide Internet users reached 1.8 billion including 360.0 million Internet users in China and 227.7 million users in the US. This statistic represents an increase of 399% compared to year 2000. With the continuous growth in Internet penetration, demographic characteristics of online population are getting to resemble the general popula-tion.

The average age of Internet users is rising in tandem with that of the general population, and racial and ethnic characteristics are more closely mirroring those in the offline population. More interesting is the fact that over 90% of people between age of five and 17 use the Internet on a regular basis. These younger people are more familiar with the Internet than other media such as radio and television.

When they grow into the economically active population, the Internet will be the most influential medium in business. Since the emergence of the Internet, travel planning has always been one of the main reasons that people use the Internet.

The top five most popular online purchases were books (66%), clothes (57%), travel arrangements (57%), gifts (51%) and CDs (45%) in the US in 2007. A study con-ducted in Britain also found that respondents' most search activity conducted online was making travel plans (84%), followed by getting information about local events (77%), looking for news (69%) and finding information about health or medical care (68%) in 2007.

The revolution of the Internet and information and communication technolo-gies (ICTs) has had already profound implications for the tourism industry. A whole system of ICTs and the Internet has been rapidly diffused throughout tourism sectors. Subsequently, online travel bookings and associated travel services are recognized as one of the most successful e-commerce imple-mentations, with estimates of sales of $73.4 billion in 2006.

It is evident that e-business is an essential prerequisites for successful organisations in the emerging, globally networked, internet-empowered business environment, especially for the tourism industry. Many tourism-related organisations had to go through a major business processes re-engineering to take advantage of the emerging technologies in order to trans-form their processes and data handling as well as their ability to operate and to compete in the emerging global marketplace.

The purpose of this review is to provide essential knowledge related to ICT developments and main implications of ICT in tourism. It illuminates the complexity of the various types of systems and demonstrates how they fit together in the production, distribution and delivery of tourism products. In addition, the utilisation of ICTs and the Internet by different functions and sectors of the industry is examined and conclusions for the future impact of ICTs are outlined.

INFORMATION AND COMMUNICATION TECHNOLOGIES (ICTS) IN TOURISM

Tourism has closely been connected to progress of ICTs for over 30 years. The establishments of the Computer Reservation Systems (CRSs) in the 1970s, Global Distribution Systems (GDSs) in the late 1980s and the Internet in the late 1990s have transformed operational and strate-gic practices dramatically in tourism.

The tourism indus-try at first focused on utilizing computerized systems to increase efficiency in processing of internal information and managing distribution. Nowadays, the Internet and ICTs are relevant on all operative, structural, strategic and marketing levels to facilitate global interaction among suppliers, intermediaries and consumers around the world. In this part, we first provide the concepts and definitions of the key terms related to the Internet and ICTs. Then we discuss benefits and limitations of the Internet and ICTs.

DEFINITIONS AND CONCEPTS

World Wide Web (WWW or the Web)

A multimedia protocol which uses the Internet to enable the near instant distribution of media-rich documents (*e.g.*, textual data, graphics, pictures, video, sounds) and to revolutionise the interactivity between computer users and servers.

Internet

The network of all networks. Nyheim, McFadden, and Connolly (2005) defined the Internet as a network which links multiple networks and users around the globe and a network that no one owns outright. The terms, the Web and the Internet, have often been used inter-changeably; however, the Web is part of the Internet as a communication tool on the Internet. Additionally, the terms, the Internet and ICTs, are often utilized in parallel; however, rigorously speaking, the Internet is part of ICTs.

Intranet

A corporate or government network that uses Internet tools, such as Web browsers and Internet protocols. Intranets are "closed," "secured" or "fire walled" net-works within organisations to harness the needs of internal business users, by using a single controlled, user-friendly interface to support all company data handling and processes.

Extranet

A network that uses the Internet to link multiple intranets. Increas-ingly enterprises need to formulate close partnerships with other members of the value-chain for the production of goods and services. As a result, extranets utilise the same principle and computer networks to enhance the interactivity and transparency between organisations and their trusted partners. This facilitates the linking and sharing of data and processes between organisations to maximise the effectiveness of the entire network.

Information and Communication Technologies (ICTs)

ICTs include not only the hardware and software required but also the groupware, netware and the intellectual capacity (humanware) to develop, programme and maintain equipment. Synergies emerging from the use of these systems effectively mean that information is widely available and acces-sible through a variety of media and locations. In addition, users can use mobile devices such as portable computers, mobile phones as well as digital television and self serviced terminals/kiosks to interact and perform several functions.

This convergence of ICTs effectively integrates the entire range of hardware, software, groupware, netware and humanware and blurs the boundaries between equipment and software. Buhalis, ICTs include "the entire range of electronic tools, which facilitate the operational and strategic management of organisations by enabling them to manage their information, functions and processes as well as to communicate interactively with their stake-holders for achieving their mission and objectives." Thus, ICTs emerge as an integrated system of networked equipment and software, which enables effective data processing and commu-nication for organisational benefit towards transforming organisations to e-businesses.

Electronic Commerce (E-Commerce) and Electronic Business (E-Business)

E-commerce is defined as the process of buying, selling, or exchanging products, services, or information via computer networks, including the Internet. In this review, the terms are used interchangeably. E-business includes not only buying and selling of goods and services, but also servicing customers, collaborating with business partners, conducting e-learning, and conducting electronic transactions within an organization.

Electronic Tourism (E-Tourism)

The application of ICTs on the tourism industry. Buhalis suggests that e-tourism reflects the digitisation of all processes and value chains in the tourism, travel, hospitality and catering industries. At the tactical level, it includes e-com-merce and applies ICTs for maximising the efficiency and effectiveness of the tourism organi-sation. At the strategic level, e-tourism revolutionises all business processes, the entire value chain as well as the strategic relationships of tourism organisations with all their stakeholders.

E-tourism determines the competitiveness of the organisation by taking advantage of intranets for reorganising internal processes, extranets for developing transactions with trusted partners and the Internet for interacting with all its stakeholders and customers. The e-tourism concept includes all business functions (*i.e.*, e-commerce, e-marketing, e-finance and e-accounting, eHRM, e-procurement, eR&D, e-production) as well as e-strategy, e-planning and e-management for all sectors of the tourism industry, including tourism, travel, transport, leisure, hospitality, principals, intermediaries and public sector organisations.

Hence, e-tourism bundles together three distinctive

disciplines: business management, information systems and management, and tourism.

Computer Reservation System (CRS)

A database which enables a tourism organisation to manage its inventory and make it accessible to its partners. Principals utilise CRSs to manage their inventory and distribute their capacity as well as to manage the drastic expansion of global tourism. CRSs often charge competitive commission rates while enabling flexible pricing and capacity alterations, to adjust supply to demand fluctuations. Airlines pioneered this technology, although hotel chains and tour operators followed by developing centralised reservation systems. CRSs can be characterised as the "circulation system" of the tourism product.

Global Distribution Systems (GDSs)

Since the mid 1980s, airline CRSs developed into GDSs by gradually expanding their geographical coverage as well as by integrating both horizontally, with other airline systems, and vertically by incorporating the entire range of principals, such as accommodation, car rentals, train and ferry ticketing, entertainment and other provisions. In the early 1990s, GDSs emerged as the major driver of ICTs, as well as the backbone of the tourism industry and the single most important facilitator of ICTs globalisation. In essence, GDSs matured from their original development as airline CRSs to travel supermar-kets. Since the late 1990s GDSs have emerged as business in their own right, specialising in travel distribution. SABRE, GALILEO, AMADEUS and WORLDSPAN are currently the strongest GDSs in the marketplace.

Intermediaries

Intermediaries (brokers) play an important role in commerce by providing value-added activities and services to buyers and sellers. The most well-known intermediaries in the physical world are wholesalers and retailers. Traditionally, intermediaries of the travel industry have been outbound and inbound travel agencies and tour operators. However, the Internet restructured the entire touristic value chain, forcing the existing intermediaries to take up the new medium and to develop corresponding business models. Intermediaries in the cyber-world refer to organizations/companies that facilitate transactions between buyers and sellers and receive a percentage of the transaction's value. Expedia, a system developed by Microsoft, has had a very rapid growth, demonstrating that the new major e-mediaries constitute not only a stronger competition but are also able to displace many companies with years of experiences in tourism, such as American Express and Rosenbluth Travel.

Infomediaries

An electronic intermediary that provides and/or controls information flow in cyberspace, often aggregating information and selling it to others. The most well-known infomediaries in the tourism industry are TripAdvisor and HolidayCheck which successfully implement a Web 2.0 approach and integrate the users as producers of trusted content. Metamediaries like travel meta-search engines appear between suppliers and consumers to aggregate and filter out relevant and pertinent information from the wealth of material. TSEs like Sidestep, Mobissimo and Kayak enable customers to compare offers and prices by carrying out live queries to suppliers, consolidators and online agencies and presenting the results transparently.

Web 2.0

The coined by O'Reilly Media at the Web 2.0 Conference held in San Francisco in 2004, refers to "the second-generation of Internet-based services that let people collaborate and share information online in perceived new ways-such as social networking sites, blogs, wikis, communication tools, and folksonomies". A Web 2.0 website may feature a number of the following techniques: Rich Internet application techniques, optionally Ajax-based; Cascading Style Sheets; Semantically valid XHTML markup and the use of Micro-formats;

Syndication and aggregation of data in Really Simple Syndication (RSS/Atom; Clean and meaningful URLs; Extensive use of folksonomies (in the form of tags or tagclouds, for example); Use of wiki software; Weblog publishing; and Mashups and REST or XML Webservice APIs. Increasingly the Internet is becoming a platform of data/views/knowledge creation and sharing which harness the network to get better information to all users. Differences between Web 2.0 and the previous generation, referred to as Web 1.0. The indicates how the Web 2.0 emphasizes online collaboration and sharing among users via various Internet application tools.

Social Media

Social media is defined as the online platform and tools that people use to share opinions and experiences, including photos, videos, music, insights, and perceptions with each other. As a powerful democratization force, social media enables people, rather than organizations, to control and use various media with ease at little or no cost; consequently, it enables communication and collaboration on a massive scale.

Social Network

A place where people create their own space, or home page, on which they write blogs; post pictures, videos or music; share ideas; and link to other Web loca-tions they find interesting. Using the Web 2.0 application tools, individuals tag contents they post with keywords they choose themselves and this process makes their contents searchable through the Internet. The social network theory, a social network is a social structure made of nodes and ties. Nodes are the indi-vidual actors within the networks, and ties are the relationships between the actors. Social networking indicates the ways in which individuals are connected through various social familiarities ranging from casual acquaintance to close familial bonds.

BENEFITS OF THE INTERNET AND ICTS

The development of the Internet and ICTs has made many

significant impacts on the operation, structure and strategy of organisations, as well as communication with consumers. The enhancements in ICTs capabilities, in combination with the decrease of the size of equipment and ICTs costs, improved the reliability, compatibility and inter-connectivity of numerous terminals and applications.

The emergence and mainstreaming of the Internet empowered the global networking of computers, enabling individuals and organisations to access a plethora of multimedia information and knowledge sources, regardless of their location or ownership, often free of charge. Summarized by Turban, displays benefits of e-commerce to organizations and individual customers. The Internet and ICTs have enabled tourism organisations to develop their processes and adapt their management to take advantage of the emerging digital tools and mechanisms to:

- Increase their internal efficiency and manage their capacity and yields better. For example an airline's reservations system allows the company to manage their inventory more efficiently and the managers to increase occupancy levels. They also incorporate sophisticated yield management systems that support organisations to adjust their pricing to demand fluctuations in order to maximise their profitability.
- Interact effectively with consumers and personalise the product. For example, British Airways has launched the Customer Enabled BA strategy to enable passengers to undertake a number of processes, including booking, ticketing, check-in and seat and meal selection, from the convenience of their computer.
- Revolutionise tourism intermediation and increase the points of sale. For example, Expedia, Travelocity, Lastminute, Orbitz and Opodo have emerged as some of the most dominant global electronic travel agencies, offering an one-stop-shop for consumers.
- Empower consumers to communicate with other consumers. For example www. tripadvisor.com,

www.virtualtourist.com or www.igougo.com supports the exchange of destination information and tips, whilst www.untied.com or www. alitaliasucks. com enables dissatisfied customers to make their views available.
- Provide Location Based Services by incorporating data, content and multimedia information on Google Maps and Google Earth.
- Support efficient cooperation between partners in the value system. For example Pegasus enables independent hotels to distribute their availability through their web sites and other partners online whilst an extranet allows hoteliers to constantly change availability and pricing.
- Enhance the operational and geographic scope by offering strategic tools for global expansion.

LIMITATIONS OF THE INTERNET AND ICTS

The Internet and ICTs provide numerous benefits to individuals and organizations. However, there are also limitations and barriers in utilizing the Internet and ICTs. Turban et al. (2008) classified barriers to e-commerce as either technological or nontechnological. One of the most concerned technological barriers is a lack of global standards for quality, security, and reliability The lack of standards in technology and its applications eventually increases the cost of system integration for effective and efficient management in distribution, operation and communication worldwide.

Large hospitality corporations have invested to transform their systems into a total netware system; however, small and medium-sized tourism enterprises (SMEs) struggle to integrate the systems due to a shortage of financial sources. Consequently, SMEs are at a competitive disadvantage and find it increasingly difficult to maintain their position in the marketplace. Payment security and privacy concerns are one of the major nontechnological barriers that prevent consumers from completing transactions online. Business organ-izations must therefore pay more attention to protect themselves and their customers from losses due to cyber-crimes, such as auction fraud, vacation fraud, gaming fraud, spamming, identity theft and hacking booking details. Additionally, the recent surge of Internet usage and availability has caused overwhelming volumes of information, some of which is inaccurate or misleading.

For this reason, the Internet has lead to a decrease in the efficient search for information. From the consumer perspective, the increasing number of alternatives or attributes in a choice set increases uncertainties and risks in consumer choices and entails higher transaction costs, such as search costs for identifying alternatives, learning costs associated with familiarizing oneself with alternatives, and activity costs involved in motivating a change.

Using ICTs as a stand-alone initiative is inadequate and has to be coupled with a redesign of processes, structures and management control systems. ICTs can support business success when rational and innovative planning and management is exercised constantly and consistently. Corporations should be able to respond to current and future challenges, by having the resources and expertise to design new processes from scratch, in a timely fashion.

As a result of the rapid ICT developments, corporations need to convert their operations from business functions to business processes, as well as re-conceive their distribution channels strategy, and even more importantly, their corporate values and culture. Perhaps the greatest challenge organisations face is to identify and train managers who will be effective and innovative users of ICTs and would lead technology based-decision making. Intellect therefore becomes a critical asset, while continuous education and training are instrumental for the innovative use of ICTs and the competitiveness of tourism organisations.

E-TOURISM: SUPPLY AND DEMAND

In this part, we provide a comprehensive review of e-tourism within two themes: supply (*e.g.*, tourism industry sectors) and demand (*e.g.*, consumers).

SUPPLY: THE TOURISM INDUSTRY SECTORS

E-tourism provides opportunities for business expansion in all geographical, marketing and operational senses. As a result of Internet developments, a number of new players have come into the tourism marketplace. Perhaps the most significant change was the proliferation of low-frills airlines that use the Internet as a main distribution mechanism for direct sales. This development has educated consumers that they can only find cheap fares if they go direct to the carrier online threatening both traditional/flag carriers as well as their entire distribution system (*e.g.*, GDSs and travel agencies).

Equally the development of major eTravel agencies such as Expedia, Travelocity, Lastminute, Orbitz and Opodo has created powerful "travel supermarkets" for consumers. They provide integrated travel solutions and a whole range of value added services, such as destination guides, weather reports and insurance.

By adopting dynamic packaging (*i.e.*, the ability to package customised trips based on bundling individual components at a discounted total price), they effectively threaten the role of tour operators and other aggregators. A thorough analysis of the various sectors of the tourism industry demonstrates the key devel-opments and the influence of ICTs and the Internet for their internal organisation, their relationships with partners and the interaction with consumers and stakeholders.

E-Airlines

Due to the complexity of their operations, airlines realised quite early the need for efficient, quick, inexpensive and accurate handling of their inventory and internal organisation. Origi-nally, reservations were made on manual display boards, where passengers were listed. Travel agencies had to locate the best routes and fares in manuals and then check availability and make reservation by phone, before issuing a ticket manually. In 1962, American Airlines introduced the SABRE CRS as an alternative to expand its Boeing 707 fleet by 50%. The growth of air traffic and air transportation deregulation stimulated the expansion of CRSs to gigantic computerised networks. As prices, schedules and routes were liberated, airlines could change them indefinitely, while new airlines entered the market. CRSs enabled airlines to compete by adapting their schedule and fares to demand. To increase competitiveness, airlines developed the "hub and spoke" systems, while their pricing became very complex and flexible. "Fare wars" multiplied the fare structures and increased the computing and communication needs, while most major CRSs installed terminals in agencies to facilitate distribution.

In addition, vendor airlines biased their CRSs screens in order to give higher display priority to their flights rather to their competitors. The remote printing of travel documents, such as tickets and boarding passes, itineraries and invoices, as well as the sale settlements between airlines and travel agencies, and the partnership marketing through frequent flyer programmes were invaluable benefits supported by the emerging ICTs. CRSs were developed to GDSs and re-engineered the entire marketing and distribution proc-esses of airlines. They essentially became strategic business units (SBU) in their own right due to their ability to generate income and to boost airlines' sales at the expense of their com-petitors. Many airlines sold their interests in GDSs enabling them to operate as independent distribution companies. Distribution is a crucial element of airlines' strategy and competitiveness, as it determines the cost and the ability to access consumers. The cost of distribution is increasing considerably and airlines find it difficult to control.

Nowadays ICTs and internal CRSs are used heavily to support the Internet distribution of airline seats. These systems are at the heart of airline operational and strategic agendas. This is particularly the case for smaller and regional carriers as well as no-frills airlines which cannot afford GDSs' fees and aim to sell their seats at competitive prices. This has forced even traditional/full-service/flag airlines, such as British Airways and Air Lingus, to recognise the need for re-engineering the distribution processes, costs and pricing structures.

Hence, they use the Internet for:

- Enhancing interactivity and building relationships with consumers and partners;
- On-line reservations;
- Electronic ticketing;
- Yield management;
- Electronic auctions for last minute available seats;
- Disintermediation and redesign of agency commission schemes; and
- Maximising the productivity of the new electronic distribution media.

The Airline IT Survey 2006 demonstrates that the vast majority of airlines have a 3-year IT strat-egy that aims to reduce costs and increase efficiency. Between 1999 and 2006 on average air-lines spend between 2 and 3% of their revenue on ICTs investment. On average 21.5% of airline bookings take place on own airline website, and 29.7% on all online sales. Airlines are investing heavily in direct sales which coupled with 'cus-tomer relations management (CRM)' and 'revenue management systems (RMSs)' will enable them to better control their distribution and strategic marketing.

E- Hospitality

Hotels use ICTs in order to improve their operations, manage their inventory and maximise their profitability. Their systems facilitate both in-house management and distribution through electronic media. 'Property management systems (PMSs)' coordinate front office, sales, planning and operational functions by administrating reservations and managing the hotel inventory. Moreover, PMSs integrate the "back" and "front" of the house management and improve general administration functions such as accounting and finance; marketing research and planning; forecasting and yield management; payroll and personnel; and purchasing. Understandably, hotel chains gain more benefits from PMSs, as they can introduce a unified system for planning, budgeting and controlling and coordinating their properties centrally. Hotels also utilise ICTs and the Internet extensively for their distribution and marketing func-tions. Global presence is essential in order to enable both individual customers and the travel trade to access accurate information on availability and to provide easy, efficient, inexpensive and reliable ways of making and confirming reservations. Although Central Reservation Offices (CROs) introduced central reservations in the 1970s, it was not until the expansion of airline CRSs and the recent ICT developments that forced hotels to develop hotel CRSs in order to expand their distribution, improve efficiency, facilitate control, empower yield management, reduce labour costs and enable rapid response time to both customers and management re-quests.

Following the development of hotel CRSs by most chains, the issue of interconnectivity with other CRSs and the Internet emerged. As a result, 'switch companies,' such as THISCO and WIZCOM, emerged to provide an interface between the various systems and enable a certain degree of transparency. This reduces both set-up and reservation costs, whilst facilitates res-ervations through several distribution channels. One of the most promising developments in hospitality is 'application service providers (ASPs)'. ASPs will be increasingly more involved in hosting a number of business applications for hos-pitality organisations.

Hotels will 'rent' the same software for a fee and will use it across the Internet. For example, some hotel firms may 'rent' their PMS software application from supplier Micros/Fidelio. ASPs are ideal for hotels, especially for smaller- to mid-sized ones, that want to leverage the best vertical and enterprise support applications on the market without having to deal with the technology or pay for more functionality than needed. As they do not have extensive ICT departments and expertise, they can easily access up-to-date applications and benefit from the collective knowledge accumulated by ASP providers without having to invest extensively in technology or expertise building.

The development of the Internet has provided more benefits as it reduces the capital and operational costs required for the representation and promotion of hotels. For example the cost per individual booking can be reduced from US$10-15 for voice-based reservations, to US$7.50-3.50 for reservations through GDSs, to US$0.25 through the WWW. Savings can also be achieved in printing, storing, administrating and posting promotional material. Chan and Law (2006) suggest that hotel websites are a basic requirement to an increasing number of communication and business strategies. The usability of a website, effectiveness of its interface, as well as its amount of information, ease of navigation, and user friendliness of its functions, are central to the success of these strategies and an Automatic Website Evaluation System (AWES) can provide objective and quantitative guidance to website design.

However, many small and medium sized, independent, seasonal and family hotels, find it extremely dif-ficult to utilise ICTs due to:

- Lack of capital for purchasing hardware and software;
- Lack of standardisation and professionalism;
- Insufficient marketing and technology training and understanding;
- Small size which multiplies the administration required by CRSs to deal with each property; and finally,
- The unwillingness of proprietors to lose control over their property

As it is estimated that one-third of bookings in hospitality in the U.S. will be generated from the Internet and another third will be directly influenced by online research, but booked offline, hoteliers gradually explore online marketing to increase their market awareness and to attract more guests and higher revenues. HeBS (2007) demonstrate that they use techniques like website design, search engine optimization, paid search marketing and e-mail blasts. In their benchmark survey of hospitality executives worldwide, including general managers, revenue managers, sales and marketing managers, and other industry professionals, they found that:

- In 2007, a remarkable 68% of hoteliers will be shifting their budgets from offline to online marketing activities, representing a huge shift from traditional methods.

- US properties rely more on direct to consumer bookings via their stand-alone websites compared to intermediary sites as a percentage of their overall Internet business (20.7% and 16.6%, respectively) than do their international counterparts (15.3% and 17%, respectively) who are still receiving, on average, more of their Internet bookings from intermediaries.
- The top three Internet marketing formats hoteliers believe produce the highest ROIs are website optimization, Search Optimization + Organic Search, and website re-design.
- Interestingly enough, more hoteliers believe new media formats as consumer generated media and blogs will generate better ROIs than traditional banner advertising.
- An average of 16.2% of Internet transactions occur through intermediary websites.
- US hotels rely more heavily on keyword search marketing (PPC) and search engine optimization (SEO) that their international counterparts who favour website re-design and optimization, and strategic linking.
- Franchised hotels seem to rely more heavily on the chain websites.

HeBS (2007) concludes that hoteliers have gradually matured and now understand that long-term, strategic objectives and formats (*e.g.*, website re-designs and optimizations, e-mail mar-keting and strategic linking) produce higher Return on Investment than "quick fix" solutions. Finally two main strategies issues emerged on online distribution for hospitality, namely price parity and brand integrity. Post Sept 11th, many hotels around the globe were having problems filling their rooms. In combination with the development of on-line intermediaries (*e.g.*, Hotels.com, Expedia) that were using the merchant model of contracting at the time, it meant that many hotels were unable to control their price effectively on the various online outlets. This not only caused revenue loss because prospective customers were shopping around, but also damaged their brands. Over a period of time major branded properties realised that control over pricing should be central to the marketing proposition and hence undertook a number of measures to address that. Key findings of O'Connor's (2002) study include that brands use multiple simultaneous routes to the marketplace, and that the rates offered over alternative routes have equalised.

E-Tour Operators

Leisure travellers often purchase "packages," consisting of charter flights and accommodation, arranged by tour operators. Tour operators tend to pre-book these products and distribute them through brochures displayed in travel agencies. Hence, until recently in northern Euro-pean countries, where tour operators dominate the leisure market, airline and hotel CRSs were rarely utilised for leisure travel. In the early 1980s, tour operators realised the benefits of ICTs in organising, promoting, distributing and coordinating their packages.

Thomson's Open-line Programme (TOP) was the first real-time computer-based central reservation office in 1976. It introduced direct communication with travel agencies in 1982, and announced that reser-vations for Thomson Holidays would only be accepted through TOP in 1986. This move was the critical point for altering the communication processes between tour operators and travel agencies. Gradually, all major tour operators developed or acquired databases and established electronic links with travel agencies, aiming to reduce their information handling costs and increase the speed of information transfer and retrieval. This improved their productivity and capacity management whilst enhancing their services to agencies and consumers.

Tour opera-tors also utilised their CRSs for market intelligence, in order to adjust their supply to demand fluctuations, as well as to monitor the booking progress and productivity of travel agencies. Tour operators have been reluctant to focus on ICTs through their strategic planning. Few realise the major transformation of the marketplace, while the majority regard ICTs exclusively as a facilitator of their current operations, and as a tool to reduce their costs. However, several tour operators in Germany, Scandinavia and the UK have moved towards electronic brochures and developed their online strategies. Successful operators report that up to 25% of their packages are booked directly by consumers online.

This enables them to concentrate on niche markets by:

- Offering customised packages;
- Up date their brochures regularly;
- Save the 10-20% commission and reduce the costs of incentives, bonus and educational trips for travel agencies; and
- Save the cost for developing, printing, storing, distributing conventional brochures which is estimated to be approximately £20 per booking.

Although a partial disintermediation seems inevitable, there will always be sufficient market share for tour operators who can add value to the tourism product and deliver innovative, personalised and competitive holiday packages. As ICTs will determine the future competitiveness of the industry, the distribution channel leadership and power of tour operators may be challenged, should other channel members or newcomers utilise ICTs effectively to package and distribute either unique or cheaper tourism products.

However, many key players including TUI have started disintegrating their packages and selling individual components directly to the consumers. In this sense they will be able to re-intermediate, by offering their vast networks of suppliers through their channels. Innovative tour operators use the Internet extensively to promote their products and to attract direct customers. They also use the Internet to de-compose their packages and sell individual products. Thomson.co.uk for example has developed a comprehensive online strategy to provide media rich information on its web site. The company supports podcasting and vide-ocasting and also has integrated Goggle Earth geographical information data on its website. It also distributes branded content on a wide range of Internet sites such as youtube.com to attract consumers to its web site and to encourage them to book. In January 2007 a total of 5.5 million people visited the Thomson.co.uk website demonstrating that the customer acquisi-tion strategy used is effective. It is evident therefore that tour operators that will use technol-ogy innovatively will be able to provide value to their clientele and safeguard their position in the marketplace.

E-Travel Agencies

ICTs are irreplaceable tools for travel agencies as they provide information and reservation facilities and support the intermediation between consumers and principals. Travel agencies operate various reservation systems, which mainly enable them to check availability and make reservations for tourism products. Until recently GDSs have been critical for business travel agencies to access information and make reservations on scheduled airlines, hotel chains, car rentals and a variety of ancillary services. GDSs help construct complicated itineraries, while they provide up-to-date schedules, prices and availability information, as well as an effective reservation method.

In addition, they offered internal management modules integrating the"back office" (accounting, commission monitor, personnel) and"front office" (customers' history, itinerary construction, ticketing and communication with suppliers). Multiple travel agencies in particular experience more benefits by achieving better coordination and control between their remote branches and headquarters. Transactions can provide invaluable data for financial and operational control as well as for marketing research, which can analyse the market fluctuations and improve tactical decisions.

The vast majority of leisure travel agencies used'videotext networks' to access tour operator and the reservation systems of other suppliers such as ferry operators, railways and insurance companies. On the plus side, Videotext systems are relatively inexpensive to purchase and operate, require little training and expertise and are fairly reliable. However on the minus side, they are slow; data has to be retyped for each individual database searched; they fail to integrate with the back office; cannot interface with multimedia applications; and are unable to take advantage of the emergent ICTs. Effectively, the type of agency and its clientele determine the type of ICTs utilised. Typically business travel agencies are more GDSs dependent, whilst leisure agencies and holiday shops are more likely to use videotext systems.

The Internet has revolutionised the travel agency industry as for the first time ever. Agencies had the ability to reach travel inventory directly without having to invest in time and costs for acquiring GDSs. They are able to search and book suppliers such as airlines and hotels online, increasing their bookable inventory. They also have the tools to sell their own services and to promote their organisations.

However, until recently travel agencies have been reluctant to take full advantage of the ICTs, mainly due to:

- A limited strategic scope;
- Deficient ICTs expertise and understanding;
- Low profit margins which prevents investments; and
- Focus on human interaction with consumers.

This has resulted in a low level of integration of ICTs and capitalisation on the Internet's potential. Many agencies still do not have Internet access and are unable to access online information or suppliers. As a result many agencies lack access to the variety of information and reservation facilities readily available to consumers and therefore their credibility in the marketplace is severely reduced. This may jeopardise their ability to maintain their competitiveness and consequently, they may be threatened by disintermediation.

Several forces intensify this threat:

- Consumers increasingly search information and make reservations on-line;
- Principals aim to control distribution costs by communicating directly with consumers and by developing customer relationship management;

- Commission cuts; and
- Travel agencies have limited expertise as they employ inadequately trained personnel.

Gradually it is becoming evident that travel agencies around the world not only will have to utilise the Internet to access travel suppliers and information online but will also have to rely on the media to communicate with their clientele, to put the offerings forward to the marketplace and to attract business. Traditional travel agencies can use the Internet to provide extra value to their clientele by integrating additional products and services to their core products. In addition, they may use the internet to specialise to particular niche markets and to offer specialised services to those markets. In contrast, new players (*e.g.*, Expedia, Travelocity, Orbitz, Lastminute, Opodo) have already achieved a high penetration the marketplace and grown spectacularly.

Through a number of mergers and acquisitions, there are effectively 5 major groups that have emerged in the marketplace:

1. Amadeus IT Group includes Vacation.com, Opodo and TravelTainment;
2. The Expedia group includes Expedia.com, Hotels.com, Anyway.com (Expedia.fr), Egencia (formerly Expedia Corporate Travel), Travelnow.com, Hotwire.com, Venere.com, ClassicVacations.com, eLong.net, TripAdvisor and SeatGuru.com;
3. The Orbitz group includes Orbitz, CheapTickets, ebookers, HotelClub, RatesToGo, the Away Network, Asia hotels, and corporate travel brand Orbitz for Business;
4. Priceline includes Priceline.com, Active Hotels.com, Booking.com and Agoda.com; and
5. The Sabre group (Sabre Holdings or Sabre, Inc.) includes Travelocity.com, Sabre Travel Network, Sabre Airline Solutions, Sabre Hospitality Solutions, Cubeless, GetThere, Holidayautos.com, IgoUgo, Lastminute.com, Moneydirect, Nexion, Trams, Travelguru, Travelocity Business, World Choice Travel and Zuji. Interestingly even in areas with low

Internet penetration, online travel agencies have taken off.

The Chinese market is one of those markets which are growing rapidly. For example in early 2007 Ctrip.com posted impressive results demonstrating both the potential and the growth of the Chinese eTourism market. Chinese online travel service provider Ctrip.com (CTRP) announced that for the full year ended December 31, 2006, total revenues were RMB834 million, representing a 49% increase from 2005. Hotel reservation revenues were RMB476 million, a 31% increase from 2005.

The hotel reservation revenues accounted for 57% of the total revenues in 2006, compared to 65% in 2005. The total number of hotel room nights booked was approximately 6.84 million in 2006, compared to approximately 5.45 million booked in 2005. Air ticket booking revenues were RMB303 million, an 83% increase from 2005. The air ticket booking revenues accounted for 36% of the total revenues in 2006, compared to 30% in 2005. The total number of air tickets sold was approximately 6.39 million in 2006, compared to approximately 3.67 million air tickets sold in 2005. Packaged tour revenues were RMB42 million, an 83% increase from 2005. The packaged tour revenues accounted for 5% of the total revenues in 2006.

For the full year ended December 31, 2006, net revenues were RMB780 million, a 49% increase from 2005 whilst gross margin was 80%, compared to 83% in 2005. For the full year 2007, Ctrip expects to continue the year-on-year net revenue growth at a rate of approximately 30%. Before share-based compensation charges, the company expects operating margin to be approximately 35%. This demonstrates clearly not only the size of the Chinese market and the huge potential but also the fact that even markets with low internet penetration experience a dramatic growth of e-Tourism. As location becomes less significant electronic travel agents will dominate global travel retailing.

Already in the USA more than 80% of online travel retailing is concentrated in the top five players. Therefore, the future of travel agencies will depend on their ability to utilise ICTs in order to increase the added-value to the final tourism product and to serve their customer. Agencies which simply act as booking offices for tourism products will probably face severe financial difficulties in the future. In contrast, knowledgeable and innovative agencies which utilise the entire range of technologies in order to provide suitable integrated tourism solutions will add value to the tourist experience and increase their competitiveness. Traditional travel agencies will have to compete on both price and service with both suppliers and online travel agencies and will only be able to survive if they offer superior service.

E-Destinations

Destinations are amalgams of tourism products, facilities and services which compose the total tourism expertise under one brand name. Traditionally the planning, management and coordination functions of destinations have been undertaken by either the public sector (at national, regional or local level) or by partnerships between stakeholders of the local tourism industry.

They usually:

- Provide information and undertake some marketing activities through mass media advertising;
- Provide advisory service for consumers and the travel trade;
- Design and distribute brochures, leaflets and guides; and
- Coordinate local initiatives.

Although ICTs were never regarded as a critical instrument for the development and management of destinations, increasingly'destination management organisations' (DMOs) use ICTs in order to facilitate the tourist experience before, during and after the visit, as well as for coordinating all partners involved in the production and delivery of tourism. Thus, not only do DMOs attempt to provide information and accept reservations for local enterprises as well as coordinate their facilities, but they also utilise ICTs to promote their tourism policy, coordinate their operational functions, increase the expenditure of tourists, and boost the multiplier effects in the local economy. Despite the fact that studies on destination-oriented CRSs have been traced back to as early as 1968, it was not until the early 1990s that the concept of'destination management systems' (DMSs) emerged. Even at this stage however most DMSs are mere facilitators of the conventional activities of tourism boards, such as information dissemination or local bookings.

Several planned DMSs have failed in their development phase, mainly due to:

- Inadequate financial support;
- Lack of long term vision of the developers;
- Lack of understanding of industry mechanisms and the interest groups;
- Expensive and inappropriate technological solutions; and
- IT leading rather following tourism marketing.

This has discouraged DMO managers to further invest in the development of suitable systems. However, by 2004 most destinations around the world had recognised the value of the DMS concept and had some type of system offering information about their region. In the last few years, DMOs have realised that it is critical for their competitiveness to develop their online presence. To the degree that tourists increasingly research their holidays online DMOs realise the need to have an inspirational web site that can encourage and facilitate tourist visitation.

Most importantly several DMS system providers-including Tiscover, World.net, Integra, and New Vision-have emerged as the leading suppliers in the marketplace. Interesting destinations are coming together to coopete-compete and collaborate at the same time. The European Portal visitEurope.com brings together 34 European destinations and creates a virtual window to the world where each destination both competes and collaborates online. This has discouraged DMO managers to further invest in the development of suitable systems. However, by 2004 most destinations around the world had recognised the value of the DMS concept and had some type of system offering information about their region. In the last few years, DMOs have realised that it is critical for their competitiveness to develop their online presence. To the degree that tourists increasingly research their holidays online DMOs realise the need to have an inspirational web site that can encourage and facilitate tourist visitation. Most importantly several DMS system providers-including Tiscover, World.net, Integra, and New Vision-have emerged as the leading suppliers in the marketplace. Interesting destinations are coming together to coopete- compete and collaborate at the same time. The European Portal visitEurope.com brings together 34 European destinations and creates a virtual window to the world where each destination both competes and collaborates online.

DEMAND: TRAVEL MARKETS AND CONSUMERS

Travellers have heavily relied on the Internet because of the information-intensive characteristic of travel products. Travel products are generally intangible (*e.g.*, products cannot be touched nor returned), inseparable (*e.g.*, products must be produced and consumed simultaneously although they are often paid for in advance), heterogeneous (*e.g.*, products are difficult to standardize) and perishable (*e.g.*, products cannot be stocked). Thus, travel products are normally purchased before the time of use, consumed (*i.e.*, experienced) after arriving at the travel site, and best evaluated after consumed. Because of all these unique characteristics, purchasing travel products is associated with a higher level of perceived risks compared to tangible products.

Consumers, therefore, search for a greater amount of information via the Internet to reduce the risks. The Internet enables travellers to access reliable and accurate information as well as to undertake reservations in a fraction of the time, cost and inconvenience required by conventional methods. Thus, they improve the service quality and contribute to a higher tourist satisfaction. Additionally, the Internet provides access to transparent and easy to compare information on destinations, holiday packages, travel, lodging and leisure services, as well as about their real-time prices and availability. Increasingly consumers utilise commercial and non-commercial Internet sites for planning, searching, reserving, purchasing and amending their tourism products. They can also get immediate confirmation and speedy travel documents, enabling prospective travellers to book at the"last minute." Experienced travellers are empowered by ICTs and use information and booking systems to improve their personal efficiency and competencies. A number of new organisations, such as Expedia, Travelocity, and Lastminute, emerged in the late 1990s on-line, empowering consumers to research their travel requirements.

They gradually assumed a leading intermediation role on a global basis. The Internet has enabled consumers to access this information rapidly and increasingly the development of domain specific search engines and meta-search engines such as Kelkoo and Kayak have introduced utter transparency in the marketplace. In addition consumer generated content, through review portals such as TripAdvisor, multimedia sharing such as Panoramio.com, and blogs also create accessible content that increase the level of information available on a global basis.

The use of ICTs is therefore driven by the development of complex demand requests, as well as by the rapid expansion and sophistication of new products, which tend to address niche market segments. There is evidence that e-tourism has already taken off in several countries. In Europe, the Internet is now more than twice as important as travel agents as an information source, although the travel trade is still very important in terms of travel distribution, IPK International's European Travel Monitor in 2006 the iinformation sources used by European outbound travellers where:

- *Internet*: 45%
- *Travel agency*: 20%
- *Friends/relatives:* 17%
- *Travel guide*: 8%
- *Travel brochure*: 7%

- *Newspaper*: 3%
- *Tourist office*: 2%
- *TV*: 2%
- *Other*: 5%

Marcussen (2009) demonstrates that the Internet European Market has increased dramatically since 1998 and in 2009 it is expected to be accounted for 25.7% of the total market. The UK accounted for 30% of the European online travel market in 2008, with Germany in second place at 18%. The direct sellers accounted for 64% of online sales in the European market in 2008, followed by intermediaries 36%.

The Internet and ICTs have furthermore changed travel markets from a customer-centric market to a customer-driven market in which consumers play a stronger role in creating and sharing travel information through community/networking websites and review websites using Web 2.0. Product information has traditionally been produced, distributed and controlled by suppliers to promote their products. Information is now easily created/recreated, distributed and fortified by consumers through the networking/review websites exemplified by Web 2.0.

Consumers are more likely to trust information generated by consumers rather than product suppliers. The tourism industry is required to treat consumers as "co-producers" and leverage network resources to successfully operate their businesses in this consumer-centric era. Looking forward, successful tourism organisations will increasingly need to rapidly identify consumer needs and to interact with prospective clients by using comprehensive, personal-ised and up-to-date communication media for the design of products which satisfy tourism demand. Thus, destinations and principals need to utilise innovative communication methods in order to maintain and increase their competitiveness.

They also increasingly need to engage in to Web 2.0 activities and engage dynamically with all stakeholders that generate content for their regions and organisations. The ICT developments have introduced new best strategic and operational management prac-tices that lead organisations to shift their orientation from product-orientation to a consumer-orientation that customises products and services and adopt flexible and responsive practices to the marketplace. Success will increasingly depend on sensing and responding to rapidly changing customer needs and using ICTs for delivering the right product, at the right time, at the right price, for the right customer. To the degree that ICTs can contribute to the value chain of products and services, by either improving their cost position or differentiation, they reshape competitiveness and thus have strategic implications for the prosperity of the organi-sation. The competitiveness of both tourism enterprises and destinations will increasingly therefore depend on the ability of those organisations to use ICTs strategically and tactically for improving their positioning.

E-TOURISM AND THE FUTURE

E-tourism represents the paradigm-shift experienced in the tourism industry as a result of the adoption of ICTs and the Internet. It is evident that all best business practices have been transformed as a result, and that the each stakeholder in the marketplace is going through a redefinition of their role and scope. There are both challenges and opportunities emerging but the competitiveness of all tourism enterprises and destinations has been altered dramati-cally. It is evident that the "only constant is change."

Organisations which compute will be able to compete in the future. Although ICTs can introduce great benefits, especially in efficiency, coordination, differentiation, and cost reduction, they are not a universal remedy and require a pervasive re-engineering of business processes, as well as strategic management vision and commitment in order to achieve their objectives. Using Porter's five forces framework Buhalis and Zoge (2007) illustrate that the emergence of the Internet altered the structure of the travel industry. Overall, consumers benefited the most as their bargaining power increased due to their ability to access accurate and relevant information instantly and to communicate directly with suppliers, while benefiting from lower switching costs.

The Internet led to the intensification of rivalry among tourism suppliers as it introduced transparency, speed, convenience and a wide range of choice and flexibility in the marketplace. Transparency enabled buyers to increase their bargaining power by facilitating price compari-sons and access to instant, inexpensive and accurate information but reduced the bargaining power of suppliers. Rivalry was further intensified because of lowered barriers to entry and because of the possibility of equal representation of small businesses. Innovative suppliers increasingly use advanced CRM to gather information on consumers' profile and to offer tai-lored and value added products whilst expanding their distribution mix widely to harness the marketplace. Suppliers should enhance their direct communications with end consumers and online intermediaries to save on costs, increase profitability and enhance their efficiency. Real time representation facilitated instant distribution and led to bypassing the traditional distribution channels.

This not only changed the structure of the tourism value system but also raised challenges for traditional intermediaries. The need for traditional intermediaries to shift their role to consumer advisors is becoming evident and unless TAs and TOs utilise internet tools for building and delivering personalised tourism products they will be unable to compete in the future. Although the tourism industry structure has been altered dramatically it is evident that both tourism suppliers and online intermediaries should apply constant innovation, in terms of marketing techniques and tech-nological advancements, in order to be able to offer differentiated, personalised, tailored and value added products. The key point for sustaining their competitive advantage is to focus on their core competencies and to exploit the opportunities that technology offers to improve their strategic position in the tourism value system.

ICTs provide innovative strategic tools for tourism organisations and destinations to improve both their operations and positioning. Hence, the visibility and competitiveness of principals and destinations in the marketplace will increasingly be a function of the technologies and networks utilised to interact with individual and institutional customers. Unless the current tourism sector utilises the emergent ICTs, and develops a multi-channel and multi-platform strategy they will be unable to take full advantage of the emerging opportunities. It is safe to assume that only creative and innovative principals and destina-tions which apply continues innovation in using intelligent e-tourism applications and adopt their processes accordingly will be able to achieve sustainable competitive advantages in the future.

13

The Effects of Online Social Media on Tourism Websites

INTRODUCTION

At the close of the 20th century–roughly between 1997 and 2000–a set of hardware and software technologies collectively known as the Internet had an enormous diffusion and radically changed most of our economic and social life. In the last few years a further "revolution" has impacted the way we communicate, work and conduct business. The buzzword for this is Web 2.0. Not really a technological advancement, since it relies on well developed and known tools, Web 2.0 rather identifies the changes occurred in the ways software developers and people make and use the Web. The applications that facilitate interactive information sharing, collaboration and formation of virtual communities form today a large part of cybernauts' daily activities and may be seen as a natural development of the original Berners-Lee's idea of "a collaborative medium, a place where we all [could] meet and read and write".

Obviously, as it happened for the first Internet revolution, Web 2.0 could not remain unnoticed in activities genetically bound to the human species such as travel. The impact of Web 2.0 on tourism has been (and is) quite important as numerous publications, scholarly and not, continue to state. Most of the analyses conducted so far assess the behaviour, the usage and the effects Travel 2.0 has as an important set of tools in the hands of a tourist and how it affects the image and the business of destinations, companies and organisations. Moreover, the adoption of such tools is considered to be quite important for improving the status of tourism websites. This generates the hypothesis that the role of OSNs in rising the number of visitors to referenced websites is significant. Aim of this thesis is to verify this impact.

Two OSNs have been considered: Facebook and Twitter. The pattern of visits to a sample of Italian tourism websites has been analysed and the relationship between the total visits and those having the two OSNs as referrals have been measured. The rest of this thesis is organised as follows. The role of Travel 2.0 and OSNs. The methods used. Results and discussion are reported. Some concluding remarks close the thesis.

BACKGROUND

The environment called Web 2.0 (or Travel 2.0) is today too well known to be further described here (would it be needed, the thesis by Constantinides and Fountain, 2008, is a good summary of the main issues on Web 2.0). A few considerations, however, are in order for better understanding the general framework in which this work has been conducted. Tourism has long been the one of most important components of the online commerce world, whose impact has profoundly changed the structure of the industry. Online travel has anticipated ever since (and partly continues to do so) the development of new market dynamics and consumer behaviours. With the introduction and the diffusion of the interactive Web 2.0 features and applications, tourism markets have become real conversations on one of the most thrilling subject for a human being.

This happens in particular with OSNs which seem to have rapidly attracted a considerable attention by Internet users of all ages. They are, almost unanimously, recognised as the busiest environments, and this is valid especially for Facebook which has become in few years by way the largest (in number of users) and the most widespread (in geographical terms) online social network in the World. As stated ten years ago by the Cluetrain Manifesto:"people in networked markets have figured out that they get far better information and support from one another than from vendors." In the Web 2.0 era, the boundaries between information producers and users is blurred, and the usual concepts of authority and control are radically changed. Among the other consequences, marketing approaches aiming at improving online reputation are being greatly affected. Brand awareness, one of the objectives of classical marketing practices transforms into brand engagement, purpose of Marketing 2.0. This engagement is created by the perceptions, attitudes, and behaviours of those with whom the different companies and organisations are communicating.

More importantly, especially for tourism, it passes necessarily through the experience (direct or indirect) a customer gains. Contents generated by users (UGCs) have an acknowledged importance in all fields, and in tourism in particular. Their positive effects have recognised repercussions on quantifiable phenomena such as e-commerce, but also on intangible matters such as those related to the image or the informational side of specific products or services (termed sometimes info-commerce).

Already in 2007, the annual Country Brand Index (CBI) measuring attractiveness of countries in several areas, stated that the Web had the highest importance (67%) as channel to collect information about a tourism destination. On the other hand, the continuing growth of UGCs' influence, due to their wideness and deepness, makes them perceived as even more reliable than official sources for a tourist. PhoCusWright (2009) nine out of ten cybertravellers read (and trust) online reviews on tourism products and services (hotels, restaurants and destinations).

Three phases are influential in this travel experience formation process:

1. Pre-experience, built on other people's travel stories, before travelling;
2. Experience during travel or stay, today increasingly shared real-time through mobile applications;

3. Post-experience, which disseminates comments, evaluations, emotions.

These issues form the foundations on which specialised Travel 2.0 tourism websites have built their success. Today, however, we see a new phenomenon that can be interpreted as starting a new trend, especially in some countries: generic OSNs are being progressively more used in travel and tourism. Italy is surely one of these countries, being at the first places in the World with regard to diffusion and usage of OSNs, Facebook in particular. Facebakers there are almost 17 million Italian Facebook users, 56% of the online population, which put Italy at the sixth place in country rankings. Italians seem to like much conversing and debating their travel experiences, tastes, perceptions and attitudes.

Recent research reports travels as the second most discussed topic on Italian OSNs and a Google Insights for Search query shows an incredible growth of Facebook searches in Italy with respect to other technologically developed countries such as USA, UK, France or Germany. The phenomenon is a social convergence trend: specialised travel websites increase their sociality by adopting applications which enable real-time sharing of contents among the visitors, while giants such as Facebook try to occupy vertical markets through dedicated services or acquisitions of specialised companies as the social travel recommendation site Nextstop. There are little doubts that the importance of Travel 2.0 features and tools, and specifically of social media environments, is growing fast. Many tourism businesses are, in one way or another, changing their approach to the manners of presenting themselves online.

However, most of the studies have assesses so far mainly the social and psychological effects, and have well confirmed the role played as sources of information and areas in which discussing various issues related to travels or stays. Some works have also discussed the effects of these tools on the image and the popularity of destinations or other tourism operators, mainly in the hospitality sector, in which the direct contact, real or virtual, with the customer and their crucial role for the good health of the companies. The general conclusion to-date in this field is that, beside the repeated statements on importance and role, tourism operators have not yet fully understood the new technological world by and still many concerns are brought forward.

Credibility of the information online, possibility to forge for particular interests by unscrupulous competitors, privacy, overload of useless information, in addition to the usual (in the technology arena) lack of resources or skill shortage are the most reported issues. These positions, however create a tension between demand (tourists, travellers, visitors) and supply (tourism businesses and organisations). As well reported by Xiang and Gretzel:

- "Social media Websites are"ubiquitous" in online travel information search in that they occur everywhere [...] no matter what search keywords a traveller uses. Certain social media Websites [...], which can be considered more comprehensive and travel-specific sites, are becoming increasingly popular and are likely to evolve into primary online travel information sources. [...]. The results confirm that tourism marketers can no longer ignore the role of social media in distributing travel-related information without risking to become irrelevant."

The rest of this thesis gives further quantitative support to this stated importance of the role played by OSNs by directly assessing their effects and influence on tourism website visits. This is a topic which has not been discussed in the literature so far, but has an important value in trying to establish the real role of OSNs in supporting the efforts of tourism operators to attract visitors to their websites and influence their attitudes and memories.

MATERIALS AND METHODS

The data analysed in this work were provided by Shiny through their Shinystat service, an online platform specialised in Internet audience analysis and website statistics. The company is well known mainly in Italy, its country of origin and well diffused. More than 275,000 Italian websites use it. Cumulative data were collected concerning the visits to 19,902 websites in the categories: Travel and tourism and hospitality and restaurants. The timeframe spans a little more than two years (26 observations from August 2008 to August 2010 included). To all extent the sample can be considered quite significant, even if a single source of data was used. The data collected consisted of the series of total visits to Italian websites (TOT) and the contributions to these visits having Facebook (FB) and Twitter (TW) as referrals. Shinystat uses a 30 minutes time window to define a visit; that is: all connections to a website coming from the same IP address in a 30 min period are considered as a single visit.

This follows the proposals of the Web Analytics Association. Although not particularly meaningful per se, for the arbitrarity in the definition, when measured consistently over a period of time, visits are a good indicator of the behaviour of website with respect to its popularity. The global series (TOT) is an example of pooled (or cross-sectional) series: a series consisting of the linear composition of a number of different contributions. In order to assess the significance of these contributions to the global series a multiple linear regression can be used. This technique is well known and has been widely used in many other studies.

In addition to the usual requirements of a regression analysis, the critical point in our case is to make sure that the independent variables do not suffer from multicollinearity (*i.e.* predictor variables are not highly correlated with each other) which may hinder the estimation of the effects of individual predictors. The significance of the contributions due to FB and TW as referrals were assessed with a multiple regression where the time period is the dependent variable and the FB and TW contributions are the predictors. Tests for multicollinearity and normality of residuals were performed. The time series was also examined by using a standard simple decomposition method to derive its main characteristics, seasonality in particular. All analyses have been carried out with SPSS version 17.

RESULTS

The time series for total visits to Italian tourism websites (TOT) and the FB component. It must be noticed that, for space limitations, the uses two scale axes (the right one is for the visits from FB) in order to better show the series' behaviour (measurement scales differ of almost two orders of magnitude, for the same reason TW is omitted due to its very low values). The maximum values for the contributions of FB and TW visits are recorded in the month of August 2010: FB = 0.329%; TW = 0.002%. When examining the series transformed into an index with the starting observation taken as base, TOT gets to 120 at the end of the period examined, while FB reaches 9438 and TW achieve 2280.

The predictor coefficients are reported along with their standard errors and statistical significance (indicated by a t statistic and its associated p-value). The last column contains the condition index for which gauges the presence and the extent of multicollinearity (as known when it value is higher than 15 multicollinearity is a concern, when higher than 30 multicollinearity is a serious problem).

The coefficient of determination is R2 = 0.523 which can be considered providing a good fit. Residuals are normally distributed, a Kolmogorov- Smirnov (K-S) test produces Z = 0.833 which has a (asymptotic) p-value = 0.492 (the K-S test has a null hypothesis of normality). The multicollinearity diagnostic does not show significant problems. The only slight effect found is for the TW component which has a condition index = 15.809, indicating a limited problem which can be ignored.

DISCUSSION

The results of the analysis lead to a number of interesting considerations. First of all the contribution of the two social media websites examined are of a low level. A higher proportion would have been expected, but this result is in agreement with other investigations, conducted on different bases, that show a limited usage of all Web 2.0 functionalities by tourism websites practically in every country. Little research has been conducted on this issue for what concerns Italy and, besides some popular press objects, no reliable data exist on how much OSNs are employed by the Italian tourism industry. In general, however, operators have seldom shown in the past highly favourable attitudes towards ICTs and, still today, make poor usage of them. Hence the advanced Web 2.0 features, OSNs in particular in this case, have a limited diffusion, at least at the present time. Despite that, the growth of the FB and TW components is quite remarkable (some thousand times), mainly if we compare with the limited increase in total visits (a little more than one).

This is an expected outcome and is in agreement with the many publications, scholarly and not, stating the quick growth in the usage of these virtual social environments. Also the seasonality effect is an expected result. The growth in usage in the first part of the year, peaking in July, is a clear indication of the role FB and TW play as important and reputed sources for travellers and tourists planning their summer travels, the most intense vacation period in Italy. This is in good agreement with other studies on the role of online social networks as information sources.

The regression analysis shows the positive importance and the significance of the FB contributions to the total number of visits to a tourism website. It must be noted here that no information has been analysed in this work regarding the ownership of these Facebook resources (a study on this topic is ongoing). Very probably these contributions come from pages not directly connected with the websites, a further confirmation of the weight and the value of online social environments for the popularity and the success of tourist operators. The usual disclaimers apply when it come to the limitations of this work.

A single country has been considered, Italy, and a peculiar one for its very large proportion of Facebook-dependent online population. More studies will have the task of falsifying the outcomes presented here or adding further confirmations to the effects described. The results presented here have an obvious importance for practitioners. From an academic point of view this work clarifies, for the first time, the role and the influence of OSNs on the popularity and traffic of tourism operators websites. In addition, it provides simple and effective methodological indications for gauging the significance of different contributions to a temporal phenomenon such as the one discussed here. One final consideration is in order. The mere fact that there are many visits to a website does not necessarily imply a good image of the website owner. Many bad realisations exist and, for example, they are used sometimes to show how not to present an organisation online.

In cases like these the websites may be visited by many. As already widely known, only good projects, well designed and carefully implemented, have a positive effect on the health of the actors presenting them online. This good consideration of the brand, then, produces a more favourable acceptance of the website which, in turn, reinforces the brand image, creating a virtuous cycle of appreciation. Also, many studies argue that a solid, rich and appreciated website is a necessary foundation for the design of an effective and worthy online social media strategy. In this preliminary analysis these aspects have been neglected, the only aim has been to show the effects an OSN may have. Further investigations, already ongoing, will take care of these issues.

CONCLUDING REMARKS

The main objective of this work was to show the effects of Web 2.0 features, and in particular of online social networks, on the popularity of tourism websites. The survey, conducted on data collected on a significant sample of Italian websites confirms this hypothesis. At the same time the outcomes also confirm the low presence of these features on the sites examined. Lack of resources, poor technical competence and sluggish management are usually claimed to explain the modest adoption of any type of information technology by tourism enterprises, for the most part very small. To these, in the case of social media, it would be possible to add also a certain level of suspicion, distrust and reluctance to share information, comments or suggestions with others. However, the demonstrated (not only by this work) impact of modern ICTs and Web 2.0 poses a big challenge to any business or organisation (private or public) working in today's tourism arena. The tourist (traveller, visitor etc.) makes extensive use of these technologies and shows to appreciate quite much the possibilities offered by the Internet today. Difficult (if not impossible) to demonstrate scientifically, most of the declining performance of the Italian tourism in the last years might find a strong component in this poor employment of modern technologies. Small and medium tourism enterprises are thus urged to rapidly move to a more favourable technological stance. Most, if not all, the adoption issues commonly quoted may find a solution in a firm increase in collaborative and cooperative attitudes which, as long shown, may overcome the weaknesses and deficiencies of single organisations.

14

Media's Strategy for Tourism

TOURISM POLICY OF INDIA: AN EXPLORATORY STUDY

The objective here is to assess the impact of Tourism Policy on the tourism sector and make a preliminary study of the possible impact such policy imperatives might have on the socio-economic fabric of the country. The study, commissioned by Equations, Bangalore, utilised a methodology involving a historical preview of the evolution of Tourism Policy since 1982, and an exploratory assessment of the impact. The study material included documentation available at Equations and relevant publications of the Union Government.

The impact assessment of the sectoral policies on the specified sector suffers from a serious methodological problem. Briefly, it may be argued that the development of a sector is not solely dependent on the factors within the sector: it is influenced by the general socio-economic environment, the political system and the overall policy framework.

Thus the study integrates within itself the dynamic aspects of historical changes that are taking place at the macro-economic level. Similarly, Tourism Policy would not have evolved on its own without being influenced by the general tenor of macro-economic policy. Tourism policy thus has a socio-political grounding as much as it has a macro-economic colouring.

The 1980s witnessed the era of liberalisation initiated by the Congress Government at the Centre. The process of liberating the Indian economy from the shibboleths of 'license-permit Raj' culminated in the initiation of the structural adjustment programme in 1992. "Objectives, Thrusts and Macro-economic Dimensions of the Eighth Plan" endorsed by the National Development Council, clearly outlines the context within which the structural reforms were initiated: "The need to restructure our systems of economic management has become an imperative if India is to emerge as a vibrant and internationally competitive economy in the 90's. Systems of control and regulation, developed for good reasons in the past have outlived their utility and some positively (sic) stand in the way of further progress.

Such dysfunctional systems have to be overhauled in the light of emerging realities." The process of structural adjustments has brought about far reaching changes in the Indian economy at a breath-taking pace. The impact of these changes over the tourism sector need to be studied in a dynamic context. Nevertheless, the above should not be taken as ignoring the fact that sectoral policy does have a direct and unambiguous impact over the concerned sector.

Tourism Policy, as a statement of intent by the Government, would form the reference point for action and criticism. Any initiative by Government in Tourism by way of legislation or direct investment is envisaged within the framework of Tourism Policy.

The debates in Parliament had taken recourse to the received policy of the Union Government while making references to particular cases. The backdrop of a policy always serves as a guideline for further executive and legislative initiatives. It would be cynical to regard these policy statements as mere exercises in eloquence and additions to the already existing volumes of wishful thinking.

Furthermore, Policy statements by Government should be viewed in their evolutionary stance. It would be a negation of the democratic content of our political system to view a Policy statement as a static and rigid formulation, at a point in time, applicable for years to come. Thus, since 1982, various initiatives undertaken by the Government need to be perceived as additions or modifications to the received Policy. While it may be argued that these changes in the policy are only marginal and superficial from the viewpoint of equity and social justice, it would be an oversimplification to view the latest policy statement as nothing but a certain version of the Policy formulated in 1982. Recognising the all-pervading inertia that looms large in matters governmental, one is often tempted to deny the scope for lobbying which makes possible the desired modifications in the policy corpus. In short, policy, as a body incorporating proactive intentions, is amenable to periodic reviews and possible modifications.

The issues stressed in the preceding paragraphs provide the framework within which Tourism Policy needs to be considered. In brief, there is more to policy in tourism than is found in the Tourism Policy. Perhaps, the links within a macro-economic framework need no special mention.

MAJOR POLICY INITIATIVES

The first ever Tourism Policy was announced by the Government of India in November 1982. It took ten long years for the Government to feel the need to come up with a possible improvement over this. Thus the National Action Plan for Tourism was announced in May 1992. Between these two policy statements, various legislative and executive measures were brought about. In particular, the report of the National Committee on Tourism, submitted in 1988 needs special mention. In addition, two five-year plans-the Seventh and the Eighth-provided the basic perspective framework for operational initiatives.

The Seventh Plan advocated a two-pronged thrust in the area of development of tourism, viz., to vigourously promote domestic tourism and to diversify overseas tourism in India. While laying stress on creation of beach resorts, conducting of conventions, conferences, winter sports and trekking, the overall intention was to diversify options available for foreign tourists. The Tourism Policy, 1982 was more an aggressive statement in marketing than a perspective plan for development. Its main thrust was aimed at presenting India to the foreigners as the ultimate holiday resort.

With a view to reach this destination, the following measures were suggested by the Policy:

- To take full advantage of the national heritage in arriving at a popular campaign for attracting tourists;
- To promote tourist resorts and make India a destination of holiday resorts;
- To grant the status of an export industry to tourism;
- To adopt a selective approach to develop few tourist circuits; and,
- To invite private sector participation into the sector.

The Planning Commission recognised tourism as an industry by June 1982. However, it took ten years to make most of the States to fall in line and accord the same status within their legislative framework. At the beginning of the Eighth Plan (1992-97), 15 States and 3 Union Territories had declared tourism as an industry. Four States had declared hotels as an industry. The National Committee on Tourism was set up in July 1986 by the Planning Commission to prepare a perspective plan for the sector. Within the broad framework of the Seventh Plan, the Committee had to evolve a perspective plan for the coming years.

The Committee, headed by Mr. Mohammed Yunus, submitted its recommendations in November 1987. The list of Members was as impressive Mr. S.K. Mishra (Secretary, Department of Tourism), Mrs. Kapila Vatsayan, Mr. K.L. Thapar, Mr. Rajan Jaitley, Mr. A.B. Kerker, Mr. R.K. Puri and Mr Pran Seth. The Committee in its Report recommended that the existing Department of Tourism be replaced by a National Tourism Board. It suggested that there be a separate cadre of Indian Tourism Service to look after the functioning of the Board. It also submitted proposals for partial privatisation of the two airlines owned by the Union Government.

By September, 1987, the Central Government declared more concessions for the sector: these included tax exemption on foreign exchange earnings from tourism (a 50per cent reduction on rupee earnings and a 100per cent reduction on earnings in dollars), a drastic reduction in tariff on import of capital goods, and concessional finance at the rate of 1 to 5per cent per annum. The Tourism Development Finance Corporation was set up in 1987 with a corpus fund of ₹100 crores. Until then, the sector was financed on commercial lines by the Industrial Development Bank of India, Industrial Credit and Investment Corporation of India and other commercial banks.

The National Action Plan for Tourism, published in May 1992, and tabled in the Lok Sabha on 5 May 1992, charts 7 objectives as central concerns of the Ministry:

- Socio-economic development of areas;
- Increasing employment opportunities;
- Developing domestic tourism for the budget category;
- Preserving national heritage and environment;
- Development of international tourism;
- Diversification of the tourism product.,
- Increase in India's share in world tourism (from the present 0.4per cent to 1per cent during next 5 years)

As per the Action Plan, foreign exchange earnings are estimated to increase from ₹10,000 crores in 1992 to ₹24,000 crores by 2000 AD. Simultaneously, the Plan aims at increasing employment in tourism to 28 million from the present 14 million. Hotel accommodation is to be increased from 44,400 rooms to 1,20,000 by 3 years. Other provisions in the Action Plan include a discontinuance of subsidies to star hotels, encouraging foreign investment in tourism and the setting up of a convention city for developing convention tourism.

The Action Plan envisages the development of Special Tourism Areas on lines of export processing zones. Special Central assistance is to be provided for the States to improve the infrastructural facilities at pilgrimage places. It proposes to set up a National Culinary Institute, and projects a liberalised framework for recognition of travel agents and tour operators.

The Eighth Plan document makes a special mention that the future expansion of tourism should be achieved mainly by private sector participation. The thrust areas as enumerated in the Plan include development of selected tourist places, diversification from cultural related tourism to holiday and leisure tourism, development of trekking, winter sports, wildlife and beach resort tourism, exploring new source markets, restoration of national heritage projects, launching of national image building, providing inexpensive accommodation in different tourist centres, improving service efficiency in public sector corporations and streamlining of facilitation procedures at airports.

The Eighth Plan aims at luring the high spending tourists from Europe and USA. It also envisages a 'master plan' to integrate area plans with development of tourism. This is envisaged to ensure employment opportunities for the local population. In April 1993, the Government announced further measures aimed at export promotion. The existing Export Promotion of Capital Goods Scheme (EPCG) was extended to tourism and related services. Against the existing 35per cent, the tourism sector would now pay an excise duty of 15per cent only on capital goods import, subject to an export obligation of 4 times the cargo, insurance and freight (CIF) value of imports. With an obligation period of five years, this came as a boon to the hotel industry. The cost of construction had also come down by 20per cent.

In addition to the above policy pronouncements by the Union Government, our planners had envisaged the possibilities of developing specific regions on a zonal plank. Special area programmes like the Hill Area Development Programme and the Western Ghats Development Programme form part of the overall national plan.

The Eighth Plan document stipulates that the strategy in such designated special areas is to devise suitable location-specific solutions, so as to reverse the process of degradation of natural resources and ensure sustainable development. This approach perhaps needs to be integrated into the project of special tourism areas, now being made popular by the Government. Administrative Control and Developmental Compromises The federal principles enshrined in the Indian Constitution require that the tourism sector be treated as a State subject. As such, the Department of Tourism (under the

Ministry of Civil Aviation and Tourism at the Centre) undertakes certain promotional and developmental activities with a view to enhance the sectoral potential. The Department has certain regulatory functions to perform involving the hotel industry, travel agencies and tourist operators. Over the years, there has been considerable erosion of powers so far as State Governments are concerned. The sustained campaign for privatisation in all the policy documents has left limited space of operation for the States. The public sector is increasingly being perceived as an agent of inertia than of change and hence the pressure for a hands-off policy.

On the other hand, the Union Government has been usurping the powers of the State with some pretext or the other. Promotion schemes, designed at the Centre, are transferred for implementation at the State level. The special Central Assistance, for example, granted for the development of infrastructure at the pilgrim centres, carries with it a pre-defined scheme and mode of execution. Furthermore, there are occasions when the Centre forces the State Governments to extend certain subsidies and concessions to the sector. The terms of such concessions would have been fixed by the Centre and the States would have no choice but to fall in line. For example, during the State tourism minister's conference in December 1991, the States were urged to freeze water and electricity rates for 10 years.

They were also asked to exempt certain hotels from local and state taxes for 10 years. Seventeen circuits and destinations were identified under the National Action Plan for development through Central assistance and investment by the States and the private sector. The centres were identified by the Centre and the States were asked to do the needful. There were also times when the federal division of power resulted in operational contradictions. For instance, by 1989, many foreign hotel chains like Hilton, Hyatt, Penta and Kempinski had applied for licenses for investing in India.

However, the revenue departments of the respective States failed to locate and allocate land for the construction of hotels. The scheme, thus, fell flat. Curiously, the Union

Government was not hesitant to make use of Constitutional provisions when it suited its interests. As has been stated earlier, the Yunus Committee had suggested the creation of the Tourism Board on lines of the existing Railway Board. (Perhaps, it was the brainchild of Mr. K.L. Thapar, then adviser to the Planning Commission, in charge of Transport and Tourism Sector.

Being from the Railway Service, it is not surprising that Thapar thought about a 'Tourism Board'). To begin with, the empowered committee of secretaries challenged the idea of creation of a Board. It was said that the Railway Board as an independent entity was created for historical reasons. It would be difficult for tourism to be looked after by a Board, because legally the sector would come under the Industrial (Development) Act. It was also found that such a Board would not be viable financially. In 1991, the think-tank on tourism created by Minister Madhavarao Scindia rejected the idea of a Board in toto.

It was emphasised that the Board cannot be in charge of a sector that is basically under the jurisdiction of the States! Scope for Federal Interventions The previous section highlights the dubious ways by which the Centre attempts to hijack initiatives at the State-level. This is achieved essentially by threatening to curtail Central assistance or by cajoling through promises of more financial aid. It is common knowledge that the resource-base of the States is very narrow, making them vulnerable at the negotiating table.

However, States have the freedom to resist the Centre's strong- arm tactics, provided State assemblies stand-by the interests of the States. For instance, State legislatures may refuse to freeze water and electricity rates on grounds of revenue generation. In that event, the concerned Chief Minister or the Minister of Tourism may convey the intensity of resistance that he is confronted with, and thus refuse to comply with the Centre's diktats. It is heartening to realise that the States have often exercised their power of self-determination and consequently refused to toe the line drawn by the Centre. This offers enough scope for possible interventions at the federal strata of our political system in matters of policy formulation. Privatisation and its Implications According to the Approach Paper to the Seventh Plan, " there is a vast potential for development of tourism in the country. Tourism should be accorded the status of an industry. Private sector investment will have to be encouraged in developing tourism and public sector investments should be focused only on development of support infrastructure". Thus the seeds of private initiatives were sown during the Seventh Plan. The Government took the matter of privatising the tourism sector seriously by 1988.

It was during the tenure of Mr. S.K. Mishra as Tourism Secretary that the talk of inviting private investment into the sector began. The Government permitted foreign equity participation up to 5 1 per centin tourism projects. Foreign charters were allowed to operate in the country for the first time. Foreign companies were allowed to repatriate their profits to the extent of 3per cent. The structural adjustment programme, initiated in June, 1992, paved the way for privatisation in almost all sectors of the economy. The Annual Plan (1992-93) document emphatically enunciated the Government's position vis-a-vis tourism: "(T)he future growth of tourism will have to be achieved mainly through private initiative.

The State will contribute to tourism by planning broad strategy of development, provision of monetary and fiscal incentives to catalyse private sector investment." The process of privatisation brought in its wake big investments and private involvement at various levels. As an offshoot, environmental considerations were thrown to the winds and there were instances of large scale human rights violation. The self- correcting nature of policy made provisions for stricter controls in this regard. More seriously, privatisation meant alienation of the majority of our population and their deprivation. Employment generated in tourism is generally seasonal and ill paid. The private sector- induced pockets of tourism had the potential of turning into centres of pollution, drug trafficking and prostitution.

Industry Status Granted to Tourism The Seventh Plan proposed that tourism be declared an industry. However, it took time for the States to implement this, even though they agreed in principle. The smokeless industry had the advantage of generating maximum value-added, because of low-cost inputs. The Tourism Policy Statement carried certain provisions in favour of the hotel industry. It stated that there should be provision for depreciation in the balance sheets of hotels. Being an export industry, hotels were to be given excise concessions. The provisions of the Monopolies and Restrictive Trade Practices (MRTP) Act were relaxed for hotels, because any hotel with 300 or more rooms would have incurred an investment of ₹25 crores.

The document also hinted at lower tariffs for power and water and regulations for easy import of equipment. As a follow-up, hotel and shipping were added to the list of 27 industries exempted from Section 22 A of the MRTP Act. The consequences of declaring tourism as an industry need to be studied in detail. It is not possible to capture its implications in an exploratory work like this.

However, it is obvious that the private sector has primarily benefited to a great extent by this measure. Importing Modifications to Policies We have earlier stated that the arena of policy formulation should be self-evaluating and self-correcting. In the case of Tourism Policy, this has proved to be the plus point. As an illustration, the Policy statement of 1982 made no mention of infrastructure development. The successive governments at the Centre failed to create proper tourism infrastructure, thus resulting in loss of traffic.

This lacuna was corrected in the National Action Plan. However, much of this change was due to intensive lobbying by such agencies like the Indian Association of Tour Operators (IATO), the Travel agents Association of India (TAAI) and the Indian Hotels and Restaurants Association (IHRA). It is for the voluntary agencies and pro-people forces to exploit the avenue of lobbying at various levels. The environmental implications of tourism development did not form part of the 1982 Policy. The consequences are too obvious to be written about. However, the NAP, 1992 did carry specific provisions for environmental protection and harnessing. From Policy to Cartooning Policy statements may also lead to justifiable flights of fantasy. Two examples would illustrate how policies were used to justify stands taken by the politicians: a. Shri Devi Lal, the then Deputy Prime Minister wanted a 50per cent discount for farmers at Five Star Hotels run by India Tourism Development Corporation.

The scheme had teething problems since it was not easy to distinguish a farmer from amongst the clients who visit such hotels. However, on his insistence, the so-called CHAUPALs recreated a village ambience to the amazement of foreign tourists, who took a liking for them. b. Pursuing the objective of the Seventh Plan to diversify overseas tourism to its logical conclusion was what prompted A and. Jagdish Tytler to float the idea of casinos.

It was an attempt to provide some entertainment for foreigners during the evenings. It was said that Indian classical music would not provide much needed entertainment for foreign guests because the artistes spend a lot of time tuning their instruments! Folk dances get over in an hour. So much for our much touted cultural diversity. It is embarrassing to believe that the consultative committee attached to the Ministry of Civil Aviation and Tourism had endorsed the idea. Conclusion Broadly, our successive policy pronouncements in the realm of tourism falls within the "liberalising" framework of the macro- economic policy environment.

The Finance Bill, 1988, had assured 50per cent tax exemption on foreign exchange earnings in the sector, and a further 50per cent exemption if re-invested. In effect, it amounts to 100per cent tax concession. Luxury hotels enjoy exemptions of all kinds with a view to encourage tourism earnings. These tax exemptions coupled with provision of soft loans to the sector led to a boom in the tourism related private investment. The Economic Survey 1991-92 aptly summarises the ultimate aim of such incentives for private sector participation: " The Government has tried to expand the economic space in which the people can exercise their initiative and ingenuity. It hopes to do more to expand their opportunities, to enhance their potential. But what shape the economy takes ultimately depends on what the people make of it. In that sense, the future is in their hands." We should not forget that tourism is an industry which emerges in the context of unresolved socio-economic structural issues, such as land distribution patterns or the take over of traditional occupations by modem mechanised capital. Tourism happens to be a source of livelihood for millions in India and aggressive privatisation does not ensure social and economic safety nets. In the face of the unhindered entry of international capital and successive alienation, perhaps, it is difficult to agree that "the future is in our hands"

ASPECTS OF TOURISM POLICY

THE WORLD SCENARIO AND INDIA'S POSITION

In recent years tourism has emerged as a major economic activity that is employment oriented and earns foreign exchange. Its share in the worlds GDP in 1994-95 was 10per cent which is more than the world military budgets put together. In global terms, the investment in tourism industry and travel trade accounts for 7per cent of the total capital investment. Today 21.2 crore people around the globe are employed in travel trade and tourism. In future, this industry is likely to see unprecedented growth. According to the World Tourism Council at Bruseels, the revenues from travel and tourism in Asia Pacific region will grow at the rate of 7.8per cent annually over the next decade.

Amongst the economic sectors, the tourism sector is highly labour intensive. A survey by the Government of India notes that the rate of employment generation (direct and indirect) in tourism is 52 persons employed per ₹10 lakh investment (based on 1992-93 Consumer Price Index). This is much higher than the rates of employment generation in most other economic sectors. Indias tourism industry has also recorded phenomenal growth. The rate of international arrivals in India in recent years has been to the tune of about 19 lakh arrivals per year. The unprecedented growth in tourism in India has made it the third largest foreign exchange earner after gem and jewellery and ready-made garments. This is not surprising since India possesses a whole range of attractive normally sought by tourists and which includes natural attractions like Iandscapes, scenic beauty, mountains, wildlife, beaches, kajor rivers and manmade attractions such as monuments, forts, palaces and havelis.

However, in global terms, inspite of such attractions, tourist arrivals in India are a mere 0.30per cent of the world arrivals. Receipts are similarly low, just a 0.50per cent of the world receipts. We are still quite far from the target of 50 lakh tourist arrivals per year.

TOURISM IN THE STATE

A separate Tourism Department was established in 1973 to identify and develop the tourism potential in the State. This was followed by the creation of Tourism Corporation of Gujarat Limited in 1978 which was entrusted with the task of undertaking and developing tourism-related commercial activities.

The Corporation is presently engaged in a variety of activities such as creation of lodging and boarding facilities for the tourists and other aspects of tourist acilitation such as transportation, packaged tours, wayside catering along the National and State Highways, arranging cultural festivals, organizing exhibitions and producing and distributing maps, posters, brochures and pamphlets. The Corporation has set up accommodation facilities at Chorwad, Ahmedpur Mandvi, Porbandar, Veraval, Hajira, Ubharat and Tithal.

Similar facilities at pilgrimage centres like Palitana, Somnath, Dwarkja, Pavagadh and Dakor have also been set up by the Corporation. One of the recent tourist attractions introduced by the Corporation in collaboration with the Indian Railways is a special tourist train. The Royal Orient Train which connects up various tourist destinations straddling the Gujarat and Rajasthan State. However, the Corporation has suffered losses due to a number of organizational constraints.

In order to minimize these losses and also to provide better services to the tourists, the Government has undertaken privatisation of some of the commercial property units of the Corporation.

In spite of possessing a variety of tourist attractions such as wildlife, scenic beauty, pilgrimage centres, exotic traditional crafts and festivals, beaches, hospitality of the region and a varied healthy and tasteful cuisine, the State has not been able to accelerate the pace of tourism in comparison to other states. In 1991, the State did declare a tourism policy but it did not elicit adequate response from the private sector since the policy contained only a handful of benefits while the implementation was tardy due to legal and administrative constraints. This was at a time when the Government of India had already declared tourism as an industry and a large number of states had followed suit. This enabled the tourism industry to avail of incentives, reliefs, benefits available to the industry in those states.

While other state Governments made successful efforts in developing tourism within their states, the relative inability of the Gujarat State to harness and develop its full tourist potential may be attributed to a combination of factors such as lack of effective policies, inadequate infrastructure, ineffective marketing and lack of decent facilities for the tourists.

The main rationale for formulating a comprehensive tourism policy is rooted, on one hand,in the convergence of socio-economic spread benefits, environment-friendliness and employment potential of tourism industry and on the other, in the growing demand for tourism products in the State, brought by a rapid industrial growth in the State during the recent years that has led to tremendous increase in number of business travellers.

OBJECTIVES

The main objective of the States Tourism Policy will be to undertake intensive development of tourism in the State and thereby increase employment opportunities.

The following related objectives are dovetailed with main objectives:

- Identify and develop tourist destinations and related activities.
- Diversifications of tourism products in order to attract more tourists through a varied consumer choice.
- Comprehensive development of pilgrimage centres as tourist destinations.
- Create adequate facilities for budget tourists.
- Strengthen the existing infrastructure and develop new ones where necessary.
- Creation of tourism infrastructure so as to preserve handicrafts, folk arts and culture of the state and thereby attract more tourists.

APPROACH AND STRATEGY

In addition to the facilitation role assigned to itself by the Government in the development of tourism, the Government will adopt the following strategy towards the private sector with the objective of securing its active involvement in leading the development of tourism in the State.

- The tourism will be given the status of industry in order that the facilities and benefits available to the industry are also made available to tourism projects.
- A special incentives package will be made available for encouraging new tourism projects as well as expansion of existing tourism units.
- Infrastructural facilities will be strengthened and developed within the State, particularly in Special Tourism Areas which will be notified latter and which will be developed by adopting an integrated-area.
- Effective mechanisms will be set up to build meaningful co-ordination with the Central Government and the State Governments agencies, the local self-government bodies and the NGOs.
- Government will encourage building effective

linkages with the relevant economic agents and agencies such as the national and international tour operators and travel agents of repute, hotel chains and global institutions connected with tourism such as WTO.

POLICY PROPOSALS

Tourism as Industry

Like other industrial projects, tourism projects too involve professional management, capital investment, special skills and training. The Government of India and a number of other states have declared tourism as an industry. Gujarat State which is at the forefront of the industrial development will also declare tourism as an industry. This will enable the tourism projects to be reliable to get benefits contained in the paras below.

Availability of land is a primary requirement of any project. The process of grant of land will be facilitated in urban areas for the projects concerning setting up of hotels, restaurants and apartment hotels etc. Existing arrangements for grant of government waste land to industrial units will be made applicable to various tourism projects.

Arrangements will be made to acquire private land under Land Acquisition Act for various tourism projects by companies registered under the Companies Act. The existing commercial rates of NA assessment applicable to land involving tourism projects would be reviewed and rates of NA assessment for industrial purposes will be made applicable to them. As one of the sets of infrastructural institutions, the State Financial Institutions have made an important contribution in creating conductive environment for industrial entrepreneurs. They will be called upon to do the same for tourism entrepreneurs in terms of making available adequate finance.

So far, the lending from the State Financial Institutions has been largely confined to hotels only. In reality, the range of activities for tourism projects is far larger than just hotels as can be seen from the following illustrative list:

Accommodation Projects

- Hotels
- Resorts
- Motels
- Apartment Hotels
- Heritage Hotels

Food Oriented Projects

- Restaurants
- Wayside Facilities on the State Highways.

Other Tourism-Related Projects

- Amusement Parks and Water Sports
- Handicraft Village Complexes
- Fairs and Festivals.
- Camps and Facilities Encouraging Adventure
- Train Travel Projects
- Sea/River Cruise Projects
- Sound and Light Shows
- Museums
- Natural Parks/Zoos
- Safari Projects
- Ropeways
- Sports/Health Facilities Complexes
- Training Schools for the managerial expertise for Hospitality Industry.
- Golf Courses.

Service Oriented Projects

- Travel Agency
- Tour operation
- Transport Operation
- Linkage with the International Hotel Chains (Franchise)
- Human Resources Development (HRD) for Tourism Industry and necessary training facilities.

Most of the projects on this illustrative list are not eligible for loans from the banks or the State Financial Agencies. It will be necessary to make suitable changes in the lending criteria for viable projects in the listed activities in order than their financial requirements are met. The modification of the lending criteria of the State Financial Agencies will be made with regard to the financial ceiling, debt equity ratio, recovery period, moratorium etc. Necessary arrangements will be made to ensure that the State Financial Agencies and the banks attach adequate priority to the financing requirements of tourism projects.

A new incentive package will be made available to replace the existing incentive policy instituted in 1991. A tax holiday of 5-10 years in respect of following taxes will be made available upto 100per cent of capital investment to various tourism projects located in Special Tourism Areas whether declared by the Central Government or the State Government, located in designated areas and located on National and State Highways. The scope and the extent of the benefits of tax holiday will vary according to certain considerations such as the admissible expenditure, the size of the capital investment etc.

The benefit of tax holiday will also be made available for the purpose of expansion of the existing tourism projects in these areas:

- Sales Tax
- Purchase Tax
- Electricity Duty
- Luxury Tax
- Entertainment Tax

Necessary administrative arrangements will be made at the State and District Level to operationalize the incentive schemes. Suitable schemes will be designed to market tourism products, and particularly wide publicity will be secured in respect of various facilities being offered by the travel agents, tour operators etc.

Special paying guest scheme will be formulated for providing adequate and inexpensive lodging and boarding facilities too take care of seasonal flows of tourists to the pilgrimage centres during festivals. Financial assistance will be provided for the preparation of feasibility reports by consultants in respect of tourism projects. Structure of the taxes and tariffs, *e.g.* luxury tax, entertainment tax, sales tax, etc., will be reviewed with reference to developmental needs of tourism sector and necessary amendments will be made.

Redefining the roles of the State and the Market

Since the approach of the Tourism Policy focuses on market-led developments, the role of the State would be as follows: The Government proposes to make commercial services available entirely through private sector or in association with it. The States role will primarily focus on strengthening and upgrading existing infrastructure and development of new infrastructure. Reputed consultants will be hired to prepare area development master plans/feasibility studies in respect of important tourist destinations and areas of tourism potential, *e.g.* Sardar Sarovar Project Area, Kutch, Beach sites and area covering Porbandar,Gir Forest, Veraval, Somnath, Ahmedpur-Mandvi, Saputara, Modhera etc.

Efforts will be made to get funding for development of infrastructure for these destinations/areas from national and international agencies. In conformity with States promotional role in the development of tourism sector, all competitive and commercial activities of Tourism Corporation of Gujarat Limited will be privatised except where no entrepreneur is coming forward to meet the existing need. This privatisation would help strengthen the financial position of the corporation and also help provide qualitative services to the tourists.

Tourism Corporation of Gujarat Limited will assume a catalytic role focused on acting as clearing house of information, production and distribution of promotional literature, policy advice etc. The Tourism Corporation will assist entrepreneurs and agencies in tourism sector and will try to help alleviate their difficulties particularly vis-a-vis the Government and its agencies. A Computerized Information Centre will be set up at the State level to make available necessary information to the agencies/entrepreneurs who wish to set up tourism projects. In addition to its existing offices in Bombay, Delhi and Madras, the Tourism Corporation will also open its offices in other major cities of India to give wide publicity and disseminate information on Gujarat Tourism and market tourism products through these offices and through reputed travel agents in other big cities. Thus, the information about Gujarat's tourist destinations and related information would be made available to tourists from outside the State in their own cities.

There is already a scheme of 50per cent matching grant from the State Government to the local self-governing bodies for the development of local tourist destinations. This scheme will be made more effective and attractive and necessary provisions in the budget will be made. This will help centralize the process of developing tourist destinations. The process of decentralization will be further strengthened by delegation of administrative and executive powers of approval of incentives to small tourism projects to District Level Bodies headed by the Collector. These bodies, in addition, will also secure co-ordination from other departments/agencies of the Government in development and promotion of tourism. Representation will be given on this body to the experts, individual agencies and individuals connected with the tourism.

A Single window clearance system will be instituted for speedy clearance of various permissions, approvals required under different laws and rules. Necessary modification/amendment will be made to various administrative arrangements and laws which are not consistent with the approach of this Policy. Care will be taken to ensure that prospective investors do not have to suffer protracted and complex administrative process.

Intensive efforts will be undertaken to attract investors from outside the State as well as from other countries including non-resident Indians to invest in tourism sector on large scale. Tourism Corporation of Gujarat Limited and Directorate of Tourism will play active role to ensure that investors get various permissions easily and are provided with all the necessary facilities. A High Powered Committee under the Chairmanship of Chief Secretary with Director of Tourism as the Member Secretary will be constituted with the objective of securing effective co-ordination among various Government departments and agencies as also to speed up decision making proceeds concerning tourism. The committee will meet regularly and enjoy full powers of Government, provided the approval of the Chief Minister and the Council of Ministers will be obtained wherever required.

In order to create a participate forum for deliberation and discussion concerning tourism industry, a Tourism Advisory Council headed by the Chief Minister will be set up. The Ministers and Secretaries of administrative departments concerned will be the members. The representatives of tourism industry, experts and related organisations will be nominated as members. The Additional Chief Secretary (Tourism) will be the Member Secretary of this Council. The Council will meet periodically to deliberate upon policy as well as individual issues and offer suitable advice to the Government.

PERSPECTIVE PLANNING

Perspective plan for tourism development will be prepared in consultation with experts. An overview of possible tourism products is offered below:

Religious (Pilgrimage) and Archaeological Tourism

Gujarat has a preponderance of pilgrimage centres as in some other states. Somnath and Dwarka-some of the well known and revered sites of ancient Hindu temples are situated in the State. The temple architecture has reached heights of excellence in Jain temples at Shetrunji, Girnar and Taranga. The temple of Ambaji situated in Aravalli range in North Gujarat is an important religious centre for devotees in the country. Dakor, Pavagadh, Bahucharaji, Shamlaji, Narayan Sarovar, Sudamas Porbandar, Kabirvad Shuklatirth, Kayavarohan, Bhadrakali Temple Ahmedabad and Tankara-Maharshi Dayanand Saraswatis birth place are also important pilgrimage destinations which have kept alive the religious sentiments of the people. Lakhs of pilgrims visit these places every year. These places are visited not only by the devotees from all over the country but also by non-resident Indians and travellers especially from the eastern part of the world. Necessary accommodation facilities and related services will be created on these sites. For ensuring orderly and planned development of pilgrimage centres, the State Government has constituted Pavitra Dham Vikas Board chaired by the Chief Minister. The Board will prepare and implement plans to provide necessary facilities to the devotees and also ensure conservation of cultural atmosphere consistent with sentiments of visiting devotees.

Shamlaji is an ancient site for Buddhists. The excavated relies of Buddhist period at the site are now kept in a museum at Baroda. There are a number of places of archaeological importance is such as the temple-town of Palitana, Modhera with its Sun temple, historical Ranki Vav at Patan with relics of an ancient capital, the Girnar Hills with Hindu and Jain temples, Junagadh with a historical fort, Dabhoi, Champaner, Pavagadh, Shaking Minarets, Gandhi Ashram, Siddi Sayed Jali etc. These can be developed by providing necessary infrastructural facilities and marketed as tourist destinations to attract tourists.

HERITAGE TOURISM

A large number of old palaces, havelis, darbargadhs exist in the State. These historical buildings can be converted into hotels, restaurants or museums by providing suitable incentives to owners. Wildlife and Pilgrimage Tourism circuits can be linked to heritage properties exploiting the geographical congruity. Development of this sub-sector will not only attract foreign tourists but also provide encouragement and support to local art and craft. Government will take necessary steps to promote Heritage tourism in the State.

Wildlife Tourism

There is substantial scope for development of tourism based on wildlife in the State. Gir Forest of Gujarat is the last stronghold of Asiatic Lions. The Bear Sanctuary at Ratan Mahal (Dist.Panchmahal, Black Buch Sanctuary at Velavadar (Dist. Bhavnagar), Bird Sanctuary at Nalsarovar (Dist.Ahmedabad),

Wild Ass Sanctuary at Kutch etc. can be effectively developed into tourist destinations by providing infrastructural facilities. In order to facilitate visitors to these areas, coordination among various agencies will be established.

Coastal and Beach Tourism

The Gujarat State has the longest coastline among Maritime States of the country. Identified stretches of coastline can be developed into beaches from tourism point of view. It will be the endeavour of the State to develop beach potential by providing such facilities as may attract foreign tourists. Various tourist destinations easily accessible from the coast will be linked through coastal shipping circuits.

Tourism based on Traditional Art and Craft and Cultural Activities

Banni in Kutch, Khambhat, Junagadh etc. are known for their craftsmanship. Similarly, there are hundreds of fairs that are celebrated through out the year with enthusiasm. Tarnetar Fair in Surendranagar District, Chitra Vichitra Fair at Poshina (Sabarkantha District), Kanwat Fair at Chhota Udepur (Panchmahals District), Dang Darbar in Dang. Bhavnath Fair of Junagadh, Vautha Fair of Ahmedabad etc. have immense tourism value. By developing accommodation, transport and other facilities, these fairs and festivals will be promoted nationally and internationally. The places of importance from art and craft point of view will be included in the tourist circuits and necessary facilities provided to tourists.

Corporate Tourism

Private sector will be encouraged to build the state of the art convention centres, seminar halls etc. so as to attract corporate events like seminar, workshops and annual general meetings. Participants in such events generally have high purchasing power and provide a boost to local economy.

Adventure Tourism

This is also a territory with possibility of development as

a sub-sector which will be examined and new activities like Camel Safari in Kutch, Horse-riding in Aravalli hill ranges, Parachuting in Saputara, Trekking in Dang, Pavagadh, Palitana etc. will be promoted. Such activities will create large scale employment opportunities for guides, coolies, traders for hire of tents and equipments etc. and will also encourage paying guest accommodation in such areas. Private entrepreneurs and institutions will be encouraged to develop such facilities.

Highway Tourism

There is a good network of State and National highways which criss-cross the State and a large number of travellers prefer road journey. Because of large geographical expanse of the State, these journeys tend to be quite long and boridng. There is a need for creating necessary facilities like hotels, restaurants, picnic spots, water parks etc. along the highways at suitable intervals for the highway travellers to relax. In fact, travellers can be induced to follow certain traffic routes if such facilities are better developed. Highway facilities and wayside amenities are so well developed in some states that this has become the mainstay of tourism. State shall encourage private investors to create such facilities on highways.

Various sub-sectors of tourism activities listed above will be encouraged by marking new tourism units eligible for incentives under Tax Holiday incentive scheme in designated areas. As mentioned earlier, the State Government intends to designate certain areas having significant tourist potential as Special Tourism Areas. To this end, reputed consultants and institutions will be engaged to prepare area development plans in respect of various areas such as Kutch District, areas around Sardar Sarovar project area, South Saurashtra areas covering Gir, Porbandar, Veraval, Somnath, beaches and areas of pilgrimage/heritage towns.

These areas will be developed by following integrated area development approach. The State Government will make efforts to tap all the source of national and international funding for development of these areas and provide special encouragement to tourism projects being established therein. For ensuring faster development of these areas, area development committees will be constituted.

Human Resources Development

Human Resources Development is an important aspect of service industries. Tourists depend upon travel agents, guides and hence trained manpower is a sine qua non of tourism industry. On the basis of available statistics, training facilities can be safely said to be totally inadequate. If trained manpower is not available locally, the objective of local employment will not be achieved. Keeping in view the approach of market-led development, the State Government will encourage and support creation of training facilities in the private sector by private agencies/individuals.

Hotel Management course, courses meant for guides, caterer and other supervisory and non-supervisory staff of hotel will be introduced in Industrial Training Institutes (I.T.Is). Approved hotel associations and private entrepreneurs will be encouraged to create new training facilities by making available land to them for this purpose and by giving other appropriate incentives. The Government will consider setting up a Hotel Management Training Institute at the State level preferably in private sector. Residents of Gujarat, especially local youths, would be encouraged and facilitated to take part in such training courses.

The Institute of Hotel Management, Catering and Nutrition which is working under the administrative control of the Central Government will be utilized to start new training courses so that the residents of Gujarat can get admission and manpower requirement of this sector is met., The residents of Gujarat undergoing such training will be reimbursed a part of the tuition fees through scholarships.

FEEDBACK AND MONITORING

To make the New Tourism Policy result oriented, implementation will be monitored by a High Powered Committee under the Chairmanship of Chief Secretary. A

Management Information System will be set up to assist the Committee to make available information on various aspects of implementation on a continuous basis. The Committee will also review the policy from time to time.

NATIONAL TOURISM POLICY 2002

A national policy on tourism highlighting the importance of the sector and the objectives of tourism development in the country was presented in the Parliament in 1982. The policy was formulated in an environment of a closed economy with rigid licensing procedures. The policy did not emphasize the role of private sector, and foreign investment was not envisaged. The policy also did not lay adequate emphasis on domestic tourism and the need for product development. In the Chief Minister's Conference held on October 30, 2001, the Prime Minister of India Shri Atal Bihari Vajpayee had stated.

"Tourism is a major engine of economic growth in most parts of the world. Several countries have transformed their economies using the tourism potential the fullest. Tourism has great capacity to create large scale employment of diverse kind – from the most specialised to the unskilled and all of us know that generation of massive productive employment opportunities is what India needs the most".

The Ministry of Tourism had prepared a draft National Tourism Development Policy with the objective of positioning tourism as a major engine of economic growth and to harness its direct and multiplier effects for employment and poverty eradication in an environmentally sustainable manner. This draft was circulated to all the stakeholders in the Tourism sector, the Private sector, the industry Associations, the State Governments, Departments and Ministries of Government of India.

The draft on National Tourism Policy-2002 was also discussed at the three day Tourism Conclave comprising of:

- Meeting of all foreign and domestic officers of Tourism Ministry.
- Meeting of State Tourism secretaries and
- Meeting of the State Chief Ministers and Tourism Ministers.

The Policy rests upon the following basic principles:

- Account should be taken of the fact that for the last four decades or so, a tourism revolution has been sweeping the world. In 1964, the number of tourists leaving their homes, worldwide, was 100 million. This number increased to 200 million in 1974, 500 million in 1992 and 700 million in 2001. And this number is likely to swell to 1.5 billion by 2020 and receipts from it are estimated to cross $2000 billion.

  If India has to partake in this revolution in a meaningful way, it must change its strategies as well as the techniques and tools of its machinery of implementation. In this connection, it has to be noted with concern that during the last decade or so, India's share of world tourist traffic has remained static at 0.38 per cent.
- At the institutional level, a framework would have to be evolved which is Government-led, private-sector driven and community-welfare oriented. Government have to provide a legislative framework to regulate tourism trade and industry, ensure safety and security of the tourists and create basic infrastructure and health-care facilities. The private sector has to act as a main spring of the activities and impart dynamism and speed to the process of development as well as conservation. Both Government and the private sector would be required to safeguard the stability and also the social and economic advancement of the local communities and the communities in the neighbourhood.
- The deep-rooted relationship of tourism and our cultural assets should be fully recognised and provided for. Improvements and environmental upgradation of the protected monuments and the areas around them should be considered as a linchpin of the tourism industry.
- Effective linkages and close coordination should be established with such Departments as Civil Aviation, Environment, Forest, Railways, Home, etc.

- Sustainability should serve as a guiding star for the new Policy. The development and management strategies should be so worked out as to ensure that tourism largely acts as a smokeless industry and its ecological footprints remain as soft as possible. No one engaged, directly or indirectly, in the tourism industry, should be allowed to secure short-term gains by resorting to what has been called the darker side of tourism. Neither over-exploitation of natural resources should be permitted nor the carrying capacity of the tourist-sites ignored.
- Greater emphasis should be laid on eco-tourism whose parameters should be broader than those of nature tourism alone. It must help in eliminating poverty, in ending unemployment, in creating new skills, in enhancing the status of woman, in preserving cultural heritage, in encouraging tribal and local crafts and in improving overall environment and facilitating growth of a more just and fair social order.
- Special thrust should be imparted to rural tourism and tourism in small settlements, where sizeable assets of our cultural and natural wealth exist.
- Due importance should be given to domestic tourism, particularly tourism connected with pilgrimage, and it should be so designed that the infrastructure created under it serves as a backbone of international tourism in times to come.
- A new class of young tourists, with marked preference for adventure and distant destinations, in hills, caves and forests, is emerging. This class is not looking for 5-star accommodation but only for simple and clean places to stay. The requirements of this class of tourists should be met and guest tourism encouraged through Panchayats and local bodies and associations.
- Special attraction of tourist for the Yoga, Siddha, etc., as well as for the Indian cuisine should be made use of and effectively encouraged.

- The tourist industry and travel agents should be persuaded to evolve and adopt voluntarily a Code of Ethics and its infringement should be firmly dealt with by Tour and Travel Associations.
- A section of the State police should be earmarked to act as tourist police and special training should be imparted to it.
- At the international level, India should play a dynamic role and make its presence felt at the World Tourism Organisation, World Tourism and Travel Council and Earth Council. Its unique cultural values and spiritual heritage should be projected with dignity and elevation befitting a great nation, whenever suitable opportunity comes our way.
- The civilizational issues as well as issues pertaining to civic administration and good governance must be attended to and made an effective part of the tourism policy. It should be ensured that good policies are not shipwrecked in the sea of half hearted implementation.

The policy document seeks to enhance employment potential within the tourism sector as well as to foster economic integration through developing linkages with other sectors.

Broadly the policy paper attempts to:

- Position tourism as a major engine of economic growth;
- Harness the direct and multiplier effects of tourism for employment generation, economic development and providing impetus to rural tourism;
- Focus on domestic tourism as a major driver of tourism growth.
- Position India as a global brand to take advantage of the burgeoning global travel and trade and the vast untapped potential of India as a destination;
- Acknowledges the critical role of private sector with government working as a pro-active facilitator and catalyst;

- Create and develop integrated tourism circuits based on India's unique civilization, heritage, and culture in partnership with states, private sector and other agencies;
- Ensure that the tourist to India gets physically invigourated, mentally rejuvenated, culturally enriched, spiritually elevated and " feel India from within".

The policy document takes into consideration seven key areas that will provide the thrust to tourism development. These are: Swagat (Welcome), Soochana (Information), Suvidha (Facilitation), Suraksha (Safety), Sahyog (Cooperation), Samrachana (Infrastructure Development), and Safai (Cleanliness).

TOURISM AND NATIONAL DEVELOPMENT IN INDIA – CURRENT SITUATION AND PROSPECTS

In its modern form since the end of the Second World War, tourism has grown into one of the world's largest industries with a growth rate in excess of 5 per cent per annum over the past twenty years. International tourism flows across frontiers in the year 2000 reached 698 million while receipts from these flows reached US$ 595 billion (including receipts from international transport fares). Estimates prepared by the World Tourism Organization indicate that global domestic tourism flows are at least ten times greater than international tourism flows indicating that there were at least 6,980 million domestic arrivals in 2000. Globally, tourism accounts for 11per cent of the global GDP and 8per cent of the world trade employment

In most countries with a large population, domestic tourism is the foundation of a viable and sustainable tourism industry. Much of the growth of global tourism has been generated by domestic tourism, which tends to be more focused on rural destinations. With a growing interest in the intangible culture of different countries (*i.e.* lifestyles, cuisine, ceremonies, music, religious beliefs, traditions, customs, and history), there is a strong potential to encourage international tourism to the rural areas as well. India's share of global international tourism at 2.64 million foreign arrivals through its borders in the year 2000 is relatively small in volume (about 0.38 per cent) but almost twice as high in terms of US$ receipts (about 0.69 per cent)

On the other hand, India's share of global domestic tourism is much higher (around 4.6 per cent of estimated global domestic tourism). While the proportion of global US$ receipts from international tourism increased from 0.57 per cent in 1990 to 0.69 per cent in 2000, this compares with a share of 1.37 per cent in 1981. In contrast, India's neighbours in South and South–East Asia have more effectively utilised tourism for economic growth and employment creation

A forecasting study undertaken by the World Tourism and Travel Council estimated that in 2001, tourism would account for 10.7 per cent of global Gross Domestic Product, 207.1 million jobs; US$ 1,063.8 billion in export value, and US$ 657.7 billion in capital investment. A study on the economic impact of tourism conducted by the World Tourism and Travel Council estimated that in 2001, the consumption activity arising from domestic and international tourism will contribute 5.3 per cent of India's Gross Domestic Product. Tourism will also sustain 25 million equivalent full time jobs or 6 per cent of India's workforce, and contribute more than US$ 3 billion in gross foreign exchange receipts.

Separate estimates prepared by the Department of Tourism using a multiplier based on 1980 research suggests that the actual employment generation effect of (direct and indirect) tourism in India is around 42 million (includes full time/part time/casuals).

The forecasting study undertaken by the World Tourism and Travel Council further indicates that between 2001 and 2011:

- Global Gross Domestic Product will increase from 10.7 per cent to 11 per cent;
- Global employment contribution will increase from 207.1 million to 260.4 million jobs or 9 per cent of total global employment;
- The global value of tourism related exports will increase from US$ 1,063.8 billion to US$ 2,538.3

billion or 12.8 per cent of global export value; and

- Global capital investment in tourism will increase from US$ 657.7 billion to US$ 1,434 billion or 9.3 per cent of global investment.

Forecast data from the World Tourism Organization shows that the share of tourism volumes and related receipts, Gross Domestic Product, employment, and export earnings is expected to move away from the developed countries towards the less developed countries as a result of favourable economic, motivational, technological, and policy factors. WTTC's status paper, "The India Imperative" has analysed India tourism in the light of the latest Tourism Satellite Accounting Research TSA (2001) and projections for the year 2011.

Subject to addressing key policy issues highlighted in the paper, WTTC has identified India as one of the foremost growth centres in the world in the coming decade:

- The development priorities of the Government of India up to 2012 are to place the economy on a significantly higher growth path that will deliver greater economic benefits in the context of the new global economic and security order, but also enhance human well-being, achieve social equity, sustainability, and efficiency. To achieve this overall development goal, the Government of India has embarked upon a strategy that involves a radical departure from past policies, and institutional arrangements in order to optimize and release the potential of its natural, human, financial, and technical resources.

  One of the sectors of the economy considered to have particular potential is tourism. Tourism is seen to be a priority sector because it is:

- Able to maximize the productivity of India's natural, human, cultural, and technical resources, and are sustainable development.
- Labour intensive and cottage or small industry based, providing employment that is of a high quality thus contributing to higher quality of life;

- Capable of being primarily focused on rural areas with appropriate and relatively low cost programmes;
- Has extensive forward and backward economic linkages that build overall income, employment (especially for women, youth, and disabled persons bringing greater social equity, and justice), investment, and raises central, state, and local government revenue;
- Is able to deliver significant levels of hard currency as an export industry;
- Able to promote understanding, peace, and contribute to national unity and regional stability.

There is great potential for creating enormous number of new jobs through travel and tourism. The employment potential is the highest in the tourism sector as compared to any other sector and India has the potential to more than triple its travel and tourism jobs. The tourism industry has a very strong linkage to socio-economic progress of the country. It has a very high revenue capital ratio. It is estimated that an investment of ₹1 million creates 47 direct jobs and 11 indirect jobs, which far surpasses the employment potential from Agricultural and Industrial sector.

SWOT Analysis

The tourism sector's contribution to the national development priorities and strategies has so far been relatively limited. A review of the sector's competitive strengths and weaknesses, opportunities, and threats indicates that it has considerable growth potential.

The main results of the analysis are:

- India's great competitive strength from a tourism point of view is its ancient and yet living civilization that gave rise to four of the worlds great religions and philosophies, and brought travellers and trade millennia ago. The rich natural and rural landscape of India is punctuated with the built heritage of its ancient past and more modern structures of the present and its hopes for the future. India's contacts with other civilizations is reflected in the rich cultural diversity of its people through its language forms, cuisine, traditions, customs, music, dance, religious practices and festivals, its holistic healing traditions, art, and craft.

- The main competitive constraints facing the tourism sector are the low priority that the sector has been given by government
- In the past it was unable to effectively link its role in relation to national development priorities, undue focus was laid on the international market at the expense of domestic tourism, the poor quality of the environments surrounding many of India's main tourist sites, the security scenario in the region that affects the perception of India as a safe and secure destination, the quality of facilities and services at attractions
- The quantity and quality of transportation service, and related infrastructure, facilitation of entry to India by international tourists, the multiplicity and high level of taxation
- Limited availability of tourist information in-source markets and at destination, limited scope, accuracy and reliability of market data for planning and management, insufficient marketing of India in its domestic and international markets, lack of attractive project financing, restrictive land use policies that limit the availability of suitable land for tourism development, limited and poor facilities and services outside the major cities, especially in rural areas, and the lack of community participation leading to in some cases hostility to tourism. The low priority accorded to tourism has meant that it has played only a marginal role in India's development programmes to date and this is reflected in the limited budgets, limited cooperation and coordination capabilities, and an inability to implement strategic initiative and projects.

- Notwithstanding the constraints (which themselves present opportunities), the key competitive opportunities are:- (1) leverage the huge potential of its domestic urban population to develop rural tourism
- The main internal threats to the development of the tourism sector are failing to effectively resolve the constraints identified above. These are security, safety and health situation; failing to involve communities in the decision making process for tourism development; and failure to adopt and implement sustainable development and management principles and practices at tourism sites, especially in the rural and natural areas of the country. From an external point of view, the main threats are not effectively addressing the fierce and ever-increasing competition from competing countries, over-reliance on a few well worn international and domestic travel markets, unbridled growth of international tourism that is characterized by high volumes, low economic yields, and high levels of adverse socio-cultural, and environmental impacts, and further regional conflicts such as that resulting from the September 11 event of 2001.

India possesses a rich and diverse range of unique tangible and intangible cultural, natural, and man-made tourism resources, many of which are world class in quality, and most of which are located in rural areas. The tourism resources of the country have the potential to attract significantly higher levels of market demand from the domestic and international markets provided that sustainable site management practices and principles are adopted and applied, and the other constraints identified above are effectively resolved. Provided that the identified constraints and opportunities are addressed, and appropriate plans prepared to handle the internal and external threats, then it is considered that India Tourism focus should be to:

- Substantially increase the proportion of the urban resident leisure and pilgrimage tourism to rural areas not just in terms of volume but also in terms of length of stay and expenditure. For example, the total urban resident leisure and pilgrimage domestic market is estimated to increase from 22.5 million in 2001 to 50.5 million by 2012 and it would be a key objective to encourage these to visit the rural areas through appropriate strategies; and

- Substantially increase the volume of high-yielding (high average per capita expenditure) international tourists from the priority regional and long haul source markets based on the identified travel interests.

Tourism Development Goals, Objectives, and Strategies

The tourism industry, unlike many other industries is a composite of several service providers. These service providers are generally in the private sector. In, addition, public sector institutions such as the national or state departments of tourism are involved in the planning, development, and management of tourism. The participation of different private and public agencies makes tourism industry a complex phenomenon requiring a strong cooperation and coordination for it to be developed and expanded along lines that will contribute to the overall national development objectives.

Left to itself, the industry will develop naturally, but not necessarily optimally or sustainable, and without any clear links to the broad development objectives of the country. Uncontrolled tourism growth could damage India's socio-cultural structure, degrade its tangible and intangible cultural and natural heritage, and lead to adverse economic impacts such as high importation costs, and weakening inter-industry linkages. On the other hand, when the industry is properly planned, developed and managed at all levels of government in partnership with the private sector, it will strengthen India's socio-cultural structure. It would valorize its tangible and intangible cultural and natural heritage, and lead to positive economic impacts including enhanced employment and income opportunities in rural areas, lower importation costs, and stronger inter-industry linkages. The vehicle for achieving the positive benefits of tourism, mitigating the negative effects, and delivering sustainable industry development framework of India's national development priorities is the preparation and implementation of a comprehensive national tourism policy. The overall goal and strategy for the development of the tourism industry is to ensure that its development is closely tied to the national development priorities of the country. In this context the Government of India's vision for the development of the tourism sector is: "Achieve a superior quality of life for India's peoples through Tourism which would provide a unique opportunity for physical invigouration, mental rejuvenation, cultural enrichment and spiritual elevation".

Key Objectives

To achieve the overall vision for the development of tourism, five key strategic objectives need to be achieved.

They are:

1. Positioning and maintaining tourism development as a national priority activity;
2. Enhancing and maintaining the competitiveness of India as a tourism destination.
3. Improving India's existing tourism products and expanding these to meet new market requirements;
4. Creation of world class infrastructure
5. Developing sustained and effective marketing plans and programmes.

Positioning Tourism as a National Priority

- Inclusion of Tourism in the concurrent list of the constitution of India. This will provide a constitutional recognition to the tourism sector, help in channeling the development of tourism in a systematic manner and enable central government to legislate for tourism development. The proposal for including tourism in the concurrent. List was circulated to the State Governments and discussed at the Chief Ministers' Conference. Majority of the States have agreed to the proposal.

- To provide effective linkages and close coordination between Departments, a Group of Ministers on Tourism has already been constituted.
- Constitution of a Tourism Advisory Council with key stakeholders to act as a "think tank".
- Prepare the basis for the adoption of the Tourism Satellite Account system based on SN3 protocol for the national accounts;
- Plan, and implement a professionally managed integrated communications strategy to be called the 'National Tourism awareness campaign';

Enhancing India's Competitiveness as a Tourist Destination

- Visa on Arrival-Implement visa on arrival and consider strategies for the fast issuance of visas and permits including electronic visa approaches, and improved processing of arrivals by customs and immigration officials.
- Computerization of the system of issue of visas by Embassies/High Commission.
- Air capacity available to India is woefully short during peak travel months ranging from October to March and specially from main tourism originating destinations like North America, Western Europe and South East Asia. Additional seat capacity from the major destinations would provide a major impetus to tourism and economic development. An analysis by Indian Council for Research on International Economic Relations (ICRIER) reveals that the benefits of the additional seat capacity whether provided by the national carrier or any other international carrier would have a significant benefit for national economy.
- The model strengthens the argument for opening India's sky for enhancing tourism through increased capacity.

- Improve the standard of facilities and services at the nations international and major domestic airports by employing professional property management agencies to manage the physical premises on an outsource basis, and speeding up the privatization/ leasing of airports.
- There is a need for creation of special tourism police force for deployment at major tourism destinations. This will provide travellers security through a sprit of courtesy and hospitality.

Improving and Expanding Product Development

In relation to the development of products that are related to the special interests of the target markets, the product development strategy should be to:

- India has a unique cultural heritage. It has a vast array of protected monuments spread throughout the length and breadth of the country. India has 22 world heritage sites (16 are monuments). The conservation, preservation and integrated development of the area around these monuments provides a rare opportunity for growth and *expansion of cultural tourism* in India.
- Develop sustainable *beach and coastal tourism* resort products based on a more flexible approach to developments in the coastal zone. There is a need for identifying a series of government sites on the West Coast of India, free of encroachments, for the development of beach resorts by the private sector, with sites to be offered on long term lease at preferential terms. These sites should primarily be in the regions of Goa, Kerala, and North Karnataka, for reasons of air access.
- Develop and position the Cochin and Andaman and Nicobar Islands as *international cruise destination*. This positioning is supported by their proximity to international cruise routes, their exotic appeal and the need for high quality, low impact eco-tourism activities in the islands, and develop a dedicated cruise terminal;

- Capitalize by packaging India's unmatched variety of *traditional cuisines* that are today becoming increasingly popular in the world. The linkages and ripple effects created by a rapidly expanding restaurant sector can have dramatic implications for the Indian economy, implement private public partnership of the Culinary Institute of India that will research and document ancient culinary traditions, create a highly skilled workforce of culinary professionals that can populate not only hotel and catering establishments in India, but also internationally, serving to promote India internationally through a non-traditional medium, and encourage Indian entrepreneurs to establish restaurants of Indian ethnic cuisine internationally, by conceiving a innovative incentive scheme;
- Actively promote the development of *village tourism* as the primary tourism product to spread tourism and its socio-economic benefits to rural and new geographic areas. Key geographic regions for the development and promotion of endemic tourism. The optimum locations appear to be: Northeast states, Uttaranchal, Rajasthan, Ladakh, Kutch, Chattisgarh, and the Plantation regions (tea, coffee);
- India has some of the greatest variety of fauna in the world that has perhaps not been exploited to its full potential for tourism. In this context, the wildlife sanctuaries and national parks needs to be integrated as an integral part of the India tourism product, and priority needs to be given to the preparation of site and visitor management plans for key parks, after a prioritization of parks. Tentatively, these would be: Corbett National Park, Kanha National park, Bandhavgarh National park, Ranthambhore, Mudumalai, Nagarhole, Kaziranga, Periyar, Bharatpur, Little Rann of Kutch, Chilka, and Sundarbans. The quality of tourist facilities available at the parks should be enhanced, in particular

improve visitor information/interpretation centres, and the tiger and the elephant should be the 'brands' if Indian wildlife tourism;

- India perhaps has one of the greatest *adventure tourism* assets in the world in the form of the *Himalayas,* as well as in its mighty rivers. Mountain based adventure (soft and hard) activities in the Himalayas, creating the 'Himalayas' as the brand and icon of Indian adventure tourism should be developed and promoted. White water and more sedate great river rafting offers a unique tourism product, while regulations and certification for adventure tourism operators should be introduced so they meet minimum safety and conservation standards;
- That the domestic tourism market is mostly local or regional in nature and prefers recreational pursuits and that recreation and leisure is a vital component of the quality of life, particularly in urban areas, and needs to be recognized.
- India, despite its size, significance and attributes with world cities such as New Delhi and Mumbai, receives a minuscule proportion of the global *meetings, incentives, convention, exhibition* market with only 97 international conventions bringing approximately 25,000 people in the previous year. It is imperative not just for India's tourism development, but also for the development of international and domestic trade and commerce, that India construct a world class international convention centre in Mumbai.
- India is a region of the world's greatest bio-diversity, with a variety of unique natural locales, and is therefore, a perfect candidate for ecotourism. In this context, ecotourism should be made a priority tourism product for India with the focal points located in the Himalayas, Northeastern states, Western Ghats, Jharkhand, Andaman and Nicobar Islands, and the Lakshadweep Islands. Tour

operators needs to be encouraged to promote ecotourism, which should also be made a grassroots, community based movement, though awareness, education and training of the local community as guides and interpreters;

- India is today being 're-discovered' by the world at large for the depth of its understanding of the physical, mental, emotional and spiritual manifestations of the world and humankind. In particular, India has traditions that focus on the holistic healing of individuals and on elevating the individual to a higher plane of consciousness and awareness. This can be India's most unique tourism product – *holistic healing and rejuvenation* of the individual from every dimension – physical, mental, emotional and spiritual, and in doing so, it will capture the essence of the best of Indian philosophy and culture for international and Indian visitors alike.
- India has come to have a series of unique lodging products that can become one of India's immediate unique selling propositions (USPs). In this context, steps should be taken to eestablish a scheme for providing seed capital to entrepreneurs for the development of such unique accommodation products to be funded and administered at the State level, with adequate controls;
- India is a veritable *shopper's paradise* and the retail trade provides enormous forward and backward linkages throughout the economy. In this context, shopping should be recognized as an integral part of the tourism experience and a most valuable contributor to revenues. The development of dedicated shopping centres for traditional crafts, designed along the lines of ethnic village *haats* such as Dilli Haat and Shilpagram needs to be encouraged, the availability of information on where to procure specific crafts and produce reliable, unbiased shopping guides enhanced, funding support to

reputed NGOs promoting the handicrafts sector should be provided, a directory of traditional crafts persons should be produced and promoted, touting should be controlled through regulation and legislation, and the "Made in India" brand should be promoted;

- India has unique events, fairs and festivals, some of which are well established, such as Pushkar, Desert Festival at Jaisalmer, Kumbh Mela, etc. In this context, this sector should be promoted as a unique product of India, the "Festivals of India" programme should be reintroduced in the top 12 future markets for India. Initially, there should be an annual event in UK and USA, followed by triennial events in each of the other markets;
- Business travel is also a form of tourism and typically occurs in urban environments and should be recognized accordingly. Urban quality along the lines specified for regional and site master plans, including tourism interests and requirements in the urban planning process should be improved, and New Delhi and Mumbai should be positioned as "World Cities" and the level of physical infrastructure, urban ambience, and public services developed befitting such a status; and
- A series of themed cultural attractions should be developed based on outstanding site planning and design, a National Register of key cultural sites for tourism should be prepared and published, and Delhi should be positioned as the cultural capital of India supported by an ongoing and vibrant calendar of cultural events.

The development of this recommended niche based special interest product mix will position India as a unique world-class destination.

Creation of World-Class Infrastructure

India's physical infrastructure is the very foundation on

which tourism is to be built, and this ranges from ports of entry, to modes of transport to destinations, be they airways, roads, railways, or waterways, to urban infrastructure supporting tourism facilities such as access roads, power and electricity, water supply, sewage, and telecommunications amongst others. In this context, the strategic actions in relation to road, railways, waterways, and airport facilities are identified below.

Development of Integrated Circuits

Ministry of Tourism's financing assistance to the states has not been able to create an impact in terms of creation of international standard tourism infrastructure. The emphasis therefore has to be on identifying up travel circuits and converging all resources and expertise for development of these circuits as International Standard destinations.

Roads

The road network is particularly vital to tourism, for almost 70 per cent of passenger travel in India is by roads. Many tourist circuits too, are entirely dependent on roads. The current government plan for the road system in the country, covering both inter-state highways and improvements to rural roads directly supports tourism development. There is an urgent need to construct and improve highways linking the World Heritage Sites and places of tourism significance. Ministry of Road Transport and National Highways will collaborate with Ministry of Tourism in this effort.

Railways

The Indian Railway system can be an enormous asset in the development of the tourism and hospitality industry in the country. India has 7,000 railway stations and 11,000 trains. The railways have a special fascination for foreign tourists who wish to experience the country both at leisure and close personal contact with the indigenous people. The unqualified success of the "Palace on Wheels" substantiates the contention. For the vast majority of domestic tourists it is the railways, which is the main affordable means of travel linking the length and breadth of the vast and often enhancing sub-continent. Railway services are equipped not only to meet the travel needs of domestic and foreign tourists, but also have the infrastructure and land resource to contribute significantly to the growth of hotel accommodation in the country.

The following measures are necessary:

- Introduction of Special Tourist Trains with a preset itinerary and with private sector participation.
- *Tourist Trains* – experienced private sector organizations need to be encouraged to introduce special tourist services between important destinations. In concept these special coaches may be privately owned by organizations who will design, build manage and market the product. To improve the financial viability and promote investment, accelerated depreciation should be allowed on such investments.
- *Railway Hotels* – the Indian Railways have a plan for establishing 100 hotels at railway stations serving specific tourist centres. The Private Sector should be incentivised to operate these hotels on long-term leases. These hotels could provide clean inexpensive accommodation for the budget tourists. The proposal to construct 100 hotels of 100 rooms in three years will add 10,000 rooms and help significantly to reduce the gap between supply and demand for hotel rooms.
- *Heritage Railway Buildings* – the Indian Railways owns a number of heritage structures. Effectively maintained and marketed these would not only serve as railway stations but also as places of tourist attractions. Some of these structures are Mumbai CST and Chruchgate and Lucknow railway station.
- *Hill Railways* – India is the proud possessor of five hill railways, which can compare with the best hill railway system in the world. These railways (Darjeeling, Nilgiri, Matheran, Kangra and Shimla)

are slated to be encrypted by UNESCO as world heritage. It is essential to tap the enormous tourist potential of these products by developing these special tourist trains.

- *Railway Heritage Tourism* – Special tourism trains like Royal Orient, Budh Parikrama, Palace on Wheels and Fairy Queen are extremely popular with tourists, as they are steam hauled tourist trains. Stem traction is still operative in India and for special tourist segment it should be continued in perpetuity, otherwise skills to operate this kind technology could die.
- *Other Trains* – More trains like Shatabdhi and Rajdhani with a special tourism and hospitality focus should be planned both for the foreign and domestic tourists.

Waterways

India's 7,000 kms coastline remains untapped for the promotion of cruises. There is immense potential for this activity in the East, South and West of India. Apart from Ocean-going Cruise Lines (a circuit being contemplated by potential Indian operators in Mumbai – Goa – Lakshadweep – Cochin – Colombo – Maldives), the potential for River cruises in India needed to be developed for the North-Eastern States, (Brahmaputra and Ganges) and Kerela. India is blessed with a vast coastline as well as several navigable rivers that have extreme tourism significance.

To capitalize on this, the strategic actions are to:

- Liberalise after due study the regime governing operation of passenger services along India's coastline, as this can form both a means of transport as well as a tourist attraction.
- Harness the potential of India's mighty rivers, especially the Ganges and the Brahmaputra as a means of transport as well as unique tourism products.

Strategies for Effective Marketing

The competition for travellers from the source markets

identified for India is fierce, and to effectively compete in these markets, India will have to shift its current traditional marketing approach to one that is more aggressive and competitive.

In this context, India will have to use an array of marketing tools and strategies to:

- Differentiate itself from the competing destinations including developing a unique market position, image, and brand that cannot be held by a competitor;
- Undertake an extensive qualitative and quantitative market research programme in the target source markets;
- Identify and assemble a highly attractive product offering tailored to the interests of each source market, and develop and implement on-going cost-effective promotion programmes in each source market in partnership with the States and the private sector of the tourism industry in India and the source markets. Of special importance is the formulation and implementation of a village tourism programme that would be primarily targeted at the domestic urban market in India but which could also attract the international market;
- Establish an effective and on-going market representation presence with the travel trade in each source market; and
- Establish an Internet portal in various languages to service the information, product description, and product sales requirements of the target market segments in each source market, and to connect these directly with the preferred suppliers.

Creating an India Tourism Brand Position

In the international market, India requires a positioning statement that captures the essence of its tourism product to convey an "image" of the product to a potential consumer and which will become the India "brand". A good example of this positioning approach is Thailand's "Amazing Thailand" brand, Malaysia's "Malaysia, Truly Asia" brand, The Philippine's "Festival Islands" brand, and Egypt's "The Land of the Pharos" brand. These more or less powerful positioning statements serve to effectively differentiate each of these destination countries from their competitors, and provide an effective umbrella under which the whole marketing effort may be organized and implemented on a partnership basis. The India's positioning statement and branding should focus on what makes India unique and unmatched in the tourism world.

This is almost certainly related to its great competitive strength, *i.e.* its ancient Vedic civilization with a cultural heritage that continues to live in a largely unchanging and vibrant manner even today, especially in its rural areas. In the domestic market, where the focus of interest is rural or village tourism, a different positioning statement is required. This has to be related to the concept of "returning to or rediscovering ones roots" in order to escape the complexities and pressures of India's cities for the calm green of the rural countryside and the simplicity of the traditional village. The development of a powerful positioning image and brand position for India in its international and domestic markets requires adequate research by a professional agency, and industry "buy in" if it is to be successful. This research is being undertaken.

Market Research

An extensive programme of market research in India's primary source markets is an essential first step to:

- Establish the present image of India as a destination in relation to its competitors;
- The ensemble of products likely to be of interest to the markets in each primary source country;
- Issues such as pricing, concerns about security, health, safety, and quality, basic information on how to arrange a trip to India including visa issuances, currency, and telecommunications, transportation services; and

- The influence of media, Internet portals, and the buying behaviour of the customer.

The results of this market research will help to guide the formulation and implementation of the overall marketing strategy, the formulation and implementation of product development and promotion strategies, and the indicators that should be used to measure the success of the strategies.

DIGITAL TECHNOLOGY FOR MARKETING

The Internet is having a greater impact on the marketing of travel and tourism than any technology since the invention of television. It has already established itself as a crucial channel via which tourism organizations can promote their destinations and products offered by their service providers. The implications of the Internet and other growing interactive multi-media platforms are far reaching. India Tourism would be utilising both the Internet and the other emerging interactive technologies and capitalising on these new channels. The benefits to be gained include cost-effective global distribution and new opportunities for closer and eventually self-financing partnerships between public entities and private operators.

SUMMARY

India's tourism industry through the capacity of it's tourism resource, facilities and services and as yet relatively untapped market potential has considerable scope for expansion and development. The Tourism Policy elucidated above aims at setting-up a framework that will allow the various stakeholders to fully develop the potential of tourism and to harness this to the national development priorities.

TOURISM POLICIES OF UTTAR PRADESH

UTTAR PRADESH STATE TOURISM DEVELOPMENT CORPORATION LIMITED

Uttar Pradesh State Tourism Development Corporation Limited (Company) was incorporated on 5 August 1974 as a wholly owned State Government company with a view to promote tourism in the State. In March 1975, the Government restricted the role of the Company to activities of running the hotels and facilities developed by the Directorate of Tourism (DOT) and transferred to the Company for operation on commercial principles.

The objectives laid down in the Memorandum and Articles of Association of the Company inter-alia provided for takeover/purchase/operation of hotels/restaurants by way of BOT, BOOT, BOOL and BOLT methodology providing transport facilities to tourists and disposal of Central/State Government properties. As on 31 March 2003, the Company was operating 41 hotels (including one restaurant), three Advance Reservation Centres (located at New Delhi, Calcutta and Mumbai) and four travel units (located at important tourist locations within the State) offering travel facilities and package tours to tourists.

Organisational Set-up

The Management of the Company is vested in the Board of Directors (BOD) consisting of five directors nominated by the State Government. The day to day affairs of the company are looked after by a whole time Managing Director who has also been holding full time charge either as Director or as Director General of the DOT during the last five years. The Managing Director is assisted at the Headquarters by a General Manager, Company Secretary, Chief Accounts Officer and a Project Officer.

Field units like hotels and travel units are normally being looked after by the Managers working directly under the supervision of the Corporate office. The post of the Managing Director was held by eight incumbents during a period of five years up to March 2003, with terms ranging from six to 18 months. Frequent changes in the incumbency resulted in lack of initiative at the top level to formulate and implement any long term action plan for improvement in the working which is evident from the absence of any long term corporate plan with milestones for achievements there against.

Scope of Audit

Activities relating to liquor trade undertaken by the Company during 1992-93 at Agra, were reviewed by the Comptroller and Auditor General of India in the Audit Report (Commercial) for the year ended 31 March 1993 and was discussed by the Committee on Public Undertakings (COPU) during June 1998 to October 1999; their recommendations are awaited (October 2003).

Present review carried out during the period February 2003 to April 2003 generally covers the performance of the Company during the last five years ending 2002-03 with special thrust on the implementation of the Tourism Policy of the State (1998). The records maintained at the Corporate office, and out of 41 tourist hotels and four travel units, the working of eight hotels located in Agra, Varanasi, Lucknow, Allahabad and Raebareli districts and one travel unit (Lucknow) having annual turnover exceeding ₹10 lakh were selected for examination. The audit findings are discussed in succeeding paragraphs:

Financial Position and Working Results

The financial position and working results of the Company for the years 1998-99 to 2002-03 are given in Annexure-35 and Annexure-36 respectively.

The value of assets and liabilities and working results indicated in the Annexure-35 and 36 are to be viewed in the light of the following:

- Final purchase consideration of eight tourist bungalows transferred to the Company in 1977-78 by the State Government at provisional sum of ₹24 lakh, still remained undecided (October 2003) although the assets stood capitalised in the accounts at the provisional sum.
- Eighteen tourist bungalows which were transferred by the DOT in March 1991 at a total cost of ₹3.81 crore, in anticipation of State Government sanction, have not so far been approved by the Government (October 2003).The amount stood capitalised in the

Company's accounts at the above provisional sum.

- The net worth of the Company had substantially declined in 1999-2000 due to change in the basis of accounting of gratuity and leave encashment from cash to accrual basis resulting in increase in loss by ₹2.35 crore.
- The nominal profit earned by the Company during 1998-99 turned into loss from the year 1999-2000 due to continuous increase in the total operating expenses over the total income.

Operational Performance of Hotels and Restaurants

The performance of hotels in operation for the last five years ending 2002-03 are given in Annexure-37. The table below summarises the working results of the hotels (profit earning and loss incurring hotels) for the last five years ending 2002-03:

The main reasons for the losses/decline in overall profit, as analysed in audit, were:

- Operation of units contrary to the Board of Directors' directives for privatisation;
- Decline in occupancy; and
- Heavy shortfall in sale volume to achieve break even as discussed in paragraphs 2.4.6, 2.4.14 and 2.4.15 respectively.

Declining Occupancy of Hotels

Out of 21 profit earning hotels having aggregate annual turnover of ₹8.81 crore, as on 31 March 1999, the performance of seven hotels having aggregate turnover of ₹5.28 crore (60 per cent) declined over the period of five years in terms of occupancy as well as profit.

During audit the following points were noticed: The percentage of tourists staying in the Company's hotels had substantially declined over the period of five years ending 2002-03 as would be seen from the table given below: The occupancy of the above hotels had declined in spite of heavy increase in the tourist inflow (except at Sonauli). The

Management had not analysed the reasons for decline in preferences of tourists for the Company's hotels.

TOURISM POLICY OF THE STATE AND ITS IMPLEMENTATION

Tourism Policy of the State

Of the large number of activities authorised in the Memorandum and Articles of Association, the priorities of the Company are governed by the directives issued by the Government through the long term Tourism Policy of the State Government under which the Company is assigned a specific role.

The Tourism Policy (Policy), announced in December 1998, laid emphasis on development of tourism as main industry by improving the quality of the industry and expressly entrusted the following responsibilities to the Company:

- Upgradation and extension of facilities of important units located on the five circuits and making them suitable for foreign tourists by securing star status.
- Privatisation of units considering its necessity.
- Operation of only profitable units in future and privatisation of units expected to incur losses.
- Formulation and operation of profitable package tours with the assistance of other hotels and tour operators.
- Execution of agreements with domestic and foreign tour and travel agencies of repute, for attracting more tourists.
- Providing regular training to personnel, for extending better services to customers.

Implementation of the State Policy on Tourism

The Company had not identified critical areas of the Policy to effect micro level planning and had also not fixed the milestones to be achieved during the long term as well as in short term. In absence of any parameter and time frame for ensuring implementation of the Policy, the backlog in achieving the objectives remained unreviewed by the Management.

Upgradation of Facilities to Secure Star Status

In the Policy document, the State Government had not earmarked any fund for upgradation of facilities. The Policy envisaged financial assistance by way of share capital, loan and Central Government assistance on submission of proposals by the Company. The Company already secured (up to 1997-98) three star status for one of its hotel. It could further secure star status for only three hotels during the period of five years ending 2002-03.

In spite of lapse of over four years of the Policy, none of the hotels of the Company in two circuits (Buddha and Vindhya circuits) has star grade facilities to attract foreign tourists. The Company had not taken up any detailed exercise to identify the potential hotels requiring upgradation and also not analysed cost-benefit from such upgradation. The Company had, however, not made any effort in providing the facilities to secure star status in the viable star hotels nor had framed (October 2003) any plan in this regard.

Decrease in Hotel Facilities

During the period of five years ending 2002-03, only four hotels were added but effective operating hotels had declined substantially from 51 hotels in 1998-99 to 41 hotels in 2002-03 due to transfer of two hotels to Uttaranchal and closure of 12 hotels (11 hotels in 2001-02 and one in 2002-03) due to failure of the Management to run them efficiently.

Increase in Bed Capacity of Hotels

As against 596 rooms with 1506 bed capacity as on 1 April 1998, the capacity of operating hotels as on 31 March 2003 was 601 rooms with 1516 beds after adjusting the loss of capacity in units closed/transferred during 2001-02 and 2002-03 indicating thereby negligible addition in capacity over a period of five years.

Extension of Wayside Facilities

The development of tourist facilities including planning, selection of site and its construction are carried out by the DOT. After development of the facilities, the same is transferred to the Company for commercial operation. There was no coordination between the DOT and the Company as the former did not consult the Company while selecting the place and site for locating new units.

The DOT developed (between 1998 and 2001) 12 midway facilities (comprising restaurants with limited accommodation) out of Central assistance of ₹2.41 crore and State assistance of ₹35.07 lakh. The Company did not initially agree to take over the facilities on grounds of units being commercially unviable but subsequently decided (September 2001) to takeover these facilities as per the State Government directives.

It was further decided by the Company, not to run these units but to make efforts to lease them out on five years management contract basis. The facilities have, however, neither been taken over so far (September 2003) nor were any efforts made to lease them out as per the decision of the BOD. Thus, the expenditure of ₹2.76 crore incurred by the DOT could not serve the intended purpose and the entire amount remained blocked.

Progress in Privatisation of Units Prior to 1998

The Government approved (December 1993) and vested full powers in BOD of the Company to lay down and decide the terms and conditions and procedure in respect of 15 units, already identified for privatisation.

Progress in Privatisation from 1998

On the basis of response of the buyers and the constraints noticed against tenders floated in 1994-95, the Company belatedly submitted (January 1998) a proposal to the State Government seeking general approval of the guidelines and terms and conditions for privatisation. The terms of privatisation were approved (July 1998) by the Government as suggested by the Company. As per the guidelines, the

Company was appointed as an agent of the State Government for the disposal of the properties of the DOT by way of 90 years lease. In case of non-receipt of offers, the properties were to be leased out for short term of 30 years or otherwise given to the Management on contract basis for five years. The properties financed by the Central Government or developed on land belonging to other departments could be given on five years management's contract only. The procedure, for disposal of assets, were to be determined by the BOD of the Company but the Government owned properties could be disposed off only with the approval of the Government.

After approval (July 1998) of the terms and guidelines by the State Government, the Company had not floated any tender to proceed further in the matter so far (September 2003). Even the guidelines and pre-qualification criteria had not been laid down so far (September 2003) as prescribed in the Government order.

Further, the Company also did not invite any open Expression of Interest (EOI)/pre-qualification from prospective buyers to assess the responsiveness of the prospective buyers, especially for low potential units. The Company without any realistic assessment, approached (April 2000) the State Government to effect certain minor changes in the Government order along with permission for allowing two additional modes for disposal of assets, as stated below:

- Authorising the Company to enter into "Build, Operate and Transfer" and "Build, Operate, Lease and Transfer" system so as to attract capital for development of infrastructure.
- Delegation of full powers to the Board of Directors in finalisation of management contract for Government owned properties.

The approval of the State Government was awaited (September 2003). Meanwhile, the Company had not initiated any action for want of approval of the Government to the reference made by it. During the last nine years, the Company could, however, finalise lease for restaurant in hotel Taj Khema, Agra and a short term lease of two years for water sports complex at Lucknow which was too meager in relation to 20 units. Further, the Company commenced operation of two unviable hotels (Shikohabad and Chunar) taken over in 1997-98 and 1998-99 from DOT. The BOD approved (September 1998) the privatisation of these two hotels but no action was taken by the Management to explore the possibilities of leasing out. Reply of the Management (July 2003) that these hotels were taken over as per the directives of the State Government does not hold good as the inaction on the part of the Management to act as per decision of the Board of Directors resulted in operating these hotels at a cash loss of ₹25.69 lakh (aggregate income ₹13.42 lakh and aggregate expenditure ₹39.11 lakh).

Thus, the ground realities and problems to the complex issue of privatisation, remain undetermined. The negligible progress in privatisation over a period of eight years was indicative of apathy of the Company to pursue the State Policy for privatisation of loss incurring units.

Management stated (August 2003) that the procedure for privatisation would be undertaken after issue of amendment to the privatisation policy. The reply is not tenable as the Company had neither made any effort to devise modalities for privatisation before proposing the additional modes nor furnished details of units, if any, viable in the light of additional modes while submitting the proposal to the State Government so as to facilitate in taking decision.

Operation of Loss Incurring Units

The Company has been operating loss incurring units contrary to the Tourism Policy (1998) even without formulating and implementing any specific plan for improving the working of these units. As a result, in case of nine out of 20 loss incurring hotels as on 31 March 2003 the Company incurred losses aggregating ₹73.73 lakh during 1999-2000 to 2002-03. The indiscriminate continuance of operation of loss incurring units without seeking approval of the State Government was not only violative of Government policy but also resulted in loss to the Company.

Operation of Newly Acquired Unviable Units

In terms of State Government directives, the Company acquired four units from the DOT between April 1999 and January 2003. Out of these four units, two units (Tourist Bungalow Sankisa and Yatri Nivas, Ayodhya) were found (January-February 2001) unviable for operation by the Management while the viability of other two units (Tourist Bungalow, Bateshwar and Yatri Nivas, Allahabad) were not assessed.

The Company, however, put all these units on commercial operation in contravention to the Policy to operate only profitable units in future and privatise units anticipated to incur loss. The operation of these units proved to be loss incurring venture and that too without making any meaningful contribution for tourists.

Formulation and Operation of Package Tours with the Assistance of other Hoteliers and Tour Operators

The Company had formulated 42 package tours to facilitate the tourists in accessing various destinations.

In this connection following points were noticed:

- The Company had not maintained package-wise income and expenditure to review the profitability and growth in case of each package with a view to taking remedial action.
- The operation of the tours has been confined to five packages only. Of these, two local site-seeing and one package operating from Lucknow, Agra and Delhi were managed by the local units of the Company located at originating stationswhereas two remaining packages were operated within the state of Uttaranchal by the Company's agent. The rest of the 37 packages were not operated at all during the last five years in absence its own marketing network and tie up with any hotel and tour operator.

Management stated (September 2003) that these packages were offered to tourists on their demand. The reply is not tenable since the Management did not make any effort to market the package tours formulated by it. Moreover, this approach of the Management was not in consonance with the Tourism Policy.

- The Company had never floated any tender for appointment of local travel agents of resource and proven capability for promoting unoperated packages.

  Even the travel agent for the two packages, which were the main contributory to the income under this head, was appointed against its suo motto offer to the Company.
- Although, the Company had eight marketing agents outside State to procure bookings for its hotel accommodation, the Company had not considered tie up with them for procuring package tours. In September 2001, the Management decided that booking for the tour packages would be obtained through its marketing agents but such an arrangement has been finalised with only one party so far (September 2003).

  The operation of tour packages to attract tourists and promote tourism, remained localised and could make little headway in view of Company's failure to appoint tour operators/agents for promoting the business as contemplated in the Tourism Policy.

Execution of Agreements with Domestic and Foreign Agencies of Repute for Attracting more Tourists

Travel and marketing agents play a pivotal role in promotion of tourism by providing facilities of advance reservation of accommodation and travel facilities for tourist destinations. Accordingly, the Policy also laid emphasis on extension of marketing network through domestic and foreign agents of repute to attract tourists.

Procurement of Business Through Internal Sources

The Company had a network of six Advance Reservation Centres (ARC) (reduced to three from July 2002) located outside the state and four travel units operating in the name of UPTOURS within the state to provide advance booking of accommodation in the hotels of the Company and also operate tour packages assigned by the Corporate office.

A review in audit of the performance of ARCs, revealed that the Company closed down (July 2003) three ARCs (Chandigarh, Ahemdabad and Chennai) on the grounds of poor business secured by them as well as the fact that their income (by way of commission @ 10 per cent of the booking amount) failed to meet their overhead expenses. The ARCs were closed without any alternative arrangement like entering into marketing tie up with agents so as to tap potential customers and to make good the loss of business.

Procurement of Business Through External Sources

The Company has not so far (September 2003) floated any tender for appointing marketing agents. All the eight agents were appointed by the Company at the suo motto offer of the agents. Such agents, appointed without any publicity and without determination of pre-qualification criteria, could contribute only nominal business during the period May 1999 to December 2002.

In this connection following were noticed:

- The dismal performance of the agents failed to invite attention of the Management for taking any remedial action by appointing domestic and foreign agents of repute through open tender after laying down pre-qualification criteria.
- The network of marketing agents outside the State was confined to eight agents in three States (five in West Bengal, two in Pune and one in Uttaranchal). No action had been initiated to procure business from other States/Districts either by extending its own marketing network or through appointment of marketing agents in such unrepresented States.
- Although, the Company executed Memorandum of Understanding with State Tourism Corporations of seven States between March 2001 and August 2002

for providing business on mutual basis for a period of two years, the arrangement failed to work as none of the party could muster and provide business. Meanwhile the Memorandum of Understanding with West Bengal Tourism Corporation had already expired in March 2003 without any effort for renewal of the term.

Thus, the Company had failed to take initiative in terms of the Policy, which authorised appointment of domestic and foreign agents of repute to attract tourist. The Company has so far (September 2003) not even finalised pre-qualifications for eligibility of tenderers, leaving aside, the floating of tenders.

DECLARATION OF NEW HOTEL POLICY BY GOVT. OF UTTAR PRADESH

The Government of Uttar Pradesh has declared an effective hotel policy very recently.

The salient features of the hotel policy are:

- At the time of drafting of master plan, related regulated area and authorities by taking cooperation from Deptt. of Tourism will earmark the land for hotels and this land will be given for hotels. Where master plan has been finalised this action should be taken for vacant space. In authorities (development authority, industrial development authority, housing and development board) where master plan has not been finalised, with the help of Department of Tourism action to be taken to reserve suitable land for hotels keeping in mind the possibilities for tourism and whenever master plans are received then at that time also by taking help from Deptt. of Tourism the land will be reserved for hotels.

  The land earmarked for industry in the master plan should be kept reserved for tourism/hotel for a period of 5 years after the date of advertising the scheme. If no hotel entrepreneur comes forward in the time span of 5 years then in that case the authority will be free to convert the use of this land.

- If the land use conversion of the authority's land is necessary to grant the earmarked plot to hotel industry then the work regarding conversion of land use to be done at a competent level under the rules and regulations of authority on case to case basis.
- In places where there is no development authority, there as per requirement the land of village committee/town area body should be resumed and transferred to Deptt. of Tourism. Deptt. of Tourism can establish a land bank of such lands received from village committee/town area bodies. Deptt. of Tourism will provide this land to tourism industry/ hotel, as per requirement. But under the rules there will be a binding that if the land is not used for tourism industry within a period of 5 years then this land will be automatically transferred to the village committee.
- In above places where are no development authorities but municipal bodies are formed, there the District Magistrate may provide the land to entrepreneurs on fixed circle rate or lease.
- Since Tourism has been granted the status of industry in which hotels are also included hence plot should be earmarked and allotted similarly like industries on industrial rates. This policy will be implemented in each district of the state.
- Whenever development authorities form their plans under the purview of Deptt. of industry development then they should also earmark the necessary land for hotels at the appropriate places.
- Hundred per cent rebate in luxury tax for next 5 years be given to new hotels from the starting date. Other rebates will be applicable as per industrial policy.
- The allotment of earmarked land for hotel industry will be done only to hotel entrepreneur.
- Hotel entrepreneurs will be provided land on industrial rates by all authorities (Housing Deptt. and Industrial Development Deptt., Noida, Greater

Noida). It will be ensured that all hotel entrepreneurs are benefited by this provision, for this above mentioned all authorities will make necessary order/ revision in their rules. So that it becomes possible that the land can be made available to hotel entrepreneur on industrial rate.

- Department of Tourism will derive the number of plots as per the city wise need based on star rating of hotel.
- To identify plot a committee will be formed under the Chairmanship of the commissioner.
- Applicant entrepreneurs/society will not get more than one plot in a city.
- At places where more than one authority/society have land, there only one concern department will be made nodal deptt. by the Deptt. of Tourism which will invite application on behalf of all concern department but the final decision regarding allotment/auction, will be taken by the concerned departments only.
- After identification of land for hotel, applications will be invited from hotel/tourism entrepreneurs to provide them land on industrial rates.

Eligibility terms will be fixed for application, which will be following:

- Only those companies/societies will apply who are registered and connected with the hotel industry and have earlier experience in this regard.
- In hotel policy eligibility terms have also been fixed in which 5 star and other level project will be given to those hotel entrepreneurs who have an average turn over of ₹100 crore or above in the last 3 years, positive net worth and minimum 10 years experience in hotel profession.
- For 4-Star and other 4-Star level project the rule will be following:-

  Average turn over of ₹75 crore or above in the last 3 years, positive net worth and minimum 10 years experience in hotel profession. Like wise for 3-Star and other level project an average turn over of ₹50 crore on above in the last 3 years, positive net worth and minimum 5 years experience in hotel profession will be required.

- In authorities where there is provision of industrial plots there as per the present time policy the allotment of industrial plots in case of more than one applicant will be done on the basis of suitability can be ascertained on the basis of their experience, turn over and net worth basis. And keeping eligible applicant rating in descending order on the basis of hotel plots being made available in a city, based on their priority the plot be allotted. This rating 5 star (or above), 4- Star and 3- Star categories can be done separately.
- For each hotel the applicant company's ownership or under the management will have points as under:
- Experience in hotel profession will have maximum 50 points
  - 5-Star or above-10 points per hotel
  - 4-Star-7 points per hotel.
  - 3- Star hotel- 5 points per hotel
  - If the hotel has a tie up/contract with an international chain or the applicant himself is of international chain then for each such hotel 3 additional points will be provided.
- For turn over maximum 25 points will be fixed.
  - 1 point will be fixed per 10 crore turn over.
- For net worth maximum 25 points will be fixed.
  - 1 point will be fixed per 4 crore net worth.

TOURISM POLICIES OF MADHYA PRADESH

ECO AND ADVENTURE TOURISM POLICIES

Development of Eco/Adventure Tourism in Madhya Pradesh

The Government of Madhya Pradesh had announced its

Tourism Policy in 1995, which had, as one of its major objectives, the promotion of Eco and Adventure Tourism. The importance of tourism and the benefits derived from it are well known. With changing times, interests of tourists have also changed requiring development of newer varied forms of tourism.

Today's tourist is not content with cultural or religious tourism alone-the tourist today looks for some thrill, fun, adventure and something other than the routine. In keeping with this change in attitude of tourists, the State Government has decided to actively promote Eco-Tourism and Adventure Tourism. In order to popularise and develop these forms of tourism, Government is, for the first time, seeking participation of private investors. It would be appropriate to mention here that Eco Tourism is that form of tourism in which the tourist is able to enjoy nature and see wild life in its natural habitat in quiet and serene surroundings. Adventure tourism provides the tourist with a special thrill and feeling of adventure whilst participating in sporting activities in rivers, water bodies and hills and mountains. Madhya Pradesh with its richly endowed natural environment, unexploited so far, has immense potential for such sports.

Instead of depending on its limited resources, the State Government has decided to open up this sector for private participation for optimum utilization of these natural resources. While on the one hand, with these efforts, Government hopes to attract tourists in larger numbers, on the other hand, it is expected that it would help in generating greater demand for local products, and creating new employment avenues for the local communities. In order to attract private participation, the State Government has finalised a set of simplified guidelines which are hassle free and would make it easy for an entrepreneur to conform with.

Salient Features

- The main activities connected with Eco and Adventure Tourism which are to be promoted with private participation.

- The locations, identified for launching Eco and Adventure Tourism activities initially on a trial basis. Apart from these locations, the entrepreneur is free to come up with his own sites, subject to Government approval.
- The locations determined initially for Eco and Adventure Tourism activities have been classified in three categories A, B and C, depending on their accessibility and potential viability.
- A Letter of Intent will be issued by the Govt. of Madhya Pradesh to private entrepreneurs atter taking security deposit of ₹50,000/- per hectare. This will enable the entrepreneur to carry out the pre-deter-mined Eco and Adventure Tourism activities at identified locations. The validity, of the Letter of Intent, would be one year from the date of issue.
  - The Letter of Intent issued to the entrepreneur will entitle the en-trepreneur to enter the identified location and make necessary arrangements to launch and conduct Eco and Adventure Tourism activities in accordance with Government guidelines.
  - Within 9 months from the date of receiving the Letter of Intent, the enterpreneur will have to submit a detailed project report to the Department of Tourism on the Eco/Adventure activities to be conducted and the works to be undertaken.
  - The project report submitted by the entrepreneur would be examined within a time frame of three months (before the expiry of the Letter of Intent) and a final decision taken. In the event of the ap plication being finally approved, the plot of land/ building applied for, will be given to the entrepreneur on a lease of 30 years at prescribed rates.
  - The amount of security deposit will be adjusted against the premium due only after acceptance of the application.

  - The amount of annual lease rent will be increased by 50per cent every ten years.
- While considering proposals, projects of less density would be given preference. Whilst sanctioning projects, the commercial viability ot existing projects at the same location will be taken into account.

PROCEDURE FOR PRIVATE SECTOR PARTICIPATION

- Private entrepreneurs will have to apply in the prescribed format. The application must clearly and specifically mention the activities proposed to be undertaken at the identified locations.
- The applications will be addressed to Principal Secretary, Government of Madhya Pradesh, Department of Tourism, Mantralaya, Bhopal.
- The applications will be considered on "First Come, First Served" basis.
- The applications received will be scrutinised following a prescribed procedure and selections will be made.
- The selected applicant will be issued a Letter of Intent. The Letter of Intent will be valid for a period of one year.
- A security deposit ~ ₹50,000/- (₹Fifty Thousand) per hectare for the land applied for, will have to be deposited by the applicant before receiving the Letter of Intent. This amount will not be refunded. In case the entrepreneur is finally given the lease atter his project report is accepted, the security deposit will be adjusted against the premium for the land/ building.
- The applicant will have to submit a detailed project report of the proposed scheme within 9 months from the date of issue of the Letter of Intent, failing which the LOI will lapse.
- The Letter of Intent will authorise the applicant to enter the location and also to make initial/preliminary arrangements for launch of activities as per the

proposed scheme in consonance with the instructions from the Government.

- While preparing the project report, the entrepreneur will have to make the following provisions compulsorily. "
  - Detailed description of the construction work connected with the activity in the field of Eco and Adventure Tourism
  - Clear mention of the arrangements to be made for disposing of solid and liquid waste.
  - Details of trails to be constructed for hiking, trekking, walking.
  - A clear action plan for conservation and management of the allotted land.
  - A site development plan.
  - The extent to which weightage of importance is being given to the points listed below when the project becomes operational:
    a. The extent of use of locally available foodstuffs and locally produced items.
    b. Percentage of job opportunities for the local residents
    c. Use and promotion of non-conventional energy.
    d. Measures to be taken for ensuring that ecological balance and carrying capacity is maintained and not adversely affected un der any circumstances.
- The project report will be accepted/rejected at government level.
- On acceptance of the scheme, the entrepreneur will have to deposit prescribed premium and annual lease rent. The security amount deposited earlier would be adjusted against the premium.
- The proposed site will be given on a lease for 30 years.
- Other things being equal, projects of low density tourist intake will be given preterence.
- The lease deed shall have the clause that if the

entrepreneur tails to construct the tourist facilities as per the project report, within two years, the lease will be deemed void.

Restrictions

- Except for camp fire use, the use of wood as fuel would be prohibited. The wood for making camp fires will have to be procured from depots of the Forest Department.
- The facilities constructed under the scheme and the land/building allotted for the scheme will not be allowed to be diverted for any other use.

Facilities to be given to Successful Applicants

- The vehicles mentioned in the project report for transporting tourists to visit the identified location will enjoy an exemption from transport taxes for a period of 5 years. This will be considered to be a 'sunset facility' and it will expire automatically after 5 years.
- To operate liquor shops in the identified location the following concessions will be given in FL 3 Licence fee.
  - No concessions for locations within a radius of 5 kms from the outer limit of municipal areas with population of 3 lakh and above.
  - *In areas other than the above*:
    a. *Category areas*: 10per cent discount in licence fee
    b. *Category areas*: 25 °I° discount in licence fee
    c. *Category areas*: 50 per cent discount in licence fee
- The current norm of having a minimum of ten rooms for guests in a hotel and certain other conditions applicable for FL 3 licence will be relaxed.

Selected Activities for Development of Eco and Adventure Tourism in Madhya Pradesh

- Camping
- Trekking

- Angling
- Water sports
- Elephant Safari
- Cycle Safari
- Riding Trail
- Photo Safari
- Canoeing Safari
- White Water Rafting
- Rock Climbing/Mountaineering
- Para Sailing/Para Gliding
- Hot Air Ballooning

Identified Places in the State on Experimental Basis for Development of Eco and Adventure Tourism

Proposed Activities

- Camping
- Trekking
- Elephant safari

Water Sports Places

- Area adjacent to Satpura National Park
- Area adjacent to Panna National Park
- Area adjacent to Pench National Park
    - Tawa Project, Distt. Hoshangabad
    - Kaliasot Project, Distt. Bhopal.
    - Halali Project, Distt. Raisen
    - Barna Project, Distt. Raisen
    - Gandhi Sagar Project, Distt. Mandsaur
    - Tigra Project, Distt. Gwalior
    - Harsi Project, Distt. Gwalior
    - Mohini Sagar Project, Distt. Shivpuri
    - Kolar Project, Distt. Sehore
    - Rani Avanti Bai Project, Distt. Jabalpur

Canoeing Safari/White Water Rafting

- River Narmada
- River Tons

- River Chambal
- River Ken
- River Son

Rock Climbing and Mountaineering

- Pachmarhi Escarpment Distt. Hoshangabad
- Raisen Fort
- Gwalior Fort
- Narwar Fort
- Asirgarh Fort

Para Sailing/Para Gliding/Hot Air Ballooning

- Pachmarhi Escarpment
- Tamia to Patalkot
- Mandu
- Wanchu Point
- Raisen Fort

A-Category

- Adjoining Area of Satpura National Park
- Kaliasot, Distt. Sehore
- Halali Project, Distt. Raisen
- Mohini Sagar Project, Distt. Shivpuri
- Pachmarhi Escarpment (Pachmarhi-Chouragarh Dhoopgarh-Bada Mahadeo-Rajendragiri)
- Gwalior Fort

B -Category

- Tawa Project, Distt. Hoshangabad
- Bargi Project, Distt. Raisen
- Tigra Project, Distt. Gwalior
- Kolar Project, Distt. Sehore.
- Rani Avanti Bai Project, Distt. Jabalpur
- Mandu, Distt. Dhar

C-Category

- Narwar Fort, Distt. Shivpuri
- Asirgarh Fort, Distt. Khandwa
- Raisen Fort

- Wanchu Point
- Tamia to Patalkot
- Harsi Project, Distt. Gwalior
- Adjoining Areas of Panna National Park
- Adjoining Areas of Pench National Park
- Gandhi Sagar Project, Distt. Mandsaur

TOURISM POLICIES IN RAJASTHAN

MISSION STATEMENT

A pragmatic policy designed to ensure optimum utilisation of rich tourism resources of the state to generate employmnet specially in rural areas, to develop aready market for the rich and varied handicrafts, to preserve and to accelerate contribution of tourism industry in socioeconomic development of the state by making tourism a truly People's Industry in Rajasthan.

THE PREAMBLE

Tourism has emerged as an important instrument for sustainable human development including poverty alleviation, employment generation, environmental regeneration and development of remote areas and advancement of women and other disadvantaged groups in the country apart from promoting social integration and international understanding.

The enunciation of a new pragmatic policy, taking into account the changing socio-economic and investment scenario in the State of Rajasthan and the emerging trends in the tourism phenomenon has thus become necessary. The primary agenda of Government is to promote tourism as a means to ensure sustainable economic development and positive social change through development of tourism while preserving and protecting the environment and heritage.

INTRODUCTION AND PRESENT SCENARIO

With gross out up of US$ 3.4 trillion tourism has emerged as largest and one of the fastest growing industries in the world. Global tax revenue from tourism is estimated at US$

655 bn (1999). The estimated number of world travellers per annum is over 616 million and these travellers spend over US$ 444 billion as per estimates of World Travel and Tourism Council (WTTC) for year 2000 AD. Every 9th person in the world is engaged in travel and tourism industry for livelihood as per data of World Tourism Organization (WTO). The number of world travellers would go up to 1600 million by the year 2010 AD (WTTC).

Direct employment through the world tourism industry is over 144 million persons (WTTC) and indirect is manifold more. Presently the foreign tourist arrivals in India constitute only about 0.4 per cent of the total foreign tourist movement in the world. One of the objectives of the National Action Plan for tourism announced in May, 1992 by Government of India was to increase India's share in the world tourism market to 1per cent by 2000 AD (which is still to be achieved).

Presently India ranks 44th in the list of top 60 destinations of the world. International tourism contributes substantially to foreign exchange earning. In the year 1999-2000 tourism was the second largest net foreign exchange earner sector for the country, earning ₹12000 Crores in foreign exchange. 10.6 per cent of world's work force is engaged in travel and tourism; tourism contributes 10.2 per cent of world's GDP. In India Travel and Tourism Sector supports 9.3 million jobs and by the year 2010 it would support 12.9 million jobs, thus providing 1 in 15 jobs in the country. There is a huge domestic tourism market with an estimated 240 million tourists (140 million general tourists and 100 million religious tourists) per annum, spending by them is estimated to be over ₹95,000 Crores. (Tourism Future Data).

Rajasthan has emerged during the last decade, as one of the favourite tourist destinations in India for both domestic and foreign tourists. While in the year 1973 the total arrivals of tourists to Rajasthan were about 2 million, it has increased to 6.99 million by the year 1998-99. At present the State receives 0.60 million of the 2.3 million foreign tourists who visit India annually. Additionally over 50 Lacs domestic tourists also visit Rajasthan annually. The world famous "golden triangle" comprising of Delhi-Agra-Jaipur has put Jaipur on the world tourism map. 60per cent of international tourists visiting India, come to these places. On an average a foreign tourist spends ₹800 per day and domestic tourist ₹400 per day. It is further estimated that the average stay of a foreign tourist in the State is 2.5 days. The total spending by all the tourists visiting the State is over ₹1000 Crore per annum. Every rupee spent by a tourist in the State, changes hands thirteen times and every hotel room generate direct employment to three persons and indirectly to eight persons.

Rajasthan with its rich historical, cultural and environmental heritage, coupled with colourful fairs and festivals and friendly people has become a favourite destination for tourists from all over the world. Except for a sea-beach and snow-clad mountains, it offers everything to tourists. The rate of growth of tourism in Rajasthan has been phenomenal in last few years. Annual rate of growth for domestic tourists has been 7per cent and for international tourists has been 5per cent.

Some of the tourism products of Rajasthan have become internationally famous and popular among the tourists such as Palace-on-Wheels, Heritage Hotels, Camel Safaris, Pushkar Fair, Desert Festival, Palace Hotels and Wild life Sanctuaries/ National Parks. Recognising the potential attractions that Rajasthan has to offer to domestic and foreign tourists, the Government has accorded Tourism a special status. Tourism was declared industry in Rajasthan in the year 1989.

OBJECTIVES

- Increase employment opportunities, specially in rural areas for uemployed rural youth. Optimum utilisation of rich tourist resources of the State in order to attract the maximum number of domestic and international tourists;
- To facilitate the growth of tourism in the State and to further involve the private sector in the development of tourism in Rajasthan;
- Preservation of rich natural habitat and bio-diversity,

historical, architectural and cultural heritage of Rajasthan; special emphasis on conservation of historical monuments in Rajasthan;

- To develop a ready market for the rich and varied handicrafts and cottage industries of Rajasthan; ensure welfare of artisans/artistes;
- To promote inter cultural understanding through religious/pilgrim tourism and fairs and festivals;
- To promote socio-economic development of Rajasthan through Tourism with special thrust on backward areas;
- To make tourism a "People's Industry" in the state;
- To minimise the negative impacts of tourism and promote sustainable tourism;
- To open new vistas in tourism like Adventure tourism, Eco-tourism, Camel/Horse safaris, River and Canal cruise, House boats in Rajasthan (Palace-On-Waves), Educational Tourism, Caravan Tourism and Village Tourism.

Jawahar Kala Kendra, Jaipur and other cultural institutions will be associated with Tourism development.

ROLE OF THE STATE GOVERNMENT

- Catalyst;
- Promoter, facilitator and providing infrastructure;
- Pioneer/Joint Explorer/Planner;
- Regulator;
- Law and Order;
- Tourist Police;
- Complaints Handling;
- Standaedization of goods and services;
- Enactment for Tourism.

POLICY FORMULATION FOR GROWTH OF TOURISM SECTOR

- Comprehensive Master Plan of State with regional/ sub area/circuit plans to be updated and executed in a time bound manner;

- External assistance;
- Central assistance;
- State plan resources;
- Private sector investment-for a planned development of tourism infrastructure and growth of tourism industry;
- Growth led by private sector;
- Developing rural tourism to generate employment in rural areas by launching Paryatan Rozgar Yojana with active participation of Panchayati Raj Institutions (PRIs);
- Electronic; Print and Cyber Media plan for aggressive marketing of Rajasthan as a premiere tourism destination state;
- Enhancing and diversifying tourism products of the state;
- Synergy between tourism and handicrafts, Haat, Shilpgram models to be replicated; airport facilities, rail facilities, local transport, communication links and other essential amenities become essential.

The Government as well as the private sector shall undertake both the growth of such infrastructure. While the State has to play the leading catalytic role in some sectors, there will be an endeavour to encourage private sector participation in developing infrastructure. Efforts will be made to dovetail external assistance, central assistance, and State plan resources with private investment to achieve goals set in the Master Plan.

In order to develop infrastructure, the Government will prepare an Area-based Master Plan outlining the infrastructure necessary in each such area. The plan will be based on the potential, which each destination holds for development of Tourism. An investment plan will be evolved from this Master Plan. The Investment Plan will further be translated into an Annual Action Plan in order that the goals set in the Master Plan will be achieved in a time bound manner. Tourism, by its nature is a multi-sectoral activity, requiring participation of many agencies. Efforts will be made to co-ordinate these agencies by evolving suitable administrative mechanisms.

ACCOMMODATION

The most crucial component for tourism is providing suitable accommodation for various categories of tourists. Since the tourists are not a homogeneous entity, and are highly differentiated; accommodation ranging from budget and economy class to 5 Star and Resorts will have to be augmented. Rajasthan has estimated tourist accommodation of 19000 rooms in 772 Hotels. As per requirements estimated by the state department of tourism, 20000 rooms are needed by the year 2002 AD. The State will endeavour to encourage more private investment in the hotel industry rather than engage itself in raising such infrastructure except in areas where private investment may not be forthcoming. State Tourism Advisory Board under the Chairmanship of Chief Minister of Rajasthan constituted to provide policy guidelines.

ENSURING SAFETY AND SECURITY OF TOURISTS AND PROMOTING SUSTAINABLE TOURISM

- Alleviation of rural poverty through employment generation by domestic tourism;
- Tourism to gradually become eco-tourism, responsible tourism;
- Educating the young ones toewards heritage and tourism;
- Promoting tourism in rural areas;
- Empowerment of women, improving plight of rural artisans;
- Making tourist earnings reach the Below Poverty Line threshold in villages;
- Tourist Police, Safety, Security and hassle free stay of tourists;
- Tourism regulation, institutional mechanism;
- Advisory bodies at District, Division and State level;
- Carrying capacity, code of conduct;
- HRD, R and D and documentation for Scientific tourism management.

TOURISM INFRASTRUCTURE

The State being the second largest in the country and

having perhaps the greatest potential for tourism development, the creation of adequate and suitable infrastructure like accommodation, roads, airport facilities, rail facilities, local transport, communication links and other essential amenities become essential.

The Government as well as the private sector shall undertake both the growth of such infrastructure. While the State has to play the leading catalytic role in some sectors, there will be an endeavour to encourage private sector participation in developing infrastructure. Efforts will be made to dovetail external assistance, central assistance, and State plan resources with private investment to achieve goals set in the Master Plan.

In order to develop infrastructure, the Government will prepare an Area-based Master Plan outlining the infrastructure necessary in each such area. The plan will be based on the potential, which each destination holds for development of Tourism. An investment plan will be evolved from this Master Plan. The Investment Plan will further be translated into an Annual Action Plan in order that the goals set in the Master Plan will be achieved in a time bound manner. Tourism, by its nature is a multi-sectoral activity, requiring participation of many agencies. Efforts will be made to co-ordinate these agencies by evolving suitable administrative mechanisms.

HERITAGE HOTELS

Rajasthan has been a pioneer state in launching Heritage hotels in the country by converting old palaces and havelies of erstwhile rulers in to tourist accommodations which has been extremely popular with tourists, especially foreign tourists. At present there are 39 recognized Heritage hotels in Rajasthan providing 1069 rooms for tourists and 60 hotels are operating which are yet to be recognized by the Department of Tourism. State Government would encourage Heritage hotel movement in the state in order to provide quality accommodation for the tourist and also save precious historical heritage from dilapidation.

Bibliography

Airey, D.: *Tourism Education,* New Delhi: Oxford University Press, 2001.

Altheide, D.: *Media Participation in Tourism Development,* New Delhi: Government of India Press, 2005.

Baloglu, S.: *Annals of Tourism Research,* New Delhi: Oxford University Press, 2004.

Doorne, S.: *Representing Tourism Imagery and Ideology,* New Zealand: Tilberg: Tilberg University Press, 2000.

Kasper, C.: *Tourism Marketing and Management Handbook,* New York: Prentice Hall, 1997.

Ladkin, A.: *The Profile of Tourism Studies Degree Courses,* London: The National Liaison Group for Higher Education in Tourism, 2004.

Moilliet, D.: *Media Research Journa*l, London: Macmillan, 2001.

Murphy, A.:*Regional Tourism and its Economic Development,* Kolkata: ICSP Publication, 2001.

Payne, K.: *Tourism and Media Research,* Guwahati: United Publishers, 1998.

Robinson, P.: *Tourism and Cultural Conflicts,* UK: Oxford University Press, 1997.

Shea, L. J.: *Journal of Media and Tourism Education,* Kolkata: ICSP Publication, 2001.

Timothy, D.: *Tourism and Destination Communities,* New York: Prentice Hall, 1997.

Umbreit, T.: *The Role of Education in the Tourist Industry*, Salt Lake City: University of Utah, 2002.

Vroom, J. A.: *Tourism Education: A Model Program*, New Delhi: Manas Publications, 2004.

Vukoniae, B.: *Tourism in Central and Eastern Europe: Educating for Quality*, Tilberg: Tilberg University Press, 2000.

Walsh, M. E.: *Tourism Management*, New Delhi: Government of India Press, 2007.

Watson, J.: *Developing Tourism Managers*, New Delhi: Government of India Press, 2005.

Weiler, B. *Journal of Tourism Studies*, London: Macmillan, 2001.

Index

I

J

L

M

N

O

P

R

S

T

U

V

W